ADVANCES IN MANAGEMENT ACCOUNTING

ADVANCES IN MANAGEMENT ACCOUNTING

Series Editors: Marc J. Epstein and John Y. Lee

Recent Volumes:

ADVANCES IN MANAGEMENT ACCOUNTING

EDITED BY

MARC J. EPSTEIN

Harvard University and Rice University, USA

JOHN Y. LEE

Pace University, Pleasantville, USA

2004

ELSEVIER
JAI

Amsterdam – Boston – Heidelberg – London – New York – Oxford
Paris – San Diego – San Francisco – Singapore – Sydney – Tokyo

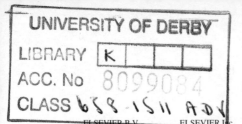
ELSEVIER B.V.
Sara Burgerhartstraat 25
P.O. Box 211
1000 AE Amsterdam
The Netherlands

ELSEVIER Inc.
525 B Street, Suite 1900
San Diego
CA 92101-4495
USA

ELSEVIER Ltd
The Boulevard, Langford
Lane, Kidlington
Oxford OX5 1GB
UK

ELSEVIER Ltd
84 Theobalds Road
London
WC1X 8RR
UK

First edition 2004

British Library Cataloguing in Publication Data
A catalogue record is available from the British Library.

ISBN: 0-7623-1139-8
ISSN: 1474-7871

⊗ The paper used in this publication meets the requirements of ANSI/NISO Z39.48-1992 (Permanence of Paper). Printed in The Netherlands.

CONTENTS

v

vi

LIST OF CONTRIBUTORS

Jacob G. Birnberg	Katz Graduate School of Business, University of Pittsburgh, Pennsylvania, USA
Clement C. Chen	School of Management, University of Michigan-Flint, Michigan, USA
Tony Davila	Graduate School of Business, Stanford University, California, USA
David P. Donnelly	Department of Accountancy, University of Missouri-Kansas City, Missouri
Marc J. Epstein	Jones Graduate School of Management, Rice University, Texas, USA
David R. Finley	Simon Fraser University, Canada
Laura Francis-Gladney	State University of New York Institute of Technology, New York, USA
Keith T. Jones	Eastern Kentucky University, Kentucky, USA
Robert Kee	Culverhouse School of Accountancy, University of Alabama, Alabama, USA
Woody M. Liao	Graduate School of Management, University of California-Riverside, California, USA
Harold T. Little	Gordon Ford College of Business, Western Kentucky University, Kentucky, USA
Nace R. Magner	Department of Accounting and Finance, Western Kentucky University, Kentucky, USA
Sharon F. Matusik	Leeds School of Business, University of Colorado-Boulder, USA
David O'Bryan	Pittsburg State University, Kansas, USA

Jeffrey J. Quirin	School of Accountancy, Wichita State University, Kansas, USA
Valerie J. Richardson	TreWyn, Inc., Maryland, USA
William E. Shafer	Department of Accounting and Finance, Lingnan University, Hong Kong
Stuart B. Thomas	Faculty of Management, University of Lethbridge, Canada
Robert B. Welker	College of Business and Administration, Southern Illinois University at Carbondale, Illinois, USA
Kristin Wentzel	School of Business Administration, La Salle University, Pennsylvania, USA

ix

STATEMENT OF PURPOSE AND REVIEW PROCEDURES

Advances in Management Accounting (AIMA) is a professional journal whose purpose is to meet the information needs of both practitioners and academicians. We plan to publish thoughtful, well-developed articles on a variety of current topics in management accounting, broadly defined.

Advances in Management Accounting is to be an annual publication of quality applied research in management accounting. The series will examine areas of management accounting, including performance evaluation systems, accounting for product costs, behavioral impacts on management accounting, and innovations in management accounting. Management accounting includes all systems designed to provide information for management decision making. Research methods will include survey research, field tests, corporate case studies, and modeling. Some speculative articles and survey pieces will be included where appropriate.

AIMA welcomes all comments and encourages articles from both practitioners and academicians.

Review Procedures

AIMA intends to provide authors with timely reviews clearly indicating the acceptance status of their manuscripts. The results of initial reviews normally will be reported to authors within eight weeks from the date the manuscript is received. Once a manuscript is tentatively accepted, the prospects for publication are excellent. The author(s) will be accepted to work with the corresponding Editor, who will act as a liaison between the author(s) and the reviewers to resolve areas of concern. To ensure publication, it is the author's responsibility to make necessary revisions in a timely and satisfactory manner.

EDITORIAL POLICY AND MANUSCRIPT FORM GUIDELINES

(1) Manuscripts should be type written and double-spaced on $8\frac{1}{2}''$ by $11''$ white paper. Only one side of the paper should be used. Margins should be set to facilitate editing and duplication except as noted:

    (a) Tables, figures, and exhibits should appear on a separate page. Each should be numbered and have a title.

    (b) Footnote should be presented by citing the author's name and the year of publication in the body of the text; for example, Ferreira (1998); Cooper and Kaplan (1998).

(2) Manuscripts should include a cover page that indicates the author's name and affiliation.

(3) Manuscripts should include on a separate lead page an abstract not exceeding 200 words. The author's name and affiliation should not appear on the abstract.

(4) Topical headings and subheadings should be used. Main headings in the manuscript should be centered, secondary headings should be flush with the left hand margin. (As a guide to usage and style, refer to the William Strunk, Jr., and E.B. White, *The Elements of Style*.)

(5) Manuscripts must include a list of references which contain only those works actually cited. (As a helpful guide in preparing a list of references, refer to Kate L. Turabian, *A Manual for Writers of Term Papers, Theses, and Dissertations*.)

(6) In order to be assured of anonymous review, authors should not identify themselves directly or indirectly. Reference to unpublished working papers and dissertations should be avoided. If necessary, authors may indicate that the reference is being withheld for the reason cited above.

(7) Manuscripts currently under review by other publications should not be submitted. Complete reports of research presented at a national or regional conference of a professional association and "State of the Art" papers are acceptable.

(8) Four copies of each manuscript should be submitted to John Y. Lee at the address below under Guideline 11.

(9) A submission fee of $25.00, made payable to Advances in Management Accounting, should be included with all submissions.
(10) For additional information regarding the type of manuscripts that are desired, see "*AIMA* Statement of Purpose."
(11) Inquires concerning Advances in Management Accounting may be directed to either one of the two editors:

Marc J. Epstein
Jones Graduate School of Administration
Rice University
Houston, Texas 77251–1892

John Y. Lee
Lubin School of Business
Pace University
Pleasantville, NY 10570–2799

INTRODUCTION

This volume of *Advances in Management Accounting (AIMA)* begins with a paper by Jacob G. Birnberg. This thought-provoking article is based on the author's keynote address delivered at the *First AIMA Conference on Management Accounting Research: New Paradigms and Methodologies* which was held in Monterey, California, May 15–16, 2003. As the title of the paper indicates, it is about expanding management accounting research frontiers in the next decade. According to Birnberg, the management accounting research cycle has been one of importing new ideas from other disciplines followed by a period of introspection when the new ideas are integrated into the fabric of management accounting research and practice. This prominent scholar claims there are good reasons to believe that management accounting is again at the point where it should look outside its own research domain for new ideas. His paper proposes several areas where management accounting researchers may find new, interesting and productive research. Within these areas a variety of specific research topics are suggested and potential research questions are raised.

In the second paper, Davila, Epstein, and Matusik address key issues involving innovation strategy and performance measures. The authors provide initial evidence on the issue of the lack of innovation in organizations and frustrated managers' attempts for better ways to implement an innovation strategy through an empirical examination. The authors contribute to the existing literature in two important areas: how managers choose what measures to pay attention to in managing the innovation process and how innovation strategy is related to the use of measures. They find that managers use measures about specific phases of the innovation process together. For example, measures that inform about the execution stage of the innovation process are grouped together rather than being grouped with measures informative about other phases of the innovation process, such as market performance. This result provides the first empirical test of how managers combine measures to filter information about business processes. The authors also find that different dimensions of strategy are positively associated with how managers use different types of measures.

The third paper by Thomas examines the performance effects of financial incentives for a simple, recurrent task designed to simulate an assembly-line setting. The study looks at early performance, improvement and overall performance and reports on a laboratory experiment whose results confirm the findings of Bailey et al. (1998) but also indicates that for both performance-based and fixed incentives, significant performance improvement takes place well beyond the initial performance of the task, declining gradually over time. This is in contrast with the suggestion of Bailey et al. (1998) that workers with performance-based incentives will choose to improve initial performance rather than subsequent performance. Findings also suggest that improvement peaks earlier for performance-based incentives than for a fixed incentive. Improvement persisted longer and there was better overall performance with the high fixed component quota and piece rate incentives than with the low fixed component quota.

Next, Kee expands activity-based costing (ABC) to incorporate the cost of capital in evaluating product mix and capital budgeting decisions. Product mix and the acquisition of the assets needed for their production are interdependent decisions. However, these decisions are frequently evaluated independently of each other and with conceptually different decision models. The model Kee develops in this paper traces the cost of capital to products and thereby measures the economic value added (EVA) from their production. The article also examines the role of ABC when product mix decisions are made at the product and portfolio levels of the firm's operations.

In the fifth paper, Richardson examines the transformation progress of the two government agencies as they attempt to convert to high-performing organizations by utilizing and establishing new and more flexible systems of performance-oriented business practices and processes. The two agencies are: the Office of Student Financial Assistance of the Department of Education and the Patent and Trademark Office of the Department of Commerce. The paper compares and contrasts the different approaches and tools used to improve management and organizational performance, as well as concentrate on human resources, procurement, budget, customer service, and internal controls. The document explores whether or not these agencies have improved their performance as a result of these flexibilities and examines the organizational and cultural challenges encountered as the agencies move from a restrictive and bureaucratic system, to a more liberal system of management and internal controls.

Next, Quirin, O'Bryan, and Donnelly incorporate equity theory into a theoretical model of budgetary participation and performance. The study develops and tests a nomological framework of budgetary participation that includes two organizational constructs, budgetary participation and budget-based compensation, and three individual characteristics, perception of equity, organizational commitment, and employee performance. Measures of these constructs were gathered from a sample of 98 employees in 15 organizations. In accordance with the proposed theory and hypotheses, results reveal that budgetary participation is associated with increased use of budget-based compensation as well as higher levels of perception of equity and organizational commitment. Budget-based compensation and perception of equity, in turn, are also associated with increased levels of organizational commitment, while elevated commitment was related to higher performance. The results provide further insight into the beneficial aspects of budgetary participation. Specifically, the results indicate that budgetary participation is positively associated with perception of equity, which in turn increases organizational commitment and, ultimately, employee performance.

In the seventh paper, Francis-Gladney, Little, Magner, and Welker address the issue of whether organization-mandated budgetary involvement enhances managers' budgetary communication with their supervisor. Large organizations typically mandate that managers attend budget meetings and exchange budget reports with their immediate supervisor and budget staff. The authors examine whether such organization-mandated budgetary involvement is related to managers' budgetary communication with their supervisor in terms of budgetary participation, budgetary explanation, and budgetary feedback. Questionnaire data from 148 managers employed by 94 different companies were analyzed with regression.

In the eighth paper, Chen and Jones extend prior participative budgeting research by examining the effects of aggregation levels of performance feedback and task interdependence on budgetary slack and the effects of different levels of feedback on group performance in a group participative budget setting. The study addresses the issue that prior experimental budgeting research has focused primarily on individuals' budget setting, rather than group setting. The results suggest that aggregation levels of performance feedback differentially impact budgetary slack and group performance. Providing both group and individual performance feedback increases group performance and reduces budgetary slack compared to providing group performance feedback only. Providing information about other subordinates' performance further increases group performance and reduces budgetary slack beyond the effects of providing individual workers information only about their own performance. The results indicate that task interdependence also affects the level of budgetary slack. Specifically, high task interdependence groups created more budgetary slack than did low task interdependence groups.

The ninth paper, by Wentzel, examines whether perceptions of fairness mitigate managers' use of budgetary slack during asymmetric information conditions. Prior research demonstrates a positive relationship between information asymmetry and managers' use of budgetary slack and thereby suggests that minimizing managers' private information is a potential tactic for reducing slack in budgets. Asymmetric information, however, often cannot be avoided when specialized technical expertise is required to operate a particular responsibility area. This study contributes to the literature by investigating whether favorable perceptions of fairness mitigate managers' use of budgetary slack during participative environments in which managers hold private information. Overall, the findings demonstrate the benefits of fair budgeting practices. In particular, survey results suggest that the presence of budgetary slack in efficiency targets is lower for mangers who hold favorable fairness perceptions. A gender effect is also demonstrated between perceptions of fairness and the presence of budgetary slack in spending targets.

In the final paper, Liao, Finley, and Shafer report the results of an experimental study examining the joint effect of two group characteristics, responsibility and cohesiveness, on escalation of commitment in an ongoing unsuccessful project. Two levels (high/low) of group responsibility and group cohesiveness were manipulated to examine their effects on group escalation decisions. Forty-eight 3-member decision groups were formed and randomly assigned to four treatment cells with 12 groups in each cell. The results of a 2×2 ANOVA reveal a significant main effect of responsibility on escalation of commitment, as well as a significant interaction of responsibility and cohesiveness. Specifically, groups with both high responsibility and high cohesiveness committed the largest amount of resources to an ongoing unsuccessful project. These results provide support for the proposition that group responsibility and cohesiveness exert significant joint effects on group escalation of commitment in an ongoing unsuccessful project.

We believe the 10 articles in Volume 13 represent relevant, theoretically sound, and practical studies the discipline can greatly benefit from. These manifest our commitment to providing a high level of contributions to management accounting research and practice.

Marc J. Epstein
John Y. Lee
Editors

EXPANDING OUR FRONTIERS: MANAGEMENT ACCOUNTING RESEARCH IN THE NEXT DECADE?

Jacob G. Birnberg

ABSTRACT

The cycle in research in management accounting has been one of importing new ideas from other disciplines followed by a period of introspection when the new ideas are integrated into the fabric of management accounting research and practice. There are good reasons to believe that management accounting is again at the point where it should look outside its own research domain for new ideas.

This paper proposes several areas where management accounting researchers may find new, interesting and productive research. Within these areas a variety of specific research topics are suggested and potential research questions are raised.

INTRODUCTION

The Post World War II MBA revolution was intended to professionalize management education and incorporate recent developments in operations research and economics. In accounting education these changes initially took place in management accounting. It can be characterized as a broadening of our intellectual frontiers to adapt a variety of ideas from other disciplines including economics,

Advances in Management Accounting

Advances in Management Accounting, Volume 13, 1–26

© 2004 by Elsevier Ltd.
ISSN: 1474-7871/doi:10.1016/S1474-7871(04)13001-3

operations research and, to a lesser degree, psychology. This was reflected in the changes that occurred in the management accounting textbooks (see Anthony, 2003; Horngren, 1962). More recently I have perceived that researchers have spent less time expanding management accounting's frontiers and more time refining and integrating existing knowledge.

This period of integration has benefited management accounting and management accounting researchers. We have been able to consolidate and integrate the innovations in management accounting. However, there also is a need periodically to expand our frontiers. This will invigorate our research and enrich practice. I believe that management accounting research is at one of these points.

With this in mind, I have chosen to encourage such an expansion by doing two things:

- Suggest ways in which researchers can identify potential areas for future research.
- Identify potentially fertile fields where researchers may find interesting topics for their research.

The reason for adopting a more general approach is simple. Specific ideas may be useful to one or two potential researchers or may be of value to no one. In contrast, broader topics offer three advantages: first, it permits me to discuss a wider range of issues; second, there is the opportunity to create a community of interest among accounting researchers in a given topic; third, you may find something of interest in the topic I discuss that did not or could not have occurred to me. This is a win-win situation. You have new topic(s) and perceive that *I* was responsible for it!

The remainder of this paper consists of six sections. The first discusses how readers can develop their own list of topics. I do this by illustrating how I arrived at the areas I have chosen to discuss. Each of the four following sections discusses a potential area of research. The final section provides a brief summary of what I have suggested.

SELECTING THE TOPICS

In selecting areas I have deliberately attempted to stretch the boundaries of management accounting research – though not as much I had initially hoped to do. My reason for wanting to stretch the boundaries is a simple one. I have noticed that too often researchers searching for new areas to explore look inward by examining what other managerial accountants have published (and journal referees and editors have accepted). This means that with the exception of the periodic innovation such as the work Chris Ittner (2003) reviewed, we typically move forward in modest increments in already established research topics.

Some of the topics I have generated are not truly innovative. You may have seen or heard of them before or they may have been active areas of research in the past but have been dormant of late. Other topics would benefit from being researched from a new perspective. Perhaps we could think of them as "new wine in old bottles." In contrast, there are topics are more innovative and amenable to knowledge transfer from other disciplines or other aspects of accounting.

The topics for the most part are behavioral or amenable to behavioral research methods as well as other approaches. This reflects personal biases. It also reflects the presence of papers discussing research from other perspectives, e.g. Ittner (2003).

The call for broadening the frontiers of management accounting parallels what is occurring in other disciplines and professions. The movement incorporating behavioral science and laboratory experiments into Economics (Camerer, 2001) and Finance (Thaler, 1993) is already well documented. Lawyers not only have discovered economics, but also are writing about behavioral issues in the law (e.g. Sunstein, 2003). Political scientists are concerned with governance issues and have a journal with that name.

HOW CAN WE ACCESS OTHER DISCIPLINES?

There are a variety of ways that research outside of accounting can be accessed. These include:

- Reading journals in the related disciplines not typically considered central to management accounting. These would include strategy and management information systems.
- Taking advantage of the various services such as the Social Science Research Network (SSRN) that provides abstracts of working papers and forthcoming papers. The SSRN's publications include a wide range of topics in economics, management and finance as well as accounting.
- Interact with doctoral students outside of accounting whose dissertation topic or method intersects your interests.
- Literature reviews which appear all too infrequently in accounting journals.

The link to strategy and information systems goes back to the work of Anthony (1965). He identified three levels of control – Strategic, Managerial and Operations. These three levels were arranged in a strict hierarchy with Strategic at the top and Operations at the bottom. Management was in the middle. Later researchers such as Lorange and Scott-Morton (1974) added the Information System to Anthony's original flow chart. Recently, all three levels of the organization's control system (OCS) outlined by Anthony (1965) have become more integrated and interdependent. Changes in one system can, and often do, impact the other system(s) (Birnberg, 1998a).

This integration and interdependence of systems reflects a potential intersection of research interests between the areas. For example, both literatures are concerned with managing joint ventures or inter-firm relationships (Birnberg, 1998b; Colletti et al., 2003; Sampler & Short, 1998).

Management information systems journals illustrate a similar intersection of interests. Many information systems researchers are concerned with issues related to the impact of the system on individuals and/or the organization. Others research the effect of data on decision makers. While the context may differ, these topics parallel research being done by management accountants.

The Social Science Research Network's (SSRN) Abstracts in areas of Economics, Law, and Management provide insight into what researchers in these areas are thinking in some areas that management accounting researchers would not otherwise follow. What issues do the authors whose papers were abstracted consider important? Often the abstract is sufficient to inform the reader about the paper. Good sounding titles may not discuss topics of interest, while other papers with less interesting titles may turn out to be of interest. If a paper is of interest, a copy of the paper can be downloaded easily from the SSRN website.

Doctoral students always have been a potential source of new ideas. Ideally, their programs require them to expand the boundaries of study. Moreover, accounting students interact with students in other disciplines. In the process, good doctoral students are introduced to cutting edge research in other areas. They can serve as conduits to faculty researchers through these interactions.

While literature reviews are included on the list, I relied less on the various literature reviews that have been appearing in the accounting literature than normally might be expected. There are two reasons for this: first, the authors' conclusions and suggestions already are readily available to you; second, while they are of value for the specific ideas they suggest as "open research questions," reviews usually are retrospective in nature and consider questions extant in the literature.

I do wish to highlight a suggestion found in Merchant et al.'s (2003) review of a portion of the management accounting literature. They argue that management accounting research would benefit by interacting with practicing managers in identifying issues that are of concern to them. The implication of this for researchers is twofold: first, managers know what problems are interesting to practitioners; second, researchers seeking cooperation from practitioners and/or real world data are more likely to receive it when they focus on issues of interest to practitioners.

ALTERED FORMS OF THE "SELF-INTEREST" ASSUMPTION

A variety of new research areas relate to the question of how well the self-interest assumption of traditional economics fits observed behavior. These questions are related to multi-actor settings (at least dyads). The studies of dyads in experimental economics and accounting have related to the role of norms, e.g. reciprocity, co-operation or fairness, and their impact on behavior (Luft, 1997). Others are related to the behavior of groups, an area that has been more popular in behavioral accounting than in economics (but see Fon & Parisi, 2003).

COOPERATION IN DECISION MAKING GROUPS

Accounting researchers already have begun to research what I would label "work groups." I would define a work group as an assembly of multiple actors who interact to perform a *physical* task. Young et al. (1993) or Drake, Haka and Ravenscraft (1999) are examples of this research. These studies are in contrast to decision making groups such as capital budgeting committees or cost reduction teams (Rowe, 2003). I believe that to management accountants the decision making groups should have a great deal of interest.

Decision making groups suggest several interesting questions:

- Rules – how do the groups decide?
- The role of power in decision making groups.
- The role of trust, cooperation and norms in committees.
- The role of accounting systems in facilitating or inhibiting cooperation and trust in decision making groups.

Rules and Trust, Cooperation and Norms

I am using the term *rule* to describe the rule(s), both formal (e.g. voting rules) or informal, that the committee uses to make decisions. The rules under which the committee operates are crucial in determining the need for cooperation and trust among group members. The critical questions in the choice of a rule would appear to relate to the nature of the decision making task. Is it one where cooperation of all members is desirable or will a subset of the group be sufficient for a successful implementation? What role does the group's history play? Is it an ad hoc committee or have the same committee members served together before (a history/reputation)? Can they be expected to serve on committees together again in the future? Is the decision in question part of a series of ongoing decisions and not an independent event?

The nature of the rule selected affects the number of members of the committee that must be included in the successful coalition. A rule that explicitly or implicitly requires a unanimous agreement can put greater stress on the committee than simple majority rule because more members of the committee must be recruited into the "winning" coalition before an agreement can be achieved. Whether unanimity is good for the organization, i.e. do they reach a better decision for the firm, will depend on the nature of the task and the relative desirability of the alternative solutions. If the cost of achieving a unanimous vote is selecting an alternative that is less efficient for the firm, then unanimity is not the most desirable rule from the firm's perspective *viewed as a one-shot decision*. In contrast, while majority rule may be more efficient from the firm's perspective in a one-shot decision, the process through which it is achieved may lead to an unhappy minority. If the same players will reassemble at a future date to make other decisions, *a series of decisions*, and the coalition with the "best" alternative varies from decision to decision, there may be a reputation effect that will be disruptive.

If the same individuals have a history or will participate in future groups, the effects of the decision rule may be reinforced by the group's norms. Individuals may be expected to behave in a particular way. In addition, in real world groups, unlike experimental studies, communication is permitted. This raises the question of the efficacy of "cheap talk," i.e. nonbinding promises to behave in a particular manner. Group members may respect the "cheap talk" by other group members, e.g. Kachelmeier et al. (1994). The issue of the cause – group norms, reputation or "cheap talk" – is a researchable issue. It could be that each of these is the cause depending on the situation and/or that there is an interaction among/between these variables.

Many years ago Birnberg, Pondy and Davis (1970) conducted a study intended to investigate certain aspects of the *process* through which groups reach decisions. Their concern was the group's decision rule. Three person groups (called committees) were required to vote sequentially on a series of proposals under three different voting rules. These rules were unanimity, majority rules and majority rules with a veto. Under the majority rules with a veto, the majority prevailed only if the individual with the veto was a member of the majority. Each trial consisted of choosing among three proposals. The proposal which resulted in the best (i.e. highest) outcome for each participant *over the entire period of experiment* was the proposal that was the most inequitable in any given trial. One committee member received five points and the other two did not receive any. The proposal that was most equitable in its distribution of the rewards among the group's members on any given trial, one point to each member, offered the lowest total payoff to the committee members over the entire experiment.

The participants were told that under each of the voting rules each individual would receive the same number of "high" and "low" payoffs. Securing the greatest individual reward over the entire experiment required the group members to recognize that the best solution was to co-operate. The best strategy during the experiment was for the participant to ignore their personal payoffs and always to vote for the option with the highest total payoff, regardless of how the payoff was divided. If the participants did this over the entire set of trials, each participant would realize the highest possible payoff and the group payoff would be maximized.

The participants in the study could not communicate, did not know each other, and received minimal feedback after each trial. All they were told after each trial was the outcome of the trial. When there was agreement on a specific option, the participants could draw inferences about the behavior of the other members of the group. However, none of the mechanisms discussed earlier, such as norms, communication or signaling, "cheap talk," or reputation, was present in this study.

In the absence of their ability to communicate and the knowledge of how others voted, the results were consistent with the hypotheses. Each participant used forward induction to understand how the other participants would behave under a given voting rule. Total payoffs under majority rules were greater than the payoffs under unanimity rules. The rule where one of the three members of the group had a "veto" was in between the results of the other two rules.

This experiment was conducted in a different research environment from that which we now experience. If we were to conduct the same study today, three interesting researchable topics arise:

- Communication, e.g. what role would communication play in such a setting? This also relates to the question of "cheap talk."
- The effect of richer feedback about the outcomes.
- Norms, e.g. what effect might group norms have on the participants' decision making/voting?
- Role of the accounting system, e.g. how would feedback on the votes of others affect the participants' subsequent behavior?

Communication alone need not have resulted in higher group payoffs because the members could not write enforceable contracts. However, there are studies that suggest that "cheap talk" (non-binding contracts) can affect subsequent behavior (Kachelmeier et al., 1994). Coupled with feedback, the cheap talk could be significant. Whether the communication takes place in a face-to-face environment or via an e-mail-like network could affect the participants' behavior as well.

Groups that had the opportunity through past interactions to develop trust, cooperation, or a norm that supported equitable *long term* treatment for all group members, could have secured a higher total payoff than Birnberg et al.'s (1970) participants did. Assuming that the structure of their experiment captured the essence of group decision making, the researchable issues that it raises relate to how a group's trust, cooperation and reciprocity will affect group decisions. The next section discusses how the accounting system can affect the behavior of decision makers.

THE IMPACT OF ORGANIZATION DESIGN AND ACCOUNTING SYSTEMS ON COOPERATION

In a recent study, Rowe (2003) showed that the accounting system under certain circumstances serves to highlight the benefits of cooperation to participants and leads to a larger total group payoff. Using a social dilemma as the task, Rowe created two types of four person groups which he called "real" and "nominal." The four members of the "real" groups sat around a table. They did not communicate in any way. Each member of a "nominal" group was in a different room with members of other groups. Rowe also varied the accounting presentation of the data. One condition received information about potential payoffs to the individual participants and the potential payoff to all the groups' members. The participants in the other condition only received information about their potential payoff. This did not vary the information actually available to the participants. The participants receiving only individual information could have calculated the group data with which the participants in the other condition were provided.

Rowe found that the real groups that also received the reports highlighting the payoffs to both the group and the individual performed better than the other three conditions. The experiment, as artificial as it may be, suggests that accounting systems can reinforce cooperative behavior. However, the accounting system must be consistent with other aspects of the firm's organization.

Combining the two studies (Birnberg et al., 1970; Rowe, 2003) illustrates how the "accounting system" could affect behavior by directing the participants' attention in particular ways. Would the participants in Birnberg et al.'s (1970) study have altered their behavior if the reporting system had provided feedback intended to inform the participants about the cost of the group's sub optimal choices? For example, the system could report after each trial the percent of the maximum payoff the group had achieved.

Rowe's (2003) study also raises research issues related to the accounting system. For example:

- Does the Balanced Scorecard and other multi-dimensional performance measures work better, ceteris paribus, when they are consistent with the firm's organizational structure and/or mission statement?
- Can the accounting system alter (i.e. increase/decrease) existing levels of trust among the organization's divisions and/or members by showing how everyone benefits from reciprocity?

FAIRNESS

Perception of fairness in wages and payoffs has been a significant topic in experimental economics. Ernst Fehr and his colleagues (e.g. Fehr & Schmidt, 1999) developed a significant portion of this literature. Experimental economics has an extensive literature exploring the extent and robustness of fairness as a norm (see Roth, 1995). It has been investigated in a wide range of environments and cultures (Henrich et al., 2001; Roth et al., 1991). Studies have examined the role of fairness from the perspective of both the recipient who expects the fair outcome and the decision maker who must decide what the recipient's expectation is (Fehr & Gachter, 2000).

Many of these studies have utilized a task in which the flow of benefits is unidirectional, usually the ultimatum game. In this task, participants are paired in dyads. One member of the dyad (the proposer) typically is given a sum of money and told to share the money with the other member of the dyad (the acceptor) however the proposer desires. The acceptor's only choice in these studies is to accept or reject the offer (thus, the name *ultimatum*). If the offer is accepted, the two members of the dyad share the money as the proposer decided. If the second member rejects the offer, neither party receives anything. It is intuitively obvious that the economic prediction, that the recipient will accept any nonzero offer, is unlikely to be correct. However, the size of the offers that the acceptors will reject (and receive nothing instead) is in the 40–50% range, significantly larger than one's intuition would lead one to expect (see Roth, 1995).

Experiments like the ultimatum game bear a resemblance to the resource allocation process and demonstrate the expectation of the (acceptor) participants in the process to be treated fairly. These differences suggest potentially interesting hypotheses for managerial accounting researchers. However, the ultimatum game does not totally capture significant aspects of the business setting. The budget setting process often results from a negotiation process between the parties. It is more of a two-sided bargaining process. After the contract/budget is agreed upon, the worker must decide how much effort to provide given the contract. Akerlof (1982) argued in such a setting a wage that is higher than required by the market (more than fair) will elicit greater levels of effort from the employee even though the higher effort level is not required by the agreement. He characterized the higher wage as a gift and referred to such settings as a "partial gift exchange." Hannan (2001) found support for this argument in an experimental market.

Fairness also relates to the means by which the decision is reached. Fairness in this context can relate to two distinct issues:

• The perceived fairness of the process by which the budget or other contract within the control system is reached, i.e. procedural fairness.
• The perceived fairness of the contract itself, i.e. outcome fairness.

Participation is an example of an attempt to achieve the former. Early researchers argued that the role of participation was to increase the worker's motivation through mutual understanding and, ultimately, goal congruence. Even in the absence of goal congruence, better communication could lead to more realistic expectations on the part of both parties. This should enhance the perception that the process and ultimately that the budget was fair (Shields & Shields, 1998). Akerlof's (1982) argument would suggest that the results of participation may be due to the worker's perception of the gift exchange wage. The attribution made by the worker also could be of importance.

It is important that the systems be perceived as fair. These systems are the rules that govern the workers' behavior. Hufnagel and Birnberg (1994), in an experiment study of outsourcing computer services, found that participants were sensitive to the potential unfairness in the rules governing computer access. Participants who were operating under a set of rules that did not affect their performance but had the *potential* to affect their performance adversely at a future date considered the rules to less fair even though the rule did not penalize them during the experiment. For a related study see Libby (2001).

Recent laboratory experiments in taxation also support the notion that perceived fairness in the way the process is administered leads individuals to cooperate and behave in ways inconsistent with the predictions of traditional economic theory. Evans, Moser and Kim (1995) and Kim, Evans and Moser (2004) established that perceived fairness in the tax structure is an important factor leading to greater tax compliance. In their experiments the participants were part of a decision making dyad. One party, the experimenters, changed the nature of the tax structure (akin to the computer access rules in Hufnagel & Birnberg, 1994). The other party was the participants who decided on the extent of their tax evasion behavior, if any. When the experimenters manipulated the change so that the participants perceived the change in the tax to be fair, the participants reported their incomes more honestly than when they perceived the change to be unfair.

ORGANIZATIONAL CULTURE

The discussion of norms and values provides a ready transition to the role of organization or corporate culture. During the past decade the term "culture" among accounting researchers has referred to national culture, e.g. Chow et al. (1999). Relatively little has been done in accounting with the idea of the culture existing in organizations. This topic never was a popular one among accounting researchers and recently has not been popular among organization theorists. For a discussion of culture in the organizations literature, see Elsmore (2001, pp. 43–77).

The organization's culture is the aggregation of the norms and values of the organization (Elsmore, 2001). If researchers find a significant role for variables such as co-operation, reciprocity, and fairness, the notion of a firm's culture, i.e. its collection of norms, could be as relevant for management accounting researchers as Hofstede's (1980) national culture profiles.

Researchers may wish to consider five potentially interesting questions:

- How do these variables, i.e. the culture, come to exist in an organization and what factor(s) are needed to maintain them? Specifically, how can the accounting information system facilitate the development and maintenance of the organization's culture and what role does accounting play in its change?
- Can Hofstede's dimensions of culture be adopted to or adapted for organizational culture research?
- How does the corporate culture affect the operation/formality of the accounting control system (budgets, etc.)?
- Which aspects of the organization's culture have the greatest influence on the choice of accounting system and/or the interaction between the members of the organization and the accounting system?
- In this regard, is there an interaction among the different norms, or do the norms act independently?

These questions are not dissimilar to those discussed in the national culture literature. For a review of this literature, see Harrison and McKinnon (1999). However, by examining them from the organization perspective, they apply to a broader set of issues and firms. For example, Birnberg and Snodgrass (1988) compared accounting systems in the U.S. and Japan, They found that the more homogenous culture (Japan) had a less formal system than the diverse culture (U.S.). Does this finding apply to firms as well?

Executing research in this area offers two advantages to the researcher over cross cultural research. First, the researcher is restricted to having to find research site(s) in only one country. That usually would be his or her home country. Second, field research is likely to be more convenient, i.e. less travel. This provides the researcher(s) with the opportunity to enhance the credibility of their findings by performing multi-method research on a specific question (Birnberg, Shields & Young, 1990).

These studies cannot blindly follow Hofstede (1980) five dimensions research as the cross-cultural studies have. However, Hofstede's dimensions may provide researchers with a framework within which the research initially can be structured. Researchers may be required to adapt existing instruments from organizational behavior or to develop their own instruments for this purpose.

A better set of characteristics for measuring organizational culture may be based on the work of Trompenaars (1993). Trompenaars, in his extensive study of national culture over 28 countries, developed five dimensions to culture. These are:

- Individualism versus collectivism.
- Universalism versus particularism.
- Neutral versus affective relationships.
- Specific versus diffuse relationships.
- Achievement versus ascription.

The individualism-collectivism dimension is consistent with the work of Hofstede. Universalism versus particularism refers to the basis used to determine what is proper. Is it rule based (universalism) or is it a specified list of acts or outcomes (particularism)? This dimension would appear to parallel procedural versus distributive justice. Is the rule fair or do we measure it by the outcome? Both neutral-affective and specific-diffuse refer to the intraorganization relationships. Neutral versus affective refers to the way and degree to which emotions are expressed in intra organization relationships. Specific versus diffuse refers to the degree of involvement in intra organization relationships. Are members part of particular subgroups (specific) or do they tend to view themselves as part of the larger group, i.e. all or a significant portion of the organization (diffuse)? Achievement versus ascription relates to the source of power. Is it based on achievement or is it attributed to an individual because of his or her position or status? The latter would be consistent with the authority of high ranking officers in the military or in an organization with a very strict hierarchical organizational structure. Trompenaar's dimension explains the basis for the respect for authority *to the extent it exists.* In contrast, Hofstede's power-distance dimension addresses the *extent* of that respect for authority.

It would appear that some mix of Hofstede's and Trompenaar's typologies would be useful for organizational culture research. However, it remains for researchers to ascertain which of the nine distinct dimensions are appropriate.

An Example of the Role Culture Plays

The organization's culture can affect the perspective of management. Management's perspective, in turn, will affect how management views the internal and external environment and the nature of the systems. It also affects the aspect of any task to which management attends, or considers of potential significance and which aspects are viewed as unimportant. The problems experienced by NASA with the Challenger and Columbia shuttle vehicles raises an interesting case of the role that culture can play in the manner in which an organization makes decisions. The shuttle crash raises two questions related to NASA's culture. First, why did the organization consider the flights to be routine and second, how did this affect the organization's subsequent behavior? Casual empiricism (which means that others should undertake the relevant systematic research) suggests that Trompenaar's dimensions of particularism and (power) ascription may have been particularly important in NASA's decision making. It was important to achieve particular goals, e.g. meeting the expectations of Congress, and the power was vested with particular groups because of their position. The group most concerned with the potential problem(s) created by the debris at liftoff was not the high power/status group in the organization. These characteristics would appear to be consistent with an organization operating in a world with a low degree of uncertainty in its environment. However, they are not appropriate for an organization whose environment is characterized by uncertainty over/within the task.

SOCIAL CAPITAL

Social capital may be the topic that has replaced organizational culture for some organizational behavior researchers. Putnam's (1995, p. 67) definition of social capital is that social capital consists of "(F)eatures of social organization such as networks, norms and social trust that facilitate coordination and cooperation for mutual benefit." Other definitions similarly stress the notion that social capital is value added to the organization through the "collective goal orientation and shared trust" of the group's members (Leana & Van Buren, 1999, p. 538).

Nahapiet and Ghoshal (1998) divided social capital along three dimensions: relational, cognitive and structural. Relational refers to what could be described as shared values, e.g. norms, trust, obligation and identification. Cognitive refers to what could be viewed as the shared intellectual development that results from shared experiences or training, e.g. the shared task-related language and understandings of events. These are skills that facilitate common understanding and ease of communication. Structural refers to the organization of the group, the formal and informal networks. The more appropriate the structure to the setting, the greater the likelihood of success. These relationships could include relations between the group with which one is concerned and other (external) groups.

It has been argued that social capital will be greater for a closed group (Granovetter, 1985). Closure is defined in terms of the density of the ties among group members. A group where each member is related to every other member would have the highest degree of density. This would facilitate the development of shared values, common expectations, and the sharing of information. An expected outcome of this would be that the shared goals, values, and knowledge will lead to better performance.

Much of the discussion of social capital inevitably leads to considering the relationship between social capital and Ouchi's (1977) clan form of organization. It would appear reasonable to view this literature of one way of making operational Ouchi's clan concept.

However, a closed group is not without its potential risks. A closed group could have greater difficulty recognizing changes in the environment or the incorrectness of its knowledge or beliefs. In the absence of strong connections to other groups, it may have difficulty recognizing the inaccuracy of its information and the inappropriateness of its expectations. In the earlier discussion of the culture at NASA, it could have been the "density" of the management group that made it resistant to the new information about the potential for damage having occurred at liftoff that the engineers were providing. A less closed group, i.e. one with weaker intra-group ties and stronger external ties, i.e. one with stronger ties to other groups within NASA, may have had access to more diverse information. The trade-off between the degree of agreement a group requires and the extent to which it will tolerate conflict may be a function of the uncertainty of the group's task's environment.

The question for researchers is "What role do accounting systems play in a group's social capital?" This is a question that is concerned with the role of accounting in the formation and maintenance of social groups in addition to the role of accounting in providing information for decision making and evaluating performance. This is a different type of research question than many of the others raised in this paper.

COMPUTER FACILITATED DECISION MAKING

Organizational decision making and control can be characterized as the interaction of a human decision maker(s) and the task he, she or they are called upon to perform. It takes place in a particular environment (Covaleski, Evans, Luft & Shields, 2003). The typical discussion of decision making in the management accounting literature is formulated along the lines of the principal-agent (P-A) model. The presence or absence of information is a given (Baiman, 1982, 1990). In the P-A model, the quality of the principal's or agent's information may be noisy, thereby introducing some concern over the data. However, the source of the information and the manner in which the principal or agent acquires it are not of concern. Great care is taken in management accounting texts to specify the type of data required, e.g. opportunity costs or incremental costs. However, the manner in which these costs can be ascertained usually is not discussed. Yet in the end of the 20th and beginning of the 21st century, one of the most readily apparent changes in organizations has been the information technology revolution. Firms have the ability to collect, accumulate and disseminate vast and varied amounts of data potentially relevant to the firm's activities. The same firms have at their disposal the equipment (hardware and software) to analyze these data in ways that are or should be useful to decision makers.

Hodge, Kennedy and Maines (forthcoming) in financial accounting context suggest an interesting approach to this issue. They investigated the ability of naive financial statement users to search a database using Extensible Business Reporting Language (XBRL) and its impact on their decision making. They found that the participants who were provided with the financial information performed differently than those who were able to search the financial database for themselves. The result is not surprising and is consistent with one's intuition. However, it is instructive. Decision makers faced with a complex, ill-structured problem and an extensive data set may benefit from the ability to explore the available data ("playfulness") and determine which data they want for the decision. While Hodge et al.'s (forthcoming) task was not a managerial accounting task, it does raise two interesting issues:

- Decision aid that permits the decision maker to be involved actively in the data search may, through the involvement, improve the quality of the decision making.
- To what extent is the improved decision making the result of the non-routine nature of the task the participants in Hodge et al.'s (forthcoming) study performed? It would appear to be reasonable that the more routine the decision maker believes the task is, the less likely it is that he or she will consider the decision aid desirable and the less its existence will enhance the quality of the decision.

SEARCHING FORMAL DATABASES

Managers have become "information workers" (McCall & Kaplan, 1985). The balance in their jobs has shifted from managing people, i.e. human relations, toward managing the potentially vast amount of data available to them to help them perform their jobs. While standardized reports remain, the ability to go beyond the numbers on the report provides a richer decision making environment for the decision maker. At the same time it presents a much more complex task to the system designer and the management accounting researcher.

The research on the information revolution has been primarily the domain of management information systems researchers and accounting information systems researchers. There is no reason why management accountants cannot raise relevant issues. Consider the following possible research questions relating data search and cognitive research:

- What role does the decision maker's existing knowledge structure play in the decision makers' ability to adapt their information seeking and decision making to new forms of data presentation?
- What role does the decision maker's existing knowledge structure play in the decision makers' ability to adapt their information seeking and decision making to new sources of data?
- What role does the decision maker's existing knowledge structure play in the decision makers' ability to adapt their information seeking and decision making to significant increases in the amount of data available?
- Do decision makers using the database follow a search strategy that confirms a decision or searches for data rejecting it?

All of these questions relate to the interaction between the decision maker and the task. How does a particular aspect of the decision maker, his/her knowledge structure or decision style, interact with a particular aspect of the decision maker's task environment, i.e. the database?

This may sound like the functional/data/accounting fixation issue in a different context. It is not. It is a much broader question. All of the above potential research questions describe situations where the *structure* of problem facing the decision maker changes. In the typical fixation study the *measurement rule* underlying the report changes, e.g. Ashton (1976).

The decision maker's knowledge structure can vary from tacit, i.e. not well structured or understood, to explicit, i.e. a well developed decision model. The research questions listed above all relate to the degree to which the decision maker's cognitive structure about a particular task affects his/her cognitive flexibility, i.e. the ability to adapt to a new database or the same data organized in a different manner? Will it help or hinder the decision maker? We might ask, for example:

- Does a well developed knowledge structure impede the decision maker's ability to adapt his/her knowledge structure to a richer database?
- Does a well developed knowledge structure impede the decision maker's ability to effectively search the new database for new relevant information?

Intuitively, it would appear that individuals who understand the problem ("experts") should benefit from a new and richer database. These are the individuals who not only know *what they know*, but also are keenly aware of what they do *not* know but would benefit from knowing. We would expect that these individuals should search a new database to ascertain if they are trying to "fill in the blanks" in their decision models or provide better measures of variables and parameters in their models.

However, as Simon and Hayes (1976) demonstrated with abstract problems, many problem solvers solve problems based on surface characteristics rather than the underlying structure of the problem. It is possible that redesigning the database may serve to confuse the previously successful decision maker. Without training in how to use the new data base, the decision makers' performance could deteriorate even though the new data base has the potential to improve their performance.

Individual with a less well structured model representation ("novice") could respond in one of two ways. If they are aware of the need to improve the model, the new database could result in renewed search activity ("learning"). If they are satisfied with the model, the new database could yield no improvement in their decision making and could lead to poorer decisions. This would be the old problem of information overload.

Researchers interested in this area may find that the Lens model research so popular with behavioral accounting researchers doing financial decision making and auditing research in the 1980s to be a useful paradigm. It would permit the researchers to examine the decision models of the participants (Ashton, 1974). The research also may be amenable to using the Chow test used in data fixation research (Libby, 1976). The Chow test would permit researchers to assess any changes in the decision models the participants use.

INFORMATION SYSTEM DESIGN TO ENCOURAGE PLAYFULNESS BY DECISION MAKERS

Hedberg and Jonsson (1978) raise the problem of the interaction between the decision maker's knowledge structure and the design of the database in an indirect way. They argue in their paper on "semi-confusing information systems" that the information system should be designed to encourage *playfulness* on the part of the manager. Playfulness can be defined as exploratory behavior or "out of the box" thinking intended to identify new problems facing the organization, or new, creative solutions to an existing problem. Their paper discussed why and when such an information system would be desirable, but it did not discuss how the information system might be designed to encourage this behavior. In 1978 the idea of such a system was appealing, but there were real issues of feasibility. In the first decade of the 21st century, such an approach may now be feasible.

Hedberg and Jonsson's (1978) paper raises two related questions that address the ability or willingness of the decision maker to follow Hedberg and Jonsson's injunction:

- If the decision maker's expertise takes the form of a thorough understanding of the existing problem (explicit knowledge), does this affect his/her ability to consider alternative formulations of the problem?
- How does the reward system impact the desire and/or willingness of a manager to consider radical solutions even if they are suggested by the database?

INFORMAL DATA SEARCHES

The previous discussion has its own implicit assumption. The assumption is that all data are acquired though the organization's information system. In the traditional manufacturing firm where managers are concerned with relatively routine processes, this may be the case. It is what Anthony (1965) characterized as control at the operations level. P-A models and approaches related to residual income have attempted to create the appearance of structure in tasks at the managerial control level. There are, however, situations where the decision maker is better off if he/she is able to anticipate the problem and have the appropriate data available rather than have to react to the problem when it occurs. Information of this sort is likely to come from sources outside of the formal information system. Feldman and March (1981) suggest that information of this type is acquired informally, e.g. through interacting with other members of the organization. In the information age, the informal interaction with other individuals has been supplemented by the world-wide-web and organization wide intranets (see Lekse, 2003). Data acquired through informal searches of informal sources may be stored by the decision maker in case they should become relevant at a later date.

Clearly, this raises many more questions than one can readily answer, but it does not deny the relevance of the central question they raise: To what extent do decision makers rely on informal information sources/searches? This question is of particular importance for the question of the way managers deal with qualitative data which we will address later.

LEARNING

It could be argued that the earlier discussion of the impact of accounting information systems on managers' cognitive structures could be considered to be learning. However, this change in the decision maker's model could have taken place for a variety of reasons. One set of reasons would reflect confusion from or random adjustment to the new database. It also could reflect systematic attempts by the decision maker to improve his or her decision model/cognitive structure.

This is only one aspect of learning in management accounting research. The topic can be divided into two broad categories – organizational learning and learning by individuals and groups. There is an extensive literature on organizational learning – and a fair amount of controversy – in the organizational behavior literature. See Argote and Ophir (2001). I will not discuss it here.

Individual and group learning is of potential interest to management accounting. However, much of the existing literature focuses on production learning curves. This type of learning is useful in measurement of costs for forecasts or standards. However, a more interesting set of questions related to learning focus on learning as an outcome, a dependent variable. They are interested in identifying those activities that result in learning taking place and, by implication, which do not. Examples of questions of interest include:

- What role do incentives play in encouraging learning? Do incentive schemes differ in their ability to stimulate learning?
- Does the complexity of the task affect the extent to which individuals attempt to learn?
- Is there an interaction between task difficulty and the incentive system?

The basic concern of all three of these questions is the extent to which learning is a natural response to a task, i.e. a natural desire to do better, or whether it is the result of a rational allocation of cognitive effort? A question that one of our students is exploring is the relative effectiveness of a piece rate versus a tournament in motivating the participants to expend effort to understand a task. It would appear reasonable to assume that greater potential rewards do lead to greater effort. The effectiveness of the that effort may be related to the amount of learning taking place. It is the issue of working smarter not just working harder.

A second set of questions relate to how we can better understand what facilitates or impedes learning.

- What is the role of decision aids in learning?
- Is there any personality typology that helps to identify those more able to learn in complex tasks?
- Issues in the human-computer interface from the perspective of accounting data.

The impact of decision aids has been researched by behavioral accounting researchers in auditing. The other two questions are potentially interesting questions that have not been extensively investigated in accounting. Undoubtedly Information Systems researchers have investigated these issues.

QUALITATIVE MEASURES

The question of the role of qualitative measures is one with which we, as academics, should not consider lightly. In the tenure and/or promotion decision we are asked to be a referee for someone in that position and are asked to deal with a variant of this problem – the need to rank journals or accept the school's ranking of them. Different schools have different lists. The quality of a paper as you may review it is less important than the ranking of the journal in which it is published. My intention in raising this issue is not to discuss the merits of this approach or any given list. Rather, I offer it as a familiar example of this issue with which we all are too familiar.

Many recent developments in management controls have involved the need to integrate qualitative measures into the performance evaluation process (see Banker, Potter & Srinivasan, 2000; Kaplan & Norton, 1992). This integration is most easily accomplished if the qualitative measures can be integrated with the quantitative measures. The answer quite often takes the form of quantifying the qualitative measures through a variety of procedures such as Likert scales, e.g. scales reflecting how satisfied a customer is with the service on a scale from "1 to n" or how likely the customer is to return on such a scale.

I suspect that the act of quantifying a subjective "feeling" raises some questions we have not researched in management accounting. Examples include:

- How well do the quantified measures (the surrogate) predict future behavior (the principle)?
- Do the users of these quantified measures react the same way to the reported Likert scale scores, e.g. 5 on a 7 point scale, as they would to verbal anchor, e.g. "moderately likely to return"?

- How does the quantification of the variable affect the users' perceptions of the measure's accuracy, relevance and their confidence in it relative to a qualitative (verbal) reporting of the same property?

This is not a new problem for accounting researchers. Auditors have been forced to interpret verbal descriptions of risk in financial reporting rules. Typically these problems have involved contingencies facing the firm and risk of loss. Research in this area may provide a model for management accountants to follow when undertaking research in this area. For examples, see Harrison and Tomassini (1989) and Hoffman and Patton (2002).

In a recent archival study, Leidtka (2002) examined which financial and non-financial measures contribute to explaining performance in the airline industry. He utilized a variety of publicly available financial and non-financial data to create factors measuring financial and non-financial performance measures. His data showed that two of the three non-financial performance measures did meet the Cronbach alpha test and added information about firms in the airline industry beyond that provided by the financial factors. The two non-financial factors that did provide added information were related to passenger safety and passenger volume. Both of these factors relied on relatively objective quantitative measures. The third factor that had the lowest Cronbach alpha (0.44; next lowest was 0.61) was customer satisfaction. Two of the three elements in this factor relied on customers' complaints to the U.S. Department of Transportation. This means that the third factor is a much more subjective (qualitative) measure than the other two non-financial measures used in this study.

INTER-FIRM CO-OPERATIVE ARRANGEMENTS

Inter-firm co-operative arrangements include a variety of inter-firm agreements. These relationships range from outsourcing to jointly owned and managed ventures. By definition, these arrangements would include simple contractual agreements for one firm to provide a good or service to another, e.g. the outsourcing of information processing services. However, the concern here is with those relationships where there is a significant degree of interdependence between the parties. The inter-firm relationships create what would at least appear to be a different control problem. Some of the individuals over whom a firm's management may desire to exercise control are, in fact, independent of the firm, i.e. they are employees of another firm with which the firm has a relationship.

These relationships can be described along six dimensions:

- The manner in which the relationship has evolved, i.e. the party's history.
- The extent of each party's relative and absolute levels of commitment.

- The symmetry of rewards to the parties.
- The degree of uncertainty (risk) present for each party.
- The expected duration of the agreement.
- The extent of mutual trust.

Each of these characteristics affects the way in which control problems will emerge and how the firm can and should respond to them. The manner in which the firms' interrelationship evolved is important because in certain cases this will affect the amount of perceived uncertainty and the degree of mutual trust.

The extant literature can be said to fit into three broad categories – traditional outsourcing, co-operative arrangements, and joint ventures. Traditional out-sourcing is a contract between the firm and another party to provide a particular intermediate product or service. Co-operative arrangements are those setting in which the firm and the other party work together in the preproduction phase of the process to develop the intermediate product or design the system. It differs from simple outsourcing in the degree to which the parties will work together at the design stage. In a joint venture the co-operating firms work together to establish a separate firm that will perform the desired task(s).

Cooper and Slagmulder (2004) described the evolution of a subcontracting relationship between two firms. The relationship gradually matured from one of purchaser-supplier of commodity components to a co-operative arrangement where the purchaser and supplier worked together to design a significant com-ponent for the purchaser's new product line that meets the needs of the purchaser and is designed to facilitate efficient production by the supplier.

What one learns from this case is how the prior relationship between the purchaser and supplier can create trust. This, in turn, would lead to greater symmetry in the two parties' commitment and rewards and would reduce the uncertainty due to potentially opportunistic behavior on the part of either party. As in the case of intra-firm control issues, mutual trust permitted more open and less costly control techniques.

This is not necessarily the way joint ventures evolve. Many involve firms with obvious commonality of interests but little history of past relationships. This can mean that the firms have a significant level of commitment and that the potential for mutual rewards is good. However, as Williamson (1991) argues, this is the setting that can lead to opportunistic behavior by one of the parties. What managers want to know is how our understanding of the problems inherent in the control process can help them minimize the risk of opportunism. Sampler and Short co-edited a special issue of the *Journal of Management Studies* (1998) containing papers on what they chose to call "new organizational arrangements." In this case, the new arrangements were concerned primarily with joint ventures where two or more firms organize a separate firm to undertake certain agreed upon activities.

Baiman and Rajan (2002) analyzed the problem primarily from the perspective of traditional outsourcing of components and services from the P-A perspective. The paper focuses primarily on the literature on incomplete contracts. It also introduces the notion of trust as an element in the contracting relationship. As has been the case in other formal P-A models in management accounting, their paper has the potential to provide valuable insights into how others may investigate the problem.

CONCLUSIONS

It is difficult to summarize the various topics discussed since each topic is, in itself, a summary. Rather, it is better to view each section as a potential area for future research offered for consideration. Even if the topics have merit – and there is no reason to believe that all should – you are interested only in finding that small corner of management accounting research that is of interest to you.

There are other areas that could expand our boundaries. While some may have been omitted because of space limitations, many others were omitted out of ignorance. They will be ascertained most readily by framing problems that are important to management accounting and looking outward to see if any other areas offer potentially useful solutions. The result can be exhilarating. We also can expand our boundaries by examining other areas where our tools could yield valuable insights. Many areas are calling for enhanced accountability, e.g. the case of NASA discussed earlier and in education and the No Child Left behind Act. What are the potential problems in measuring and monitoring presented by this act?

Many of the topics suggest studies that are behavioral. They are amenable to surveys, field studies, and experiments. While I have tried to avoid this bias, we all are victims of our "prejudices" and mine are well known.

One characteristic that does appear to run through the various topics suggested is a greater concern with the macro view – firm as a whole and organization. They also reflect issues of concern to managers rather than strictly a product of academic research in related disciplines such as economic, psychology, or sociology.

Like most suggestions for research, the ideas clearly are that – suggestions. I have tried to raise potentially researchable issue where I saw them. If I have identified useful areas, the ultimate benefit will be because some other researcher saw more than I did. I hope that I have not offered too many blind alleys.

ACKNOWLEDGMENTS

The author would like to thank the participants at the Advances in Management Accounting Conference on Management Accounting Research: New
Methodologies and Paradigms and the editors for many helpful comments.

REFERENCES

Akerlof, G. (1982). Labor contracts as partial gift exchange. *Quarterly Journal of Economics*, *97*(4),
    543–569.
Anthony, R. (1965). *Planning and control systems: A framework for analysis*. Boston: Division of
    Research Graduate School of Business Administration, Harvard University.
Anthony, R. (2003). Management accounting: A personal history. *Journal of Management Accounting
    Research*, *15*, 249–253.
Argote, L., & Ophir, R. (2001). Intraorganizational learning. Working Paper, Carnegie Mellon
    University Graduate School of Industrial Administration.
Ashton, R. (1974). The predictive ability criterion and user prediction models. *The Accounting Review*,
    49(4), 719–732.
Ashton, R. (1976). Cognitive changes induced by accounting changes: Experimental evidence on the
    functional fixation hypothesis. *Journal of Accounting Research-Studies in Human Information
    Processing in Accounting*, *14*(Suppl.), 1–12.
Baiman, S. (1982). Agency research in managerial accounting. *Journal of Accounting Literature*, *1*,
    154–226.
Baiman, S. (1990). Agency research in managerial accounting: A second look. *Accounting,
    Organizations and Society*, *15*(4), 341–372.
Baiman, S., & Rajan, M. (2002). Incentive issues in inter-firm relationships. *Accounting, Organizations
    and Society*, *27*(3), 213–238.
Banker, R., Potter, G., & Srinivasan, D. (2000). An empirical investigation of an incentive plan that
    includes non-financial measures. *The Accounting Review*, *75*(1), 93–114.
Birnberg, J. (1998a). The evolution of control in organizations. *Behavioral Research In Accounting-
    Research Conference Supplement to Volume*, *10*, 21–46.
Birnberg, J. (1998b). Control in inter-firm co-operative arrangements. *Journal of Management Studies*,
    35(4), 4421–4428.
Birnberg, J., Pondy, L., & Davis, C. L. (1970). An experimental study of decision-making. *Management
    Science-Applications*, *2*.
Birnberg, J., Shields, M., & Young, S. M. (1990). The case for multiple methods in empirical
    management accounting research. *Journal of Management Accounting Research*, *2*, 33–66.
Birnberg, J., & Snodgrass, C. (1988). Culture and control. *Accounting, Organizations and Society*,
    13(5), 447–464.
Camerer, C. (2001). *Behavioral economics*. Princeton, NJ: Princeton University Press.
Chow, C., Shields, M., & Wu, A. (1999). The importance of national culture for management
    controls for multi-national operations. *Accounting, Organizations and Society*, *24*(5/6),
    441–461.
Colletti, A., Sedatole, K., & Towry, K. (2003). The effects of control systems on teams and alliances:
    Trust and cooperation in new collaborative environments. Working Paper, University of Texas.

Cooper, R., & Slagmulder, R. (2004). Interorganizational cost management and relational context. *Accounting, Organizations and Society, 29*(1), 1–26.

Covaleski, M., Evans, J. H., III, Luft, J., & Shields, M. (2003). Budgeting research: Three theoretical perspectives and criteria for selective integration. *Journal of Management Accounting Research, 13*, 3–49.

Drake, A., Haka, S., & Ravenscraft, S. (1999). Cost system and incentive structure effects on innovation, efficiency and profitability in teams. *The Accounting Review, 74*(3), 323–345.

Elsmore, P. (2001). *Organisational culture: Organisational change?* Aldershot, England: Gower Publishing.

Evans, J. H., III, Moser, D., & Kim, C. (1995). The effects of horizontal and exchange equity on tax reporting behavior. *The Accounting Review, 76*(4).

Fehr, E., & Gachter, S. (2000). Fairness and retaliation: The economics of reciprocity. Working Paper, University of Zurich.

Fehr, E., & Schmidt, K. (1999). A theory of fairness, competition and cooperation. *Quarterly Journal of Economics, 114*(3), 817–868.

Feldman, M., & March, J. (1981). Information in organizations as signal and symbol. *Administrative Science Quarterly, 26*, 171–186.

Fon, V., & Parisi, F. (2003). The limits of reciprocity for social cooperation. Working Paper, George Mason University School of Law.

Granovetter, M. (1985). Economic action, social structure, and embeddedness. *American Journal of Sociology, 78*, 1360–1380.

Hannan, R. L. (2001). The effect of firm profit on fairness perceptions, wages and employee effort. Working Paper, Georgia State University.

Harrison, G., & McKinnon, L. (1999). Cross-cultural research in management control system design: A review of the current state. *Accounting, Organizations and Society, 24*(5/6), 483–506.

Harrison, K., & Tomassini, L. (1989). Judging the probability of a contingent loss: An emperical study. *Contemporary Accounting Research, 5*(2), 642–648.

Hedberg, & Jonsson, J. (1978). Designing semi-confusing information systems for organizations in changing environments. *Accounting, Organizations and Society, 3*(1), 47–64.

Henrich, J., Boyd, R., Bowles, S., Camerer, C., Fehr, E., Gintis, H., & McElreath, R. (2001). In search of homo economicus: Behavioral experiments in 15 small-scale societies. *American Economic Review, 91*(3), 71–78.

Hodge, F., Kennedy, J., & Maines, L. (forthcoming). Does search facilitating technology improve the transparency of financial reporting? *The Accounting Review.*

Hoffman, V., & Patton, J. (2002). How are contingency accruals affected by alternative reporting criteria and incentives? *Journal of Accounting and Public Policy, 21*, 151–167.

Hofstede, G. (1980). *Cultural consequences: International differrences in work values.* Beverly Hills, CA: Sage.

Horngren, C. (1962). *Cost accounting: A managerial emphasis.* Englewood Cliffs, NJ: Prentice-Hall.

Hufnagel, E., & Birnberg, J. (1994). Perceived chargeback system fairness: A laboratory study. *Accounting Management and Information Technologies, 4*(1), 1–22.

Ittner, C. (2003, May 15–16). Performance measurement: The state of the art. Paper Presented at AIMA Conference on Management Accounting Research: New Methodologies and Paradigms. Monterey, CL.

Kachelmeier, S., Smith, J. R., & Yancey, W. (1994). Budgets as credible threat: An experimental study of cheap talk and forward induction. *Journal of Management Accounting Research, 6*, 144–174.

Kaplan, R., & Norton, D. (1992). The balanced scorecard-measures that drive performance. *Harvard Business Review, 70*(1), 70–79.

Kim, C., Evans, J. H., III, & Moser, D. (2004). Economic and equity effects on reporting behavior. Working Paper, University of Pittsburgh.

Leana, C., & van Buren, H. (1999). Organizational social capital and employment practices. *Academy of Management Review, 24*(3), 538–555.

Leidtka, S. (2002). The information content of nonfinancial performance measures in the airline industry. *Journal of Business Finance & Accounting, 29*(7), 1105–1121.

Lekse, W. (2003). *Managers' knowledge exposure: Learning or technology.* Doctoral Dissertation, University of Pittsburgh.

Libby, R. (1976). Discussion of cognitive changes induced by accounting changes: Experimental evidence on the functional fixation hypothesis. *Journal of Accounting Research-Studies in Human Information Processing in Accounting, 14*(Suppl.), 16–24.

Libby, T. (2001). Referent cognitions and budgetary fairness: A research note. *Journal of Management Accounting Research, 13*, 91–105.

Lorange, P., & Scott-Morton, M. (1974). Framework for management control systems. *Sloan Management Review*, 47–56.

Luft, J. (1997). Fairness, ethics and the effect of management accounting on transaction costs. *Journal of Management Accounting Research, 9*, 197–214.

McCall, M., & Kaplan, R. (1985). *Whatever it takes: Decisionmakers at work.* Englewood Cliffs, NJ: Prentice-Hall.

Merchant, K., Van der Stede, W., & Zheng, L. (2003). Disciplinary constraints on the advancement of knowledge: The case of organizational incentive systems. *Accounting, Organizations and Society, 28*(2/3), 251–286.

Ouchi, W. (1977). The relationship between organizational structure and organizational control. *Administrative Science Quarterly, 22*, 95–113.

Putnam, R. (1995). Bowling alone: America's declining social capital. *Journal of Democracy, 6*, 65–78.

Roth, A. (1995). Introduction to experimental economics. In: J. Kagel & A. Roth (Eds), *Handbook of Experimental Economics* (pp. 3–109). Princeton: Princeton University Press.

Roth, A., Prasnikar, V., Okuno-Fujiwara, M., & Zamir, S. (1991). Bargaining and market behavior in Jerusalem, Ljubjana, Pittsburgh and Tokyo: An experimental study. *American Economic Review, 81*(5), 1068–1095.

Rowe, C. (2003). The effect of accounting report structure and organization structure on informal control and performance in cross-functional teams. Working Paper, Arizona State University.

Sampler, J., & Short, J. (1998). Special issue: Sustainability of new organizational arrangements. *Journal of Management Studies, 35*(4).

Shields, M., & Shields, J. (1998). Antecedents of participative budgeting, Accounting. *Organizations and Society, 23*(1), 49–76.

Simon, H., & Hayes, J. (1976). The understanding process: Problem isomorphs. *Cognitive Psychology, 8*, 165–190.

Sunstein, C. (2003). Moral heuristics. Working Paper, University of Chicago Law School.

Thaler, R. (Ed.) (1993). *Advances in behavioral finance.* New York: Russell Sage Foundation.

Trompenaars, F. (1993). *Riding the waves of culture.* London: Economist Books.

Williamson, O. (1991). Comparative economic organization: The comparison of discrete structural alternatives. *Administrative Science Quarterly, 36*, 269–296.

Young, S. M., Fisher, J., & Lindquist, T. (1993). The effects of inter-group competition and intra-group cooperation on slack and output in a manufacturing setting. *The Accounting Review, 68*(3), 466–481.

INNOVATION STRATEGY AND THE USE OF PERFORMANCE MEASURES

Tony Davila, Marc J. Epstein and Sharon F. Matusik

ABSTRACT

Many corporations have annual expenditures in research and development in the range of billions of U.S. dollars. Senior managers have often been frustrated by the lack of innovation in their organizations and have been looking for better ways to implement an innovation strategy. To provide initial evidence on this significant topic, we conduct an empirical examination and contribute to the existing literature in two important areas. First, we examine how managers choose what measures to pay attention to in managing the innovation process – defined as the process of creative definition, development, and commercialization of substantially new products, services or businesses. We find that managers use measures about specific phases of the innovation process together. For example, measures that inform about the execution stage of the innovation process are grouped together rather than being grouped with measures informative about other phases of the innovation process, such as market performance. This pattern "focused" around specific phases is in contrast to the alternative "balanced" pattern where managers would use measures from various phases of the process together. This result provides the first empirical test of how managers combine measures to filter information about business processes. It also provides important new evidence on the use of measures and provides guidance to the design of measurement systems. Second, this paper provides empirical

Advances in Management Accounting
Advances in Management Accounting, Volume 13, 27–58
ISSN: 1474-7871/doi:10.1016/S1474-7871(04)13002-5

evidence on the relationship between innovation strategy and the use of measures. Though previous studies have linked innovation strategy and the use of management control systems in general, there is little empirical data on the relationship of strategy and the use of measures and on the innovation process. We find that different dimensions of strategy are positively associated with how managers use different types of measures.

1. INNOVATION STRATEGY AND THE USE OF PERFORMANCE MEASURES

Innovation – the creative definition, development, and commercialization of substantially new products, services or businesses – facilitates the development of new sources of competitive advantage and, as such, it has become an important process to the success of companies (Tushman & O'Reilly, 1997). While it is commonly accepted that succeeding in this process depends heavily on intangible elements like creativity or risk-taking behavior, only recently have companies moved from a hands-off approach to innovation, where resources were invested with the hope that innovation would follow, to a more managed process (Wheelwright & Clark, 1992). This new approach relies on formal systems to manage the process from the resources required to innovate through the management of the process itself to the outputs. Within the formal systems that are used to manage innovation, measurement systems play an important role (Meyer, 1994). Measurement systems are one of the sources of information used to assess the state of the innovation process. However, little is known about how top managers use measures: (1) what is the pattern of use – in other words, which measures managers analyze together to be informed about business processes (and in particular the innovation process): do they use together measures that inform about a particular stage of the process or do they combine measures from different phases to have an overall perspective of the process; and (2) how the innovation strategy of the company affects the use of these measures. Evidence on these questions is relevant to advance our understanding of measurement systems.

The study is based on a unique database from a leading innovation consulting firm. The data includes the responses of 675 companies to a survey about their innovation practices and, in particular, to how they approach innovation measurement. The database provides a unique empirical setting to provide initial evidence on how managers use measurement systems. The paper makes several contributions to our understanding of the design and use measurement systems. First, the results of the study provide evidence on how managers use measures to monitor the innovation process. Our results indicate that managers use together measures that are informative about a particular phase in the innovation process (focused pattern) – from inputs, execution, and outputs of the process, rather than using together measures that provide an overview of the different phases of this process (balanced pattern). This result provides initial empirical evidence suggesting that managers tend to focus their attention on particular phases of a process at the expense of potentially overlooking relevant developments in other phases. Second, this paper also contributes to our understanding of the relevance of measurement systems to monitor innovation. We find that companies following an innovation-based strategy make greater use overall of their measurement systems to track innovation. Furthermore, the results indicate managers who perceive that their companies have better codification based capabilities (technology management and process management capabilities) use innovation measures more extensively. These findings extend previous research on the relationship between strategy and the use of measurement systems to the innovation process.

The rest of the paper is structured as follows. The next section reviews the theory and develops the arguments explored in our research. Section 3 describes the database and the research design. Section 4 presents the results and Section 5 concludes.

2. THEORY

Measurement systems supply managers with important information about business processes. However, not all the measures are equally relevant and managers filter them to devote more attention to the most relevant ones. Information processing theory (Tushman & Nadler, 1978) suggests that managers do not filter information from measures in a random way; rather they adopt certain patterns. These patterns help managers avoid information overload and focus their attention on information most relevant to their decision making process (Schick et al., 1990). Understanding these patterns – how managers use different measures to combine the information – is key to the design of measurement systems and to advance the knowledge about the use of these systems. Our first research question examines how managers use various innovation measures – in particular which measures are used in combination. The results provide initial empirical evidence on this relevant question. We hypothesize two alternative patterns to use measures and facilitate the filtering of the information that these measures supply. The first one suggests that managers will use measures that inform about certain phases of the innovation process together – for example the execution of innovation or the financial outcome of innovation. Multiple measures may complement each other and provide better information about critical phases in the process. We call this pattern a focused pattern. The second, that we call a balanced pattern, indicates that managers use measures from different phases of the innovation process together. This pattern provides an overview of the entire process and takes advantage of leading-lagging relationships among measures rather than emphasize a particular phase as the focused pattern suggests.

Our second research question studies the relationship between the importance of innovation strategy and how managers use measures to track innovation processes. Prior research has documented the relevance of management accounting to the implementation of strategy and has provided empirical evidence consistent with a strong association between the design of management control systems and business strategy (Govindarajan & Gupta, 1985; Langfield-Smith, 1997; Simons, 1987). These conclusions have been extended to the relationship between product strategy and the design of management control systems within product development (Davila, 2000). However, whether these theoretical predictions hold for measurement systems within the innovation process – characterized by the relevance of hard to quantify performance dimensions – is an open question. A positive association would indicate that measurement systems are relevant to the innovation process – key to the success of organizations – and efforts to better understand and design these systems are important. We further adopt two different definitions of strategy (Mintzberg et al., 1998). The first interprets strategy from a positioning perspective (Porter, 1980). The second definition adopts a resource-based view of the firm and interprets strategy as capabilities (Wernerfelt, 1984). This last interpretation of strategy is in contrast to previous management control literature that has typically focused on strategy as positioning.

2.1. The Design of Performance Measurement Systems in the Innovation Process

Individual performance measures fail to give complete information about business processes because of the noise (Banker & Datar, 1989) and lack of congruency (Feltham & Xie, 1994) that characterize them. Some measures reflect events that are outside the control of managers increasing the noise of the measure. Some other measures only capture part of managerial effort relevant to performance and suffer from low congruency. The distinction between leading and lagging measures is an example of lack of congruency; where leading indicators fail to capture the effort that affects current performance and lagging indicators fail to capture effort that affects future performance. The solution proposed is to combine multiple performance measures into a measurement system (Kaplan & Norton, 1992; Meyer, 1994). A new measure is useful to managers if its incremental information content (Holmstrom, 1979) regardless of whether the measurement system is used for contracting or information updating (Narayanan & Davila, 1998) or, alternatively, its ability to communicate strategy (Kaplan & Norton, 2001a, b) are greater than the costs associated with information processing and the possibility of information overload. Recent developments in the design of measurement systems combine financial and non-financial indicators (Epstein & Manzoni, 1998; Kaplan & Norton, 1992, 2001a, b), where non-financial information is associated with future financial performance (Banker et al., 2000; Ittner & Larcker, 1998) and provides information beyond accounting numbers.

The relevance of multiple performance measures has also been highlighted in the innovation management literature. In R&D settings, evidence indicates that several non-financial metrics are combined to track the evolution of individual projects, while a combination of financial and non-financial metrics is used at the business unit level (Donnelly, 2000). Cordero (1990) proposes a framework to measure innovation focused on the resources required for innovation and the commercial and technical outputs of the research process and highlights the importance of using these measures during the planning and execution of projects. Financial measures have also been proposed to evaluate the innovation process of platform products (Meyer et al., 1997). Within the management accounting literature, Hertenstein and Platt (1997) provide descriptive statistics on the use of different financial and non-financial measures in a particular innovation process: product development. These authors (Hertenstein & Platt, 2000) also find that managers are not satisfied with existing measures within the product development process and that the link between performance measures and strategy is weak.

Measurement systems must balance the tension between supplying a rich set of measures (Griffin & Page, 1996) that captures all the information relevant to managers (Tushman & Nadler, 1978) and avoiding too many measures that may be too costly to collect, administer, and interpret or that may lead to information overload (Schick et al., 1990). When faced with multiple measures, managers devote their attention to a subset of measures in an effort to balance the tension between relevance and information processing costs. Thus, understanding how managers use the various measures (Libby, 1981) becomes important to the design of measurement systems that are effective in managing this tension. Existing research is consistent with this conclusion and indicates that managers focus on a subset of all the measures within a measurement system rather than processing all the information that they receive (Lipe & Salterio, 2000). To analyze which subset of measures receives most attention, information processing theory suggests two alternatives. The first alternative is to choose a subset of measures that focuses on a particular phase in the innovation process. Such a subset provides a rich information set about this phase of the overall process. Multiple measures of the same phenomenon may also complement each other and provide managers with a richer picture. When several measures are reported together, the aspects that some of them are not able to capture are reflected in the other measures to give different points of view on the phenomenon of interest. Another reason for using multiple measures focused around certain aspects of the innovation process is to supply a certain degree of redundancy required to assess the reliability of the conclusions that managers obtain from the measurement system (Nonaka, 1990). This information set would allow managers to quickly react to deviations at this critical phase at the expense of having a broader perspective of the overall process. For example, if managing resources is the most critical and complex aspect of the innovation process, measures that inform about resource allocation and resource usage will receive most attention.

The previous paragraph suggests that managers examine measures that focus on certain phases within the innovation process together. The alternative view is that managers do not focus on particular phases of the innovation process but rather have an overall perspective of the process. The advantage of such an information processing pattern is that managers have a good understanding of what is happening throughout the innovation process without being narrowly focused on a single aspect. The drawback is that the information set does not provide as much depth within a particular phase of the process. If managers rely on this model, then a subset of measures that receive most attention will balance different aspects of the innovation process. For example, managers will monitor measures that track resources, processes, non-financial measures of output, and financial performance rather than actively focusing their attention on measures that provide detailed information but limited to one step in the innovation process.

The previous arguments do not suggest that one alternative is superior to the other or that a mix solution may be optimal; rather, they reflect two alternative approaches to information processing.[1] The exploratory question of whether one alternative better reflects managers' information processing pattern is the empirical question that we address. The evidence is informative to our understanding of the design of measurement systems. Because of the exploratory nature of the question, we do not translate this question into a hypothesis.

2.2. The use of Innovation Measures and Innovation Strategy

Management control literature has consistently found business strategy as relevant to the design of management control systems. Govindarajan and Gupta (1985) identify differences in the design of formal systems between companies pursuing a cost leadership strategy and companies following a differentiation strategy. Similarly, Simons (1991) reports that companies pursuing different strategies – defender, prospector, or reactor – design their formal systems differently. The strategy context also affects appraisal and compensation systems (e.g. Balkin & Gomez-Mejia, 1987; Gupta, 1987; Kerr, 1985). Langfield-Smith (1997) provides a review of this literature and presents strong evidence supporting the association between formal systems and strategy. Within the innovation process, Davila (2000) in his study of formal systems in product development finds an association between innovation strategies and the design of these systems at a product development level.

The previous findings focus on management control systems, but do not address the relevance of measurement systems to the innovation process. There are two views on the role of measurement in innovation. On the one hand, because of the intangible elements that characterize the innovation process, intense attention devoted to measurement systems will shift attention away from these elements that cannot be measured and accordingly may be counterproductive to the innovation performance. Moreover, measurement systems can be fruitfully replaced with alternative management approaches such as intense interpersonal communication. If this is the case, then measurement systems are not relevant to the innovation process whose characteristics are better suited for different management tools. On the other hand, measurement systems may provide the underlying information to support the interaction needed to understand these intangibles and frequent updating of the measures facilitate the management process.

If measurement systems are important to manage the innovation process, then companies where innovation plays a more relevant role in their strategy are expected to use innovation measures more than their less innovative counterparts.[2] Hoque and James (2000) provide preliminary empirical evidence and find that the proportion of sales coming from new products is positively related to the number of new product development-related measures. This finding suggests that measures may be important to the innovation process.

We argue that the resolution between these two views requires an understanding of the firm's innovation strategy. We examine innovation strategy in two ways to address this issue: (i) the strategic positioning of the firm's innovation strategy; and (ii) the innovation capabilities of the firm.

Strategic positioning for innovation. Within the organizational control and product development literatures, time and cost based strategies have been identified as two different approaches to innovation (e.g. Davila, 2000; Miller & Roth, 1994). Time-to-market is a recognized source of differentiation and competitive advantage (Brown & Eisenhardt, 1995; Patterson, 1993). Other companies follow a cost-based innovation approach and use innovations to produce similar products more cost effectively or to produce different, lower cost products that appeal to a different set of customer preferences. For example, target costing uses product redesign to reduce overall costs (Cooper & Slagmulder, 1999).

The specific measures used should vary based on how the firm is trying to use innovation. Managers focus on a subset of all the measures within a measurement system rather than processing all the information that they receive (Lipe & Salterio, 2000). We argue that time versus cost based innovation strategies will be associated with the use of different kinds of measures. In particular, firms that are using a time-based approach to innovation will focus on measures that will speed the time to market of innovations. Such measures will focus around inputs and execution in order to manage the speed of the development process. We also argue that such firms will focus on externally driven measures for innovation success because these firms perceive themselves to be in a race with competitors to most rapidly meet customer needs. Accordingly, these firms are oriented towards external constituencies, such as competitors, customers, and forces that may influence customer preferences. Conversely, firms taking a cost based approach to innovation will focus on different kinds of measures. In particular, these firms will assess outsourcing and financial measures in order to orient activities around meeting specific cost goals. Like firms pursuing time based strategies, we also predict these firms will use execution based metrics as well to manage the innovation process to be most cost effective. Accordingly, we expect:

Hypothesis 1a. Companies pursuing a time-based innovation strategy will use input, execution, and external focused measurement systems.

Hypothesis 1b. Companies pursuing a cost-based innovation strategy will use outsource, execution, and financial focused measurement systems.

Capabilities for innovation. Strategy is a concept that has different definitions (Mintzberg, 1998). The previous hypotheses interpret strategy as positioning (Porter, 1980) and refer to the source of competitive advantage that the firm relies on to outperform competitors. An alternative definition of strategy views competitive advantage as internal to the company and linked to its capabilities and resource endowments (Prahalad & Hamel, 1990; Wernerfelt, 1984). Capabilities allow firms to combine and coordinate resources (Amit & Schoemaker, 1993; Teece, Pisano & Shuen, 1997). Capabilities include routines that facilitate the learning process (Nelson & Winter, 1982) and the interaction required to combine tacit knowledge and explicit knowledge (Nonaka, 1994). Central to the creation and evolution of capabilities are learning mechanisms such as knowledge articulation and codification (Zollo & Winter, 2002). Codification makes for an easier transfer of knowledge (Hansen, 1999; Zander & Kogut, 1995; Szulanski, 1996) and for the recombination of knowledge stocks that may stimulate knowledge creation in the form of innovation (Nonaka, 1994). Thus, the firm's ability to codify and transfer knowledge may affect its ability to achieve a competitive advantage.

The resource based view has been applied to product development as a particular case of the innovation process (Brown & Eisenhardt, 1995; Verona, 1999). However, the product development literature generally finds a negative association between formalization and innovation activities (e.g. Aiken & Hage, 1971; Burns & Stalker, 1961; Thompson, 1965), particularly in service firms, early stages of innovation adoption, and innovations that are broad in scope (Damanpour, 1991).[3] Since formalization refers to the amount of written rules, policies and procedures in an organization, it is related to codification which refers to the ability of the firm to make explicit its knowledge, routines, and processes. Accordingly, there is an apparent disconnect in the literature. On the one hand, greater codification facilitates knowledge transfers, and the fusion of different kinds of knowledge, which may stimulate new knowledge creation. However, empirical evidence suggests that formalization undermines innovation.

We argue that what is unaccounted for in these two schools of thought is a more detailed analysis of the relationship between capabilities, strategy, and measurement systems. Historically, researchers found tradeoffs between different kinds of formal control systems (e.g. behavioral or output controls) based upon the nature of the tasks the organization is trying to control and the organizational environment the organization is trying to control (Eisenhardt, 1985; Kirsch, 1996; Ouchi, 1979; Snell, 1992). In his seminal paper, Ouchi (1979) uses the R&D setting as an example of a context in which it is difficult to identify both the precise behaviors that will lead to a scientific breakthrough and it is also difficult to identify desired outcomes in a way that lends itself to meaningful measurement of scientists' output. Accordingly, the innovation context is one in which Ouchi argues informal (clan) control is more appropriate than formal controls. His argument is based on the fact that the process of innovation is inherently uncertain, with low behavioral observability and task programmability. His arguments are consistent with most of the empirical observations discussed in the previous section but inconsistent with Cardinal (2001). She finds that within the pharmaceutical industry, a broad range of formal controls (input, output, behavioral) are associated with improved innovation performance (Cardinal, 2001). In high-technology settings, Jelinek and Schoonhoven (1990) also find that structure and formality are important for innovation.

We posit that the puzzle within the current literature stems from assuming that all innovation relies on the same type of capabilities. In Ouchi's R&D example and the empirical findings consistent with his arguments, the assumption is that innovation capabilities are of an intangible nature. In contrast, the codification literature within the resource-based view of the firm argues that capabilities that can be codified are valuable and that the innovation process can to some extent rely on formalizing these capabilities. In essence, these two schools dissent on their perceptions of the relevance of codification as a way to develop innovations.

The measurement system, which is the focus of this study, is one through which implicit knowledge is articulated or codified (Zollo & Winter, 2002). The previous discussion indicates that firms with innovation capabilities grounded in their ability to codify knowledge will rely on more formal measurement systems. However, firms that rely on intangible capabilities, such as a culture oriented around innovation or team-based skills, which are embedded within the individuals of the organization will rely to a lesser extent on formalized systems such as measurement systems. If these intangible elements are important, intense attention devoted to measurement systems may shift attention away from elements like creativity, culture, or risk taking behavior that are harder to measure – for the reasons outlined in the previous section – but are still critical to success. This shift in managers' attention may be counterproductive to innovation performance. Moreover, measurement systems can be fruitfully replaced with alternative management approaches such as intense interpersonal communication (Gersick, 1989). If this is the case, then measurement systems are not relevant to the innovation process whose characteristics are better suited for different management tools. Accordingly, we hypothesize:

H2a. Codification based capabilities will be positively related to the use of formal measurement systems.

H2b. Intangible capabilities will be negatively related to the use of formal measurement systems.

3. RESEARCH DESIGN

3.1. Sample Selection

The sample consists of 675 companies included in the 1997 Arthur D. Little Global Innovation Survey. The survey is administered periodically and works much like a trade association survey where companies submit their data and in return obtain a summary of the results to gauge their position vis-à-vis other companies. The survey covers major themes in innovation management including sources of innovation, obstacles and catalysts of innovation, and human resource practices for innovation. In particular, it addresses how companies measure innovation.

The survey was mailed in 1997 to Arthur D. Little customers. The respondent was a top manager within the company usually the chief technology officer or R&D manager. The mailing was followed up with telephone calls to the contact person at each company (typically a top manager) to encourage participation and insure that the respondent was the appropriate manager. The response rate was 23%. As presented in Table 1 (Panel A), the sample includes companies from around the world. The sample spans a variety of industries mostly in the manufacturing sector (Panel B). Companies in the sample tend to be large companies with median sales between $1,000 million and $9,000 million and a median size of 4,000 employees. The median percentage of revenues devoted to R&D is between 3 and 5.9%. These descriptive statistics reflect the type of customers that are expected from a strategic consulting firm focused on technology management. While we cannot statistically assess whether the sample is representative of the consulting company's customer base, the various managers contacted at the firm agreed that the sample was representative. The descriptive statistics of the sample are comparable in terms of sales and employees to Fortune 500 companies.

3.2. Measurement of Variables

The *measures* section of the questionnaire is designed with a simple structure and the objective of facilitating the responses rather than communicating a measurement model. This research design is important given the exploratory nature of the research. Respondents were presented with 24 measures grouped under different section headings (see Table 2 for the list of measures).[4] The measures included in the questionnaire are those that, according to the experience of the consulting firm, companies use more often. While this criterion is based on experience rather than any theoretical foundation, it provides a list of measures that encompasses the most relevant ones to the management of innovation. A comparison with previous lists of measures in product development research (Hertenstein & Platt, 2000) uncovers significant overlap and supports the adequacy of the measures selected. For each measure, the respondent is asked to evaluate the use of the measure from "indicator not used" (0) to "indicator extensively used" (5).[5]

We use two different approaches to measure *innovation strategy* when interpreted as positioning. First, eight questionnaire items are used to capture the importance of innovation to the strategy of the company. To reduce the dimensionality of this set of questions we use factor analysis. Again the questions are anchored in a 1 to 5 scale where 1 is "low importance" and 5 is "high importance." A second approach to measuring innovation strategy is the intensity of the R&D process (as percentage of sales). While innovation is a broad

Table 1.   Descriptive Statistics.

Panel A: Distribution of the Sample Across Regions

Region	Number of Companies
North America	120
Central/South America	74
Europe	191
Asia-Pacific	201
Other	89
Total	675

Panel B: Distribution of the Sample Across Industries

Industry	Number of Companies
Automotive	37
Chemicals	64
Consumer goods	73
Energy	36
Engineering and manufacturing	108
Financial services/insurance	48
Health care providers	63
Information, media and electronics	56
Metals and resources	27
Other/not reported	163
Total	675

Panel C: Descriptive Statistics

	Q1	Q2	Q3
Sales (interval scale)	2	3	3
Employees	1,500	4,000	13,000
R&D/revenue (interval scale)	2	3	3

Note: The statistics for sales are based on five interval scales (less than $100 million (1), $100–$999 million (2), $1–$9 billion (3), $10–$20 billion (4), more than $20 billion (5)). R&D over revenues is also based on interval scales (less than 1.0% (1), 1.0–2.9% (2), 3.0–5.9% (3), 6.0–8.9% (4), 9.0–11.9% (5), more than 12% (6)). Q1 indicates 25% percentile, Q2 the 50% percentile and Q3 the 75% percentile.

process that encompasses many activities in the organization, in most companies innovation is translated into a tangible advantage through R&D. Companies that invest a large percentage of their sales into R&D are perceived as companies where innovation processes have a more important role. R&D intensity is an objective measure and thus taken directly from the relevant question.

Table 2.   Descriptive Statistics: Measures.

Measure	Q1	Q2	Q3	Mean	Std. Dev
Section 1					
Revenues	3	4	5	3.7	1.6
Profit margin	3	4	5	3.8	1.5
Market share	3	4	5	3.4	1.6
Market value added	1	3	4	2.3	1.7
Customer satisfaction (e.g. periodic survey)	2	3	4	3.1	1.5
Attractiveness of company to new hires (track unsolicited applications)	0	1	3	1.5	1.5
Reputation (e.g. Fortune, Financial Times, industry surveys)	0	2	3	2.0	1.6
Percent of revenues/profits from "new" products, services or businesses	2	3	4	2.9	1.7
Section 2					
Product/service reviews (by independent organizations)	0	2	3	2.5	1.6
Net present value or discounted cash flow of portfolio	0	2	4	2.2	1.8
On-time new product/service/process innovation launch	2	3	4	2.8	1.6
Within-target performance (including unit cost)	3	3	4	3.2	1.4
Within-target cost of projects	3	3	4	3.3	1.4
Current staff satisfaction (e.g. absenteeism, staff turnover)	0	2	3	2.0	1.6
Extent of out-sourcing (e.g. percent of R&D outsourced)	0	1	3	1.5	1.4
Extent of in-sourcing (e.g. percent of technology licensed in)	0	1	3	1.6	1.6
Section 3					
Breadth and depth of market, product, and technology vision	0	3	4	2.2	1.7
Development pipeline richness (e.g. track number of ideas, concepts, technologies, etc.)	0	2	3	2.0	1.6
Staff motivation (e.g. innovation climate, competencies)	1	3	4	2.4	1.5
Networking (e.g. frequency/duration of contacts with universities, suppliers, competitors, customers)	1	3	3	2.3	1.5
Coverage of strategic goals (strength of innovation portfolio)	1	3	4	2.5	1.6
Section 4					
Improvement in return on investment	1	3	4	2.8	1.7
Reduction in break-even time	0	3	4	2.2	1.7
Increase in percent of revenues from new products or services	2	3	4	3.0	1.6

Note: The theoretical range for all variables is from 0 (indicator not used) to 5 (indicator extensively used). Number of observations ranges from 655 to 674. Q1 indicates 25% percentile, Q2 the 50% percentile and Q3 the 75% percentile. The section headings were respectively: lagging indicators, real-time indicators, leading indicators, learning indicators (in the same sequence as presented in Table 2).

Strategy defined as innovation capabilities is measured using a set of questions asking top managers about the extent to which their respective companies have certain key success factors. The questions are anchored using a 1–5 scale where 1 is "we do not have this key success factor as of today" and 5 "we have this key success factor to a great extent." The set of questions was intended to capture different types of capabilities.

In addition to the variables described above, we also control for the *size* of the organization (measured as number of employees). Size has been shown to affect the design of management control systems (Merchant, 1981) and may also affect the design of the innovation measurement system. We measure size as the number of employees. We also control for potential omitted variables. To control for the potential effect of a company's environment (Gordon & Narayanan, 1984) as well as the structure of its business process (Brownell & Merchant, 1990) on the measurement system, we include *industry* dummy variables and location dummy variables.

3.3. Statistical Specifications

Our first research question explores how managers use innovation measures to combine the information that they supply: do they focus their attention on measures that inform about a particular phase in the innovation process or do they use a balanced approach and combine measures from different phases of the innovation process. To study the existence of a pattern, we use an exploratory factor analysis approach (Johnson & Wichern, 1992). This technique allows us to identify measures that managers' use together and reveals the underlying pattern of use.

To examine our second research question – the association between types of measures and strategy, we use a regression approach. The dependent variables are the level of use of the various innovation measures; the independent variables include our proxies for innovation strategy as well as control variables. The specification is as follows:

$$\text{Use of measures} = \alpha + \sum_j \beta_j \times \text{strategy}_j + \sum_k \gamma_k \times \text{control variable}_k + \varepsilon$$

Where j indicates variables that proxy for different dimensions of strategy, and k refers to different control variables.

We use a similar specification when interpreting the concept of strategy as capabilities:

$$\text{Use of measures} = \alpha + \sum_j \beta_j \times \text{capabilities}_j + \sum_k \gamma_k \times \text{control variable}_k + \varepsilon$$

If a positive association between innovation strategy and the use of innovation measures exist, then we expect the coefficient on strategy variables to be positive and significant.

4. RESULTS

4.1. Descriptive Statistics

Table 2 provides summary statistics for the various measures included in the questionnaire. The measures used the most are financial measures (revenues and profit margin with means of 3.66 and 3.76), market related measures (market share and customer satisfaction – means of 3.40 and 3.12), and project management metrics (within-target performance, within-target cost of projects – means of 3.20 and 3.27). Using a Wilcoxon rank sum test, the two financial measures – revenues and profit margin – are used significantly (at the 1%) more than market related or project management metrics.[6] Thus, financial measures seem to attract more attention from top management than non-financial measures. This is in contrast with designers who put more emphasis on non-financial measures (Hertenstein & Platt, 1997). The measures least used capture intangible elements related to human resources (attractiveness of company to new hires, reputation, and current staff satisfaction – means of 1.54, 1.96, and 1.99 respectively) as well as R&D outsourcing (extent of out-sourcing and extent of in-sourcing – means of 1.50 and 1.56).

4.2. The use of Innovation Measures

Our first research question explores how top managers use multiple measures. We identified two potential patterns of using measures to simplify information processing – focused and balanced patterns.

Table 3 presents the results of a principal component factor analysis with a varimax rotation.[7] Five eigenvalues are above one, leading to five factors. For each factor, we highlight the measures that load more than 0.40; all but two measures load at least into one of the factors.

The pattern that emerges from the analysis is a mix between focused and balanced approaches but with more weight on focusing on the various phases of the innovation process. Managers use measures that inform about a stage of the innovation process in a similar way (and thus loading in the same factor). They combine the information in these measures rather than taking a balanced

Table 3. Factor Analysis on Innovation Measures.

Measure	Factor 1: Inputs	Factor 2: Outsource	Factor 3: Execution	Factor 4: External	Factor 5: Financial	Uniqueness
Breadth and depth of market, product, and technology vision	**0.72**	0.23	0.13	0.17	0.12	0.37
Development pipeline richness (e.g. track number of ideas, concepts, technologies, etc.)	**0.70**	0.26	0.21	0.11	0.07	0.38
Coverage of strategic goals (strength of innovation portfolio)	**0.66**	0.24	0.33	0.21	0.06	0.34
Increase in percent of revenues from new products or services	**0.63**	0.08	0.11	0.05	**0.51**	0.32
Percent of revenues/profits from "new" products, services or businesses	**0.56**	−0.06	0.00	0.16	**0.53**	0.37
Networking (e.g. frequency/duration of contacts with universities, suppliers, competitors, customers)	**0.55**	**0.48**	0.09	0.11	0.07	0.43
Staff motivation (e.g. innovation climate, competencies)	**0.53**	0.31	0.31	0.33	−0.01	0.42
Extent of out-sourcing (e.g. percent of R&D outsourced)	0.16	**0.81**	0.11	0.17	0.18	0.24
Extent of in-sourcing (e.g. percent of technology licensed in)	0.32	**0.75**	0.10	0.07	0.22	0.27
Current staff satisfaction (e.g. absenteeism, staff turnover)	0.08	**0.49**	0.39	**0.47**	−0.02	0.38
Within-target cost of projects	0.15	0.14	**0.81**	0.05	0.16	0.27
Within-target performance (including unit cost)	0.16	0.04	**0.77**	0.11	0.24	0.30
On-time new product/service/process innovation launch	0.37	0.14	**0.54**	0.19	0.15	0.49
Customer satisfaction (e.g. periodic survey)	0.09	−0.05	0.24	**0.69**	0.20	0.41
Reputation (e.g. Fortune, Financial Times, industry surveys)	0.23	0.26	0.06	**0.67**	0.06	0.41
Product/service reviews (by independent organizations)	0.24	0.33	0.03	**0.54**	0.21	0.50
Market value added	0.28	0.21	0.00	**0.49**	0.39	0.49
Attractiveness of company to new hires (track unsolicited applications)	0.25	0.39	0.09	**0.46**	0.14	0.53
Revenues	0.02	0.15	0.15	0.05	**0.84**	0.24
Profit margin	0.11	0.15	0.21	0.04	**0.82**	0.25
Market share	0.11	0.09	0.09	0.20	**0.79**	0.30
Improvement in return on investment	0.36	0.26	**0.40**	0.12	**0.41**	0.46
Net present value or discounted cash flow of portfolio	0.10	0.34	0.37	0.26	0.20	0.63
Reduction in break-even time	0.29	0.39	0.27	0.07	0.36	0.48

Note: This table reports a principal component factor analysis with varimax rotation.

approach (where measures informing about different aspects of the innovation process load together). However, the pattern identified is not a purely focused information approach but also incorporates elements of a balanced perspective. The following paragraphs analyze the pattern that emerges.

The first factor captures the input to the innovation process – the measures with the highest loadings are related to vision, pipeline richness, networking, and staff motivation. However, the factor also includes measures related to financial performance associated with new products – increase in revenues from new products and revenues from new products. This factor reflects a focused approach where managers use measures that monitor the inputs to the innovation process together. However, these measures are also combined with financial measures thus providing a somewhat balanced approach where inputs and outputs are monitored in a similar way. We have labeled this factor as "inputs" to capture the idea that the measures that load the most (but not exclusively) are related to inputs to the innovation process.

The second factor also reflects inputs to the innovation process but it is different from the previous factor in that outsourcing policies have the highest loadings. Both measures that monitor the outsourcing policies – extent of out-sourcing and extent of in-sourcing – are among the measures that receive the least attention (Table 2) indicating that this factor may not be that relevant to manage the innovation process. Staff satisfaction, while being a measure related to inputs internal to the organization also loads into this factor.[8]

The third factor captures measures that inform about the execution of the innovation process (on-time, within-target performance, within target cost). This factor reflects a focused approach to information processing where all measures that inform about the execution of innovation are monitored in a similar way. Because the focus of these measures is around the execution of the innovation process, we label this factor "execution."

The fourth factor captures measures related to how external constituencies perceive the company. The measures that load the most into this factor are customer satisfaction, company's reputation, and product reviews. Again measures that inform about a piece of the innovation process – external perceptions – are used together. Only market value added, which captures financial performance, brings a different perspective into this factor and a balanced view of the innovation process. Because of the external focus of this factor, we label it "external."

The last factor primarily focuses around financial measures (revenues, profit margin, percentage revenues from new products and increase in revenues from new products). Only market share brings a non-financial perspective.[9] We label this last factor "financial." To assess the reliability of the factors, we examined the Cronbach alphas of the measures loading at least 0.40. Even if factor analysis insures that the factors will have high intra-correlation; we estimated the Cronbach alphas for measures loading at least 0.40 to assess the reliability of the factors. They range between 0.75 and 0.86, all of them well above the typical cut-off of 0.60.

The results are most consistent with managers using several measures of a particular phase in the innovation process together. This finding is consistent with managers preferring several measures of the same phenomenon because of the limitations of individual measures – noisiness, lack of completeness, or lack of congruence, their preference for a certain degree of redundancy, or the complexity of certain phases that requires the use of multiple measures.

Measures that inform about inputs, execution, external, and financial outputs load for the most part as different factors. The evidence suggesting that managers use more of a balanced approach is limited to the use of certain financial measures together with input measures (factor 1) and market measures (factor 4).

To examine the hypotheses relating the use of measures in the innovation process with strategy, we construct five variables – each one reflecting the use of the measures captured by the five factors and built as the sum of the standardized scores for each of the questionnaire items that have a factor loading above 0.40.[10]

4.3. Innovation Strategy and Innovation Measures' Use

To examine the association between how frequently managers use measures and different dimensions of innovation strategy, we first identify the dimensions of innovation strategy. The dimensionality of the eight questions intended to capture innovation strategy is reduced through factor analysis with a varimax rotation. The results are reported in Table 4.

Two factors are extracted, one of them reflecting the importance of time (time-based innovation) and the other the importance of cost (cost-based innovation). The Cronbach alphas of both factors, based on questions with a loading greater than 0.40, are above 0.60. While innovation strategies can have more than these two dimensions, cost and time have been shown to be relevant to explain different approaches to innovation (Davila, 2000). Companies following a cost-based innovation work on improving the cost position of the company. A particular application of this strategy is target costing (Cooper & Slagmulder, 1999; Koga, 1998) that uses product redesign to reduce overall costs; alternatively cost-based innovation can also happen through the redesign of manufacturing and logistic processes. This strategy is relevant for companies following a cost

Table 4. Innovation Strategies.

Strategy Dimensions	Factor 1: Cost-Based Innovation	Factor 2: Time-Based Innovation	Uniqueness
Developing products and services that cost less and are easier to manufacture, sell, install, and service	**0.59**	0.27	0.57
Reducing costs/investments related to products and services development/introduction	**0.82**	0.05	0.33
Reducing the payback period of our new products and services	**0.74**	0.22	0.40
Improving the margin from our products and services	**0.59**	−0.03	0.65
Getting our new products and services to the market on time as planned	0.28	**0.71**	0.42
Developing our new products and services faster from concept to market introduction	0.25	**0.75**	0.37
Increasing the number of new product and services we introduce to the market	−0.14	**0.74**	0.43
Increasing the sales volume of our products and services	0.38	0.33	0.75

Note: This table reports a principal component factor analysis with varimax rotation.

strategy (Porter, 1980). The second factor is time-based innovation. Past research highlights the importance of time-to-market as a source of differentiation and competitive advantage (Brown & Eisenhardt, 1995; Patterson, 1993).

The correlation coefficients among the five measure-related factors and the main variables in the research are presented in Table 5. All of the measure-related factors are highly correlated. Thus, while measures that inform about the various phases of the innovation process are used together (as described in Table 3), managers that rely more heavily on their measurement systems do so for the various types of measures.[11] The pattern of use identified in Table 3 likely reflects an efficient approach to costly information processing rather than the more stringent condition of managing information overload. Most of the measure-related factors are correlated with R&D intensity, the two dimensions of innovation strategy, and innovation capabilities; indicating that companies for whom innovation is most important rely on measures to manage the process. Finally, R&D intensity is correlated with time strategy but not with cost strategy; companies that invest more heavily in R&D focus on competing on time.

Table 6 tests how innovation strategic positioning is related to measurement systems, as H1A and 1B predicted. Panel A shows the percentage of R&D over sales and Panel B provides information on the cost and time strategy variables

Table 5. Correlation Matrix.

	Company Size	Inputs	Outsource	Execution	External	Financial	R&D Intensity	Cost Strategy	Time Strategy	Strat. Capability	Tech. Capability	Process Capability	Team Capability	Culture
Company size		0.02	0.05	0.12***	0.09**	0.05	0.06	0.06	0.08**	-0.03	0.06	0.11**	-0.02	-0.05
Inputs	0.07*		0.69***	0.59***	0.59***	0.68***	0.23***	0.10*	0.28***	0.44***	0.43***	0.50***	0.35***	0.42***
Outsource	0.11***	0.70***		0.48***	0.68***	0.45***	0.14***	0.14***	0.15***	0.31***	0.38***	0.38***	0.21***	0.26***
Execution	0.15***	0.62***	0.51***		0.50***	0.60***	0.15***	0.22***	0.25***	0.36***	0.32***	0.41***	0.31***	0.32***
External	0.14***	0.59***	0.70***	0.53***		0.46***	0.11**	0.14***	0.18***	0.38***	0.37***	0.42***	0.30***	0.26***
Financial	0.08*	0.68***	0.46***	0.62***	0.49***		0.27***	0.17	0.33***	0.38***	0.30***	0.42***	0.32***	0.40***
R&D intensity	0.07	0.21***	0.14***	0.11**	0.14***	0.22***		-0.03	0.27***	0.23***	0.24***	0.25***	0.24***	0.24***
Cost strategy	0.03	0.11	0.16***	0.22***	0.16***	0.15***	-0.03		0.34***	0.18***	0.19***	0.16***	0.15***	0.16***
Time strategy	0.05	0.29***	0.16***	0.23***	0.19***	0.32***	0.29***	0.33***		0.26***	0.20***	0.26***	0.26***	0.33***
Strategic focus	0.06	0.45***	0.34***	0.35***	0.38***	0.37***	0.20***	0.18***	0.27***		0.57***	0.66***	0.60***	0.57***
Tech. capability	0.14***	0.45***	0.41***	0.35***	0.41***	0.31***	0.25***	0.20***	0.22***	0.60***		0.60***	0.48***	0.44***
Process capability	0.16***	0.51***	0.41***	0.41***	0.42***	0.39***	0.25***	0.19***	0.27***	0.67***	0.61***		0.54***	0.54***
Team capability	0.02	0.35***	0.24***	0.29***	0.32***	0.28***	0.20***	0.17***	0.28***	0.59***	0.50***	0.29***		0.58***
Culture	0.06	0.43***	0.27***	0.29***	0.28***	0.35***	0.22***	0.16***	0.35***	0.58***	0.44***	0.29***	0.59***	

Note: This table reports Spearman rank correlation (upper triangle) and Pearson correlation (lower triangle).
*Significant at 10% level.
**Significant at 5% level.
***Significant at 1% level.

Table 6. The Use of Innovation Measures.

Independent Variables	Dependent Variable				
	Inputs	Outsource	Execution	External	Financial
Panel A: Innovation measures and R&D intensity.					
Percentage of sales into R&D	0.067*** (0.02)	0.036 (0.03)	0.042 (0.03)	0.062** (0.03)	0.086*** (0.03)
Size (thousands of employees)	0.002** (0.001)	0.003*** (0.001)	0.003*** (0.001)	0.003*** (0.001)	0.002 (0.001)
Adjusted R^2	11.6%	6.7%	5.8%	5.8%	9.7%
# of observations	537	534	535	535	537
Panel B: Innovation measures and innovation strategy					
Time strategy	0.213*** (0.042)	0.067 (0.04)	0.186*** (0.04)	0.125*** (0.04)	0.240*** (0.04)
Cost strategy	0.032 (0.04)	0.152*** (0.05)	0.186*** (0.04)	0.105*** (0.04)	0.108*** (0.04)
Size (thousands of employees)	0.001* (0.001)	0.002*** (0.001)	0.003*** (0.001)	0.003*** (0.001)	0.001* (0.001)
Adjusted R^2	12.6%	7.4%	10.4%	8.3%	14.6%
# of observations	592	590	594	592	594

Note: This table reports OLS regression of the five measurement factors on the intensity of measures, the percentage of sales devoted to R&D – measured using an interval scale (less than 1.0%, 1.0–2.9%, 3.0–5.9%, 6.0–8.9%, 9.0–11.9%, more than 12%), and size measured as the number of employees (in thousands). In addition to the variables reported, we control for location and industry using dummy variables. This table reports OLS regression of the five measurement factors on the intensity of measures on the two innovation strategy factors. The specification controls for size measured as the number of employees (in thousands), location and industry using dummy variables.

* Significant at 10% level (2-tailed).
** Significant at 5% level (2-tailed).
*** Significant at 1% level (2-tailed).

to test our hypotheses. In all specifications we control for size as number of employees, industry, and location.

The results in Panel A indicate that companies with higher percentage of R&D over sales use input, external, and financial measures more frequently. R&D over sales is not significant for outsourcing measures (although the measures included in this variable are not extensively used) and it is neither significant for execution measures. A potential explanation for this latter observation is that measures related with the execution of innovation (execution measures) are the first ones adopted as innovation gains importance and most firms have reached a level of innovation that demands execution measures. However, attention to input and output measures, rather than execution measures, are only adopted later. A further consequence of the lack of significance of execution measures and the significance of input and output measures is that as the innovation process starts to gain importance, companies start focusing on managing the process. But companies fail to measure whether the appropriate resources are being committed nor whether the effort is paying off; only later on in the innovation curve do companies monitor inputs and outputs. Panel A also indicates that larger firms – measured as number of employees – use measures more intensively and, in particular, size is positively associated with all measurement variables except for financial measures. The regressions control for industry and region; none of the regions' coefficients was significant (at the 5% level) except for Asian companies using resource measures more extensively.[12]

Panel B reports the results for two dimensions of competitive strategy: cost and time innovation strategy. Consistent with H1A on time-based innovation strategies, the results indicate that input, execution, and external measures are important for these firms. These results lend strong support to H1A. In addition, though, these firms also used financial based measures. One possible explanation for the significant relationship between time based strategies and financial measures is that financial measures are well-accepted and so may be collected for all firms, regardless of the particular approach to innovation that they are pursuing. Financial measures may be collected as standard operation procedure. Another explanation is that financial measures reflect whether the innovation effort is being translated into value. Therefore, these measures are important in managing the innovation process. In H1B, we predicted that firms using a cost-based approach to innovation would use outsource, execution, and financial measures. Panel B indicates there is a positive and significant relationship between these three measures and cost based approaches to innovation, lending strong support to H1B. In addition, external measures are significantly related to cost based approaches to innovation. External measures include items such as customer satisfaction, product reviews, and reputation. One possible explanation is that such measures are also widely used, just as financial measures are, so that regardless of the particular approach to innovation, innovation oriented firms systematically collect these data.[13] When comparing the results for H1A and 1B, we see that both strategies are significantly and positively related to the use of execution, external and financial measures. Such measures, then, apply across a range of innovation strategies. They may be collected because they are widely accepted measures of innovation and so have high levels of legitimacy. However, time based strategies are significantly related to the use of input based measures, while cost based strategies are not. This may indicate that when time is critical, control over inputs is important. Conversely, cost based strategies are related to the use of outsource measures, while time based strategies are not. Firms may prefer to go to the market for some elements of their process in order to control costs. However, those firms competing on time may instead prefer to have control over the process and so insource (and pay attention to input measures) rather than using the market.

The findings from these two panels highlight the relevance of the measurement system to innovation strategy. The conclusion also reinforces previous evidence linking management control systems and strategy for the particular case of innovation strategy and measurement systems.

Hypothesis two predicts a positive (negative) relationship between codification based (intangible) innovation capabilities and the use of innovation measures. Using a factor analysis approach similar to the one used in Tables 3 and 4 (not reported), we identified five different capabilities (with Cronbach alphas above 0.75 in all cases). These five factors were consistent with the capabilities that managers at the consulting firm mentioned that they wanted to capture. Appendix lists the questionnaire items that load into each of the five factors. Two of the capabilities related to codification of managerial routines – process and technology management – and three related to intangible capabilities – teamwork, culture, and strategic focus. In Table 7 these five capabilities are the proxies for strategy (defined from a capability's perspective) while the proxies for strategy as positioning (time and cost proxies) are included as control variables.[14]

Codification capabilities (technology management and process management) are positive and significant for most of the types of innovation measures (only technology management is not significant for financial measures). This obser-vation suggests that developing and using these two capabilities requires more frequent use of measurement systems. However, intangible capabilities (strategic focus, team capabilities and culture) are mostly unrelated to the frequency of updating of measures and, in the case of team capabilities, the coefficients are negative (and significant in two of the regressions). Accordingly, the support for hypothesis two is mixed. On the one hand, the use of innovation measures

Table 7. Innovation Capabilities and the Use of Innovation Measures.

Capabilities	Dependent Variables				
	Inputs	Outsource	Execution	External	Financial
Strategic focus	0.091 (0.06)	0.055 (0.07)	0.089 (0.06)	0.086 (0.06)	0.154** (0.07)
Technology management	0.196*** (0.06)	0.255*** (0.06)	0.157** (0.06)	0.231*** (0.06)	0.077 (0.06)
Process management	0.264*** (0.06)	0.263*** (0.06)	0.214*** (0.06)	0.228*** (0.06)	0.196*** (0.06)
Team	−0.095 (0.06)	−0.135* (0.07)	−0.029 (0.07)	−0.016 (0.06)	−0.124* (0.07)
Culture	0.132** (0.06)	0.055 (0.06)	0.008 (0.06)	−0.048 (0.06)	0.079 (0.06)
Control Variables					
Size (thousands of employees)	0.001 (0.00)	0.001 (0.00)	0.001 (0.00)	0.001 (0.00)	0.001 (0.00)
Cost strategy	−0.031 (0.05)	0.066 (0.05)	0.093* (0.05)	0.038 (0.05)	0.114** (0.05)
Time strategy	0.152*** (0.05)	0.037 (0.05)	0.115** (0.05)	0.108** (0.05)	0.197*** (0.05)
Adjusted R^2	32.2%	21.7%	21.8%	24.5%	23.9%
# of observations	391	391	392	392	392

Note: This table reports OLS regression of the five measurement factors on key success factors identified. Control for industry and location are included but not reported.

*Significant at 10% level (2-tailed).
**Significant at 5% level (2-tailed).
***Significant at 1% level (2-tailed).

is associated with codification capabilities (consistent with H2a). In contrast, measurement systems are unrelated to the existence of intangible capabilities like culture or the ability to communicate a focused strategy; they are even used to a less extent when the information that they convey can be communicated through personal interaction as happens through team collaboration (inconsistent with H2b).

After controlling for capabilities, the size of the company that was significant in Table 6 is no longer significant. Time strategy is still significant but cost strategy is only significant in two out of the five types of measures.

5. DISCUSSION AND CONCLUSIONS

In this study, we sought to extend our understanding of the design and use of measurement systems. In doing so, we contribute to the literature in two important ways: (1) the evidence in the paper indicates that managers focus their use of measures around the phases that build a managerial process. Thus, managers use several measures to be informed about the evolution of particular phases within the process; the use of multiple measures attenuates noisiness, reduces congruency problems, provides information that is more complete, and supply the redundancy required to verify the information. This usage pattern focused around phases in the process emerges as the preferred pattern over the alternative of combining measures from various phases to have a balanced perspective over the process as a whole; and (2) The results indicate that the way managers use measures varies with the innovation strategy – whether strategy is interpreted as positioning or as capabilities. This finding is, to our knowledge, one of the first empirical evidence relating the design of measurement systems and the strategy of the firm. Recent work that includes the concept of the Balanced Scorecard or the redefinition of the Tableau de Bord relies on strategy being a key driver of the design of measurement systems. The results in this paper provide initial evidence aligned with this assumption. It also extends previous conceptualization of strategy in the management accounting literature to include a resource-based view of the firm.

The focus of the research is the innovation processes within the firm and, accordingly, the results are only valid for this particular process. However, empirical evidence informing how managers use the information conveyed in the measurement system is an important element in advancing our knowledge of the design of measurement systems.

The study suggests that measurement systems may not be relevant to the development and deployment of all capabilities that may lead to competitive advantage. Thus, while measurement systems are associated with strategy they are not necessarily associated with various sources of competitive advantage. Capabilities related to routines and knowledge management are found to be associated with the use of measures. In contrast, capabilities related to intangible elements like culture, cross-functional team, and understanding of strategy throughout the organization are not associated with the measurement system. This may indicate that the building of more informal capabilities is different from cultivating capabilities related to the coding of learning through routines.

The results of the study also have managerial implications. First, the results indicate that managers tend to focus on measures that only inform about a specific stage of the innovation process. While a fruitful approach when the specific stage is critical to success, it may have negative implications if success depends on coordinating and managing across various phases of the innovation process. Second, the findings suggest that having adequate measurement systems around the innovation process is seen as important in firms where innovation is an important aspect of their strategy. Managers planning to give more weight to the innovation processes in their firms need to invest in developing adequate measurement systems. Finally, these systems need to focus around tangible capabilities such as technology and process management.

Future research may extend this study in several directions: (1) The findings are limited to the innovation process and little is known about whether the results are generalizable to alternative settings. An important research question is to study the association between measurement systems and strategy and capabilities at the strategic level. The widespread adoption of Balanced Scorecard type measurement systems at the top of many organizations may be a fruitful way to execute such a study; (2) The findings in this study are limited to the association between measures and firm characteristics; a useful extension would be to study the performance implications of the alignment of the measurement systems with firm characteristics; (3) This research focuses on evolutionary or incremental innovation. Future research may explore the link between measurement systems (and management control systems) and revolutionary or radical innovation; in other words, how do companies monitor their efforts towards creating revolutionary change; (4) Future research can also expand the link between measurement systems and strategy beyond the selection of measures to explore its relevance to the various phases of the strategic process (strategy implementation and strategy definition and redesign); (5) In the innovation literature, Leonard-Barton (1992) highlights the need to design systems that monitor core competencies and provide early warning signals of these competencies becoming core rigidities; at this point, we do not know how measurement systems can work within this role; and (6) Finally, the intersection between measurement system design and compensation systems within innovation processes is an important line of research in the area.

NOTES

1. Information processing theory does not indicate whether one of the information processing patterns is being preferred to the other nor if such preference depends on the particular environment. The answer is thus an empirical question. Variables that may separate these environments (if indeed such different environments exist) have not yet been identified. Therefore, this study identifies a dominant pattern.

2. By "use" of measures, we refer to managers accessing measures for their day-to-day operational work. We do not make any attempt to study how the measures are used from a strategic perspective – interactively or diagnostically (Simons, 1994).

3. In a meta-analysis, Damanpour (1991) fails to find support for a direct relationship between formalization and innovation adoption. The study results do, however, indicate that there are significant interaction effects between formalization and the type of organization, innovation type, stage of adoption, and scope of innovation. The negative interactions listed above are consistent with earlier studies; however, the meta-analysis also finds positive interactions for some types of organizations and innovations.

4. The section headings are described in Table 2.

5. The questionnaire itself was focused on the innovation process (it was entitled "Global Innovation Survey"). The measures-related questions emphasized the focus around the innovation process (the wording of the questions was: "To what extent does your company use the following indicators to track the effectiveness of its product/service/process innovation activities?"

6. Wilcoxon rank sum test does not impose the ratio scale assumption on the Likert-type scales that parametric test do.

7. The results are comparable using alternative factor analysis techniques or oblique rotation. We also ranked the variables before performing the factor analysis to assess the robustness of the analysis to an alternative specification that does not assume a ratio scale. The result was identical.

8. The results are informative about measures within the innovation process. Whether these results can be generalized beyond this process is an open research question.

9. Although market share has been considered a financial measure in previous research (Hertenstein & Platt, 2000).

10. For example, the "input" variable is estimated as follows. All the measures that load into this factor –measures loading more than 0.40 are included – (see Table 3) are standardized to have mean zero and variance of one; then the "input" variable is estimated as the sum of these standardized scores. Notice that the new variables are not the factors themselves, they only include certain measures, they are standardized, and they are equally weighted. As a consequence, these new variables are not orthogonal anymore even if the original factors were so. This research design approach is favored in most survey-based research. The main conclusions in Tables 6 and 7 remained unchanged if we use the factors themselves as the dependent variables.

11. In support of this conclusion, all measures loaded above 0.45 (with positive) in the first factor in the factor analysis of the measures (before the varimax rotation) (not

reported). This main factor seems to reflect the level of use of measures. This factor explained 37% of the variance.

12. To assess the robustness of the results in Panel A, we used alternative specifications. First, we characterized R&D percentage using dummy variables where the first dummy took value of one if R&D percentage was less than 3%, the second dummy took value of one for companies with R&D percentage between 3 and 8.9% and the third dummy took value of one when R&D percentage was above 8.9%. This test was intended to evaluate whether the assumption of continuous R&D spending implicit in Panel A. The results were similar for input and financial metrics, external and outsource metrics – the latter one insignificant in Panel A – were significant for companies spending more than 9% of sales in R&D, process metrics were significant for companies with R&D spending between 3 and 8.9%. The second approach we examined was intended to assess the robustness to the implicit assumption of a ratio scale for the dependent variables. For each measure within a measure-related factor (Table 3), we assigned a one if it was above the median and zero otherwise. For example, for input metrics that comprise seven different measures (Table 3), we counted for each company how many of these measures were above or below the median, the range of this new input metric variable was zero (all variables below the median) to seven (all variables above the median). We used an ordered logit specification to test hypothesis 1. The results were similar to Panel A, the only difference being R&D percentage being marginally significant (at the 10% level) for execution metrics. A third robustness check was to replace the number of employees as the proxy for size (that imposes a linearity assumption on size) by dummy variables reflecting the various sales brackets (Table 1). The results regarding R&D percentage remained unchanged.

13. To assess the robustness of the results in Panel B, we used alternative specifications similar to the ones described in the previous Note. In particular, we replaced the dependent variables by count variables capturing the number of measures within a measure-related factor that were above the median and used an ordered logit. The objective of this robustness test was to evaluate the sensitivity to the ratio assumption implicit in the OLS approach. The conclusions from this test were identical to the ones presented in Panel B. As a second robustness test, we replaced the cost and time strategy variables using a procedure similar to the one used to estimate the count variable for the measure-related factors. For each questionnaire item used to construct a strategy variable we assigned a one if the observation was above the median and zero otherwise. For each observation, we counted the number of questionnaire items that had a one assigned. These new variables – a new variable for cost strategy and another one for time strategy – were used. The conclusions were identical to the one presented in Panel B. Finally, we also examined an alternative proxy for size; instead of using the number of employees (that imposes a linearity assumption), we used dummy variables reflecting the various sales brackets. The results for innovation strategy remained unchanged.

14. Table 7 reports the results from an OLS specification. We obtained very similar results using alternative tests similar to the ones described for Table 6. In particular, we checked the robustness of the results to using dummy variables for different size brackets (rather than the linear assumption included in Table 7). We also defined the dependent variables by first determining whether each particular observation was above the median for each measure, adding the number of measures that scored above the median, and using an ordered logit as the statistical specification. We also used percentage of R&D as a proxy for innovation strategy.

REFERENCES

Aiken, M., & Hage, J. (1971). The organic organization and innovation. *Sociology, 5*, 63–82.
Amit, R., & Schoemaker, P. (1993). Strategic assets and organizational rent. *Strategic Management Journal, 14*, 33–46.
Balkin, D. B., & Gomez-Mejia, L. R. (1987). Toward a contingency theory of compensation strategy. *Strategic Management Journal, 8*(2), 169–183.
Banker, R. D., & Datar, S. M. (1989). Sensitivity, precision, and linear aggregation of signals for performance evaluation. *Journal of Accounting Research, 27*(1), 21–39.
Banker, R. D., Potter, G., & Srinivasan, D. (2000). An empirical investigation of an incentive plan that includes nonfinancial performance measures. *The Accounting Review, 75*(1), 65–92.
Brown, S. L., & Eisenhardt, K. M. (1995). Product development: Past research, present findings, and future directions. *Academy of Management Review, 20*, 343–378.
Brownell, P., & Merchant, K. A. (1990). The budgetary and performance influences of product standardization and manufacturing process automation. *Journal of Accounting Research, 28*(2), 388–397.
Burns, T., & Stalker, G. M. (1961). *The management of innovation.* London: Tavistock.
Cardinal, L. B. (2001). Technological innovation in the pharmaceutical industry: The use of organizational control in managing research and development. *Organization Science, 12*(1), 19–36.
Cooper, R., & Slagmulder, R. (1999). Develop profitable products with target costing. *Sloan Management Review, 40*, 23–34.
Cordero, R. (1990). The measurement of innovation performance in the firm: An overview. *Research Policy, 19*, 185–192.
Damanpour, F. (1991). Organizational innovation: A meta-analysis of effects of determinants and moderators. *Academy of Management Journal, 34*(3), 555–590.
Davila, T. (2000). An empirical study on the drivers of management control system' design in new product development. *Accounting, Organizations and Society, 25*, 383–409.
Donnelly, G. (2000). A P&L for R&D. *CFO* (February), 44–50.
Eisenhardt, K. M. (1985). Control: Organizational and economic approaches. *Management Science, 31*, 134–149.
Epstein, M., & Manzoni, J. F. (1998). Implementing corporate strategy: From tableaux de bord to balanced scorecards. *European Management Journal, 16*(2), 190–204.
Feltham, G. A., & Xie, J. (1994). Performance measurement congruity and diversity in multi-task principal agent relations. *The Accounting Review, 69*, 429–453.
Gersick, C. J. G. (1989). Making time: Predictable transitions in task groups. *Academy of Management Journal, 32*(2), 274–310.
Gordon, L. A., & Narayanan, V. K. (1984). Management accounting systems, perceived environmental uncertainty and organizational structure: An empirical investigation. *Accounting, Organizations and Society*, 33–47.
Govindarajan, V., & Gupta, A. L. (1985). Linking control systems to business unit strategy: Impact on performance. *Accounting, Organizations and Society, 11*, 51–66.
Griffin, A., & Page, A. L. (1996). PDMA success measurement project: Recommended measures for product development success and failure. *The Journal of Product Innovation Management, 13*, 478–496.
Gupta, A. K. (1987). SBU strategies, corporate-SBU relations, and SBU effectiveness in strategy implementation. *Academy of Management Journal, 30*(3), 477–501.

Hansen, M. T. (1999). The search-transfer problem: The role of weak ties in sharing knowledge across organization subunits. *Administrative Science Quarterly, 44*(1), 82–112.

Hertenstein, J. H., & Platt, M. B. (1997). Developing a strategic design culture. *Design Management Journal, 8*, 10–19.

Hertenstein, J. H., & Platt, M. B. (2000). Performance measures and management control in new product development. *Accounting Horizons, 14*(3), 303–323.

Holmstrom, B. (1979). Moral hazard and observability. *Bell Journal of Economics*, 74–91.

Hoque, Z., & James, W. (2000). Linking balanced scorecard measures to size and market factors: Impact on organizational performance. *Journal of Management Accounting Research, 12*, 1–18.

Ittner, C. D., & Larcker, D. F. (1998). Are nonfinancial measures leading indicators of financial performance? An analysis of customer satisfaction. *Journal of Accounting Research, 36*, 1–35.

Jelinek, M., & Schoonhoven, C. B. (1990). *Innovation marathon: Lessons from high technology firms.* Cambridge, MA: Basil Blackwell.

Johnson, R. A., & Wichern, D. W. (1992). *Applied multivariate statistical analysis.* Englewood Cliffs, NJ: Prentice-Hall.

Kaplan, R. S., & Norton, D. P. (1992). The balanced scorecard – Measures that drive performance. *Harvard Business Review, 70*(1), 71–79.

Kaplan, R. S., & Norton, D. P. (2001a). Transforming the balanced scorecard from performance measurement to strategic management: Part I. *Accounting Horizons, 15*(1), 87–105.

Kaplan, R. S., & Norton, D. P. (2001b). Transforming the balanced scorecard from performance measurement to strategic managment: Part II. *Accounting Horizons, 15*(2), 147–160.

Kerr, J. L. (1985). Diversification strategies and managerial rewards empirical investigation. *Academic Management Journal, 28*, 155–179.

Kirsch, L. J. (1996). The management of complex tasks in organizations: Controlling the systems development process. *Organization Science, 7*(1), 1–21.

Koga, K. (1998). Determinants of effective product cost management during product development: Opening the black box of target costing. Working Paper, Harvard Business School.

Langfield-Smith, K. (1997). Management control systems and strategy: A critical review. *Accounting, Organizations and Society, 22*, 207–232.

Leonard-Barton, D. (1992). Core capabilities and core rigidities: A paradox in managing new product development. *Strategic Management Journal, 13*, 111–125.

Libby, R. (1981). *Accounting and human information processing: Theory and applications.* Engelwood Cliffs, NJ: Prentice Hall.

Lipe, M. G., & Salterio, S. E. (2000). The balanced scorecard: Judgmental effects of common and unique performance measures. *The Accounting Review, 75*, 283–298.

Merchant, K. A. (1981). The design of the corporate budgeting system: Influences on managerial behavior and performance. *The Accounting Review, 56*(4), 813–828.

Meyer, C. (1994). How the right measures help teams excel. *Harvard Business Review* (May–June), 95–103.

Meyer, M. H., Tertzakian, P., & Utterback, J. M. (1997). Metrics for managing research and development in the context of the product family. *Management Science, 43*, 88–111.

Miller, J. G., & Roth, A. V. (1994). A taxonomy of manufacturing strategies. *Management Science, 40*(3), 285–305.

Mintzberg, H., Ahlstrand, B., & Lampel, J. (1998). *Strategy safari: A guided tour through the wilds of strategic management.* New York, NY: Free Press.

Narayanan, V. G., & Davila, A. (1998). Using delegation and control systems to mitigate the trade-off between the performance-evaluation and belief-revision use of accounting signals. *Journal of Accounting and Economics, 25*(3), 255–282.

Nelson, R., & Winter, S. (1982). *An evolutionary theory of economic change.* Cambridge, MA: Harvard University Press.

Nonaka, I. (1990). Redundant, overlapping organization: A Japanese approach to managing the innovation process. *California Management Review, 32,* 27–38.

Nonaka, I. (1994). A dynamic theory of organizational knowledge creation. *Organization Science, 5*(1), 14–38.

Ouchi, W. G. (1979). A conceptual framework for the design of organizational control mechanisms. *Management Science, 25*(9), 833–849.

Patterson, M. L. (1993). *Accelerating innovation: Improving the process of product development.* New York, NY: Van Nostrand Reinhold.

Porter, M. E. (1980). *Competitive strategy: Techniques for analyzing industries and competitors.* New York, NY: Free Press.

Prahalad, C. K., & Hamel, G. (1990). The core competence of the corporation. *Harvard Business Review, 68,* 79–91.

Schick, A. G., Gordon, L. A., & Haka, S. (1990). Information overload: A temporal approach. *Accounting, Organizations and Society, 15*(3), 199–221.

Simons, R. (1987). Accounting control systems and business strategy: An empirical analysis. *Accounting, Organizations and Society, 12*(4), 357–375.

Simons, R. (1991). Strategic orientation and top management attention to control systems: New perspectives. *Strategic Management Journal, 12,* 49–62.

Simons, R. (1994). *Levers of control: How managers use innovative control systems to drive strategic renewal.* Boston, MA: Harvard Business School Press.

Snell, S. A. (1992). Control theory in strategic human resource management: The mediating effect of administrative information. *Academic Management Journal, 35,* 1–36.

Szulanski, G. (1996). Exploring internal stickiness: Impediments to the transfer of best practice within the firm. *Strategic Management Journal, 17*(10), 27–44.

Teece, D. J., Pisano, G., & Shuen, A. (1997). Dynamic capabilities and strategic management. *Strategic Management Journal, 18,* 509–533.

Thompson, V. (1965). Bureaucracy and innovation. *Administrative Science Quarterly, 10,* 1–20.

Tushman, M., & Nadler, D. (1978). Information processing as an integrating concept in organizational design. *Academy of Management Review, 3,* 613–624.

Tushman, M. L., & O'Reilly, C. A., III. (1997). *Winning through innovation: A practical guide to leading organizational change and renewal.* Boston, MA: Harvard Business School Press.

Verona, G. (1999). A resource-based view of product development. *Academy of Management Review, 24,* 132–142.

Wernerfelt, B. (1984). A resource-based view of the firm. *Strategic Management Journal, 5,* 171–180.

Wheelwright, S., & Clark, K. (1992). *Revolutionizing product development: Quantum leaps in speed, efficiency, and quality.* New York, NY: Free Press.

Zander, U., & Kogut, B. (1995). Knowledge and the speed of the transfer and imitation of organizational capabilities: An empirical test. *Organization Science, 6*(1), 76–92.

Zollo, M., & Winter, S. G. (2002). Deliberate learning and the evolution of dynamic capabilities. *Organization Science, 13*(3), 339–351.

APPENDIX

Questionnaire Items Measuring Capabilities

Strategic focus capabilities
1. Strong alignment between innovation initiatives and business strategy
2. Common vision for new product, service, or process
3. Widely understood product or service strategy
4. Very clear strategic understanding of customer needs

Technology management capabilities
1. Strong, well-developed technology platforms
2. Clear and strong approach to valuing technology projects
3. Effective technology sourcing strategy
4. Whatever title, the role of Chief Technology Officer is effectively executed

Innovation process capabilities
1. Strong intelligence gathering
2. Explicit process to gather customer needs
3. Visioning and idea generation processes
4. Screening process to be sure that only the best ideas go into development
5. Good milestone and project management discipline

Team capabilities
1. Marketing and technology departments in the same location
2. Strong, cross-functional teams effectively do most of the innovation work
3. Teams created using the most appropriate staff rather than using staff that happens to be available
4. High degree of interaction and cooperation across functions, especially marketing, R&D, and manufacturing/operations
5. Effective global R&D/marketing communication

Culture-based capabilities
1. Clear top management support and commitment for innovative activity
2. Passion for new products
3. Sense of urgency
4. A corporate climate that encourages and rewards people for initiative and risk taking

---

COMPARING THE PERFORMANCE EFFECT OF FINANCIAL INCENTIVES FOR A SIMPLE, RECURRENT TASK

Stuart B. Thomas

ABSTRACT

The current study examines the performance effects of financial incentives for a simple, recurrent task designed to simulate an assembly-line setting. The study looks at early performance, improvement and overall performance. For a new task, performance-based incentives appear to improve the initial performance of the task but not subsequent improvement rate (Bailey et al., 1998). The current paper reports on a laboratory experiment whose results confirm the findings of Bailey et al. (1998) but also indicates that for both performance-based and fixed incentives, significant performance improvement takes place well beyond the initial performance of the task, declining gradually over time. This is in contrast with the suggestion of Bailey et al. (1998) that workers with performance-based incentives will choose to improve initial performance rather than subsequent performance. Findings also suggest that improvement peaks earlier for performance-based incentives than for a fixed incentive. Improvement persisted longer and there was better overall performance with the high fixed component quota and piece rate incentives than with the low fixed component quota implying that

Advances in Management Accounting
Advances in Management Accounting, Volume 13, 59–75
ISSN: 1474-7871/doi:10.1016/S1474-7871(04)13003-7

incentives that impose higher risk (e.g. a low fixed component quota incentive)
on workers result in de-motivation and lower performance.

INTRODUCTION

The introduction of a new task typically requires a period of improvement in which workers' productivity is less than will be the case after improvement has taken place. The current study examines the effects of different pay incentives on early performance, improvement and overall performance for a simple, recurrent task. Understanding these issues will assist management in determining the role of incentives and task characteristics on the performance of workers when undertaking a new task.

Research has provided mixed results when examining whether overall performance is higher with performance-based (PB) incentives than fixed incentives. Some studies indicate a positive effect, (e.g. Berger et al., 1975; Bonner et al., 2000; Bushhouse et al., 1982; Farr, 1976; Gaetani et al., 1985; Locke et al., 1980; Nebeker & Neuberger, 1985; Orphen, 1982; Sprinkle, 2000; Terborg & Miller, 1978; Yukl et al., 1972) while others do not (e.g. Ashton, 1990; Libby & Lipe, 1992; McGraw, 1978; Young & Lewis, 1995). An extensive review of the literature indicates that the effectiveness of incentives depends on the nature of the task and the type of financial incentive that is used (Bonner et al., 2000). As tasks become more cognitively complex, financial incentives have less effect.

Consistent with the findings of Bonner et al. (2000), the current study argues that a simple task will have a close link between effort and performance, resulting in PB incentives providing a greater motivation to effort than a fixed incentive. For a new task, this greater motivation is expected to lead to higher early performance, earlier improvement peaks, greater improvement persistence and higher overall performance for PB incentives than a fixed incentive. Improvement rates however, are not expected to differ between the two types of incentives since this requires extreme effort on the part of workers (Bailey et al., 1998).

The current study also compares the performance effects of imposing risk on workers using two PB incentives: piece rate and assigned quota. Bonner et al. (2000) suggested that for simple tasks, quota incentives that provide difficult but attainable goals outperform piece rate incentives because of the motivation that goals provide (e.g. Locke & Latham, 1990). The current study argues that this is dependent on the nature of the quota incentive. It is suggested that a low fixed component (LF) quota incentive places a higher risk on workers than a high fixed component (HF) quota or a piece rate incentive since the non-attainment of the quota results in greater loss of compensation under the LF incentive. This will result in greater de-motivation of workers with an LF quota incentive leading to lower performance than with a HF quota or piece rate incentive.

Research indicates that sometimes assigned quota incentives outperform piece rate incentives (e.g. Bailey et al., 1998) and at other times piece rate outperforms quota incentives (e.g. Chow, 1983; Farh et al., 1991). The current study argues that this difference is due to the nature of the quota incentive. Bailey et al (1998) used a HF quota incentive which imposed less risk on workers than the LF component quota incentives used in the Chow (1983) and Farh et al. (1991) studies.

The remainder of the paper proceeds as follows: (1) related literature and hypothesis development; (2) research method; (3) results; and (4) discussion and conclusions.

RELATED LITERATURE AND HYPOTHESIS DEVELOPMENT

Improvements

Theorists have long proposed the use of goals and financial incentives as effective inducements for individuals to persist in improvement and demonstrate improvement with increased output (Bandura & Simon, 1977; Hilgard & Bower, 1975). Laboratory studies employing assembly tasks (Bailey et al., 1998; Gershoni, 1971; Globerson & Seidmann, 1988), a proofreading task (Huber, 1985), and a transcribing task (Chung & Vickery, 1976) have compared the effect of various monetary incentives on improvement rates. However, a review of the literature by Bailey et al. (1998, p. 122) indicates "extant research has presented an unclear picture of workers' response to incentives." Some of these studies did not statistically test the differences in improvement rates for the various incentives (Chung & Vickery, 1976; Gershoni, 1971). Others introduced incentives after initial improvement had already taken place so that workers were not given the opportunity to allocate their efforts between initial performance and subsequent improvement (Globerson & Seidmann, 1988; Huber, 1985).

The Bailey et al. (1998) study was the first to simultaneously examine the effect of different incentives on initial performance and subsequent improvement rate. They found that PB incentives (quota and piece rate) resulted in higher initial and overall performance than a fixed incentive, but that there was not a significant difference in improvement rates. They suggested that the lack of difference between performance rates was attributable to workers choosing to allocate their efforts on high initial performance rather than the more difficult task of improving subsequent performance (p. 128). The current study reexamines this relevant issue because the

Bailey et al. (1998) study is the only one that has so far examined this question. The current study uses a task that is less complex than the one used in the Bailey et al. (1998) study. Although the tasks fall under the same Bonner et al. (2000) classification, the current task did not require the detailed explanations described in the Bailey et al. (1998) study. The first hypothesis is therefore:

H1. Performance-based incentives and a fixed incentive have a similar influence on improvement rates between successive sessions.

The current study extends Bailey et al. (1998) by also comparing the behavior of performance improvements for PB incentives and a fixed incentive. They suggested that since the incentives did not reward improvements directly, workers chose to allocate effort to improving initial performance rather than the more difficult task of improving subsequent performance. In contrast to this suggestion, the current study argues that by providing an economic incentive for good performance, PB incentives motivate workers to work harder than would be the case with a fixed incentive (Bailey et al., 1998; Bonner et al., 2000; Young & Lewis, 1995). Their underlying assumption is that increasing pay potential will motive increased performance. Thus, Demski and Feltham's (1978) "bang-bang" quota incentive pays "high income" for goal attainment and "low income" for non-attainment. This is consistent with Locke and Latham's (1990) "high performance cycle" model that manipulates contingent incentives to reinforce goal commitment. The current study argues that PB incentives will motivate higher exertion resulting in improvements between successive performance sessions peaking earlier and improvement persisting over more sessions than with a fixed incentive. These types of improvements are expected to require less exertion than increasing improvement rates. These arguments lead to the following hypotheses:

H2a. Performance improvements between successive sessions peak earlier with performance-based incentives than with a fixed incentive.

H2b. Performance improvements between successive sessions persist longer with performance-based incentives than with a fixed incentive.

Performance-Based Incentives

A review of the literature reveals a variety of quota incentives rewarding goal attainment with rewards ranging from 25% (Bailey et al., 1998) to 600% (Erez et al., 1990; Pritchard & Curtis, 1973) of the base amount. Numerous studies have also utilized both assigned and self-set quota incentives. Three general forms of assigned quota incentives are usually examined. One form is a quota/piece rate hybrid in which workers are compensated for reaching a goal and then paid a piece rate for additional output (e.g. Frisch & Dickinson, 1990; Huber, 1985). Another form sets more than one goal and rewards workers depending on which goal they attain (e.g. Erez et al., 1990; Huber, 1985; Jorgenson et al., 1973). A third form, the form used in the current study, pays workers a fixed incentive that is increased if they reach a set goal. This is the form usually used in accounting studies (e.g. Bailey et al., 1998; Chow, 1983).

The use of quota incentives is intuitively appealing since they incorporate the findings of goal theory that proposes that difficult, attainable goals improve performance (e.g. Locke & Latham, 1990). A potential drawback of quotas however is that they impose risk on workers. They may not be able to meet the quota because of factors outside of their control such as lack of ability or poor weather. With quota incentives therefore, there is the chance of worker de-motivation. This is consistent with expectancy theory which proposes that motivation is determined by perceptions of the likelihood of various outcomes associated with task performance and the utility derived from these outcomes (Ronen & Livingstone, 1975). Workers who fall behind in their goal attainment will become de-motivated, reducing their effort and consequently their performance. Workers with high ability will also not have an incentive to work hard on the task if they are keeping up with the required goal since performance exceeding the quota is not rewarded. Quota incentives therefore impose risk on the compensation of both low and high ability workers. This is particularly true of the form of quota incentive chosen for this study. It imposes the most risk on workers, and so facilitates examining the research question: Does imposed risk on workers lead to reduced performance?

Quota incentives that have a lower fixed portion are expected to be more de-motivating than those having a higher fixed portion. This study compares the incentive effects of a lower fixed quota incentive with a higher fixed quota incentive. Chow's (1983) interpretation of the Demski and Feltham (1978) "bang-bang" incentive rewarded goal attainment with 300% more compensation than for non-attainment and is an example of a low fixed component (LF) quota incentive. The current study used an LF quota incentive that rewarded goal attainment with 400% more compensation than non-attainment. The quota incentive used by Bailey et al. (1998) rewarded goal attainment with 25% more compensation than for non-attainment, an example of a high fixed component (HF) quota incentive. This was the other quota incentive used in the current study. Although LF quota incentives provide a strong motivation to attain goals, they are also a relatively more risky incentive for workers since non-attainment of the goal results in significantly less compensation than attainment. In both the Chow (1983) and the Bailey et al. (1998) studies, the quota was set based on the average performance of workers using a fixed incentive, the same procedure used in the current study.

A review of the literature indicates that the current study is the first to look at performance effects of different fixed component proportions for assigned quota incentives. Understanding this issue is important for optimizing the use of performance targets within organizations. In a similar study, Frisch and Dickinson (1990) compared the effect of varying the fixed proportion of a quota/piece rate hybrid incentive. Subjects received an incentive for assembling 50 parts per session of $4, $3.63, $3.07, $2.50, or $2 depending on their assigned incentive along with a piece rate incentive for performance beyond 50 parts per session that paid $0, $0.37, $0.93, $1.50, or $2 respectively depending on subjects' performance. There were 15, 45 minute sessions. Subjects with the fixed incentive underperformed the other subjects. There was no difference among the subjects with the performance-based incentives.

The quota used in the Frisch and Dickinson (1990) study was not chosen as an incentive to high performance but rather to motivate workers to "meet minimum performance levels" (p. 18). Thus the quota was one standard deviation below the mean performance with a fixed incentive. Despite setting a low quota, 14 subjects "never or only rarely" met the quota and of these 11 withdrew from the experiment. This is consistent with the potentially de-motivating effect of quota incentives.

The current study therefore argues that quota incentives incorporate the performance enhancing benefit of goal setting but that LF quota incentives also impose a high level of risk on workers that de-motivate performance. Piece rate incentives motivate workers to work harder for more compensation without the motivating benefit of a goal. Consistent with this, studies using simple tasks have found that piece rate incentives outperform LF quota incentives (Chow, 1983; Farh et al., 1991). Furthermore, Bailey et al. (1998) found that a HF quota incentive outperformed a piece rate incentive. The third hypothesis is therefore as follows:

H3. Overall performance is greater with a high fixed quota and piece rate incentives than with a low fixed quota incentive.

Early session performances under PB incentives are not expected to differ since greater effort increases workers' chances of higher compensation. Furthermore, the de-motivating effect of quota incentives will have less effect on early session performances since workers have received relatively little feedback on how their performances match up with the quotas. The remaining hypothesis is therefore as follows:

H4. There is no difference among the incentive effects of performance-based rewards in the first session performance.

PROCEDURE

Ninety two undergraduate business students were randomly assigned to one of four incentives. Students were taken from a number of second and third year business courses having different instructors. Participation was voluntary. Although subjects were free to abandon the task or take breaks at any time, they all worked steadily at the task.

Subjects translated symbols into alphabetic letters using a decoding key that was found at the foot of each page (adapted from Chow, 1983; Chow et al., 1988) in eight, eight-minute sessions. After each session, subjects recorded the number of symbols decoded. Performance was measured as the number of symbols correctly decoded. This task was chosen for four reasons. First, it was considered to be a simple task with a close link between effort and performance. This close link is essential since it is the context in which the current study is investigating the effectiveness of various incentives. Second, the experimenter's experience with the task suggested that improvement that could be measured would take place over succeeding sessions. Third, the task was adapted from the one used by Chow (1983) which was designed to simulate an assembly-line setting where workers verify the location of integrated circuits on circuit boards for small business computers. Fourth, the task was designed so that subjects' performances for each session could be recorded and compared for the different incentives. Eight sessions were used since pilot tests using the fixed incentive suggested that subjects' performances ceased improving after this number of sessions. Using eight sessions was therefore necessary to examine whether PB incentives would continue to result in improvements after the fixed incentive. Subjects then completed a post-test questionnaire that requested demographic information and subjects' opinions of the task and incentives.

Incentives

The four incentives that were used each had expected pay of Canadian $15.00 per subject based on subjects' performances using the fixed incentive. The fixed incentive was used first to establish standards for the other incentives. The incentives were as follows:

(1) Fixed incentive: A flat fee of $15.00 for the eight sessions.
(2) High fixed component quota incentive: A flat base amount of $13.35 plus a bonus of $3.30 for achieving the standard set using the fixed incentive.

(3) Low fixed component quota incentive: A flat base amount of $6.00 plus a bonus of $24.00 for achieving the standard set using the fixed incentive.
(4) Piece rate incentive: $0.0103 for each symbol decoded.

RESULTS

Subjects were randomly assigned to one of the four financial incentives. F and chi-square statistics indicate that there were not significant differences among the four incentives with respect to gender, age and hours worked per week (Table 1). Subjects were asked to respond using 11-point scales (ranging from 0 to 10) about whether the task was easy or difficult, boring or interesting, whether the compensation was low or high, and tiredness at the end of the task. F-tests also indicated no differences ($p > 0.20$) among the incentives. Table 2 presents the total (overall) and session performances for the four incentives. Overall and session performances were best for the piece rate incentive, followed by the HF quota, the LF quota and then the fixed incentive with one exception. For Session 1, the LF quota outperformed the HF quota incentive.

Figure 1 illustrates mean plots for the four incentives for the eight sessions. Relative to other incentives, the quota incentives show a downward trend with successive sessions. This is particularly true of the LF quota incentive. This is consistent with the explanation that quota incentives provide a disincentive for low ability workers who believe they cannot meet their quota and for high ability workers who believe they are already meeting their quota so high exertion is not necessary. These effects are expected to be more pronounced for LF than for HF since non-attainment of the quota has a more extreme effect on their compensation.

Consistent with Bailey et al.'s (1998) findings, H1 hypothesized that improvement rates between successive sessions would not differ significantly

Table 1. Subjects' Descriptive Information.

	Fixed	Low Fixed	High Fixed	Piece Rate	F	p
Males	10	11	8	12		
Females	13	12	15	11		
Average age	24.1	25.7	24.3	22.5	1.052	0.431
Ave. work week hrs.	7.8	7.3	11.8	5.6	0.444	0.962

Note: The chi-square statistic indicated that there was not a significant difference in the number of males in each of the incentives ($p > 0.15$).

Table 2.   Mean (Standard Deviation) Performances of the Incentives ($n = 23$).

	Fixed	Low Fixed	High Fixed	Piece Rate
Total	1379.1739	1446.7391	1523.4348	1590.3913
	(289.8915)	(286.7088)	(235.5749)	(237.7429)
Session 1	105.1304	120.0435	117.8261	121.6957
	(25.9673)	(25.3117)	(20.2297)	(26.1541)
Session 2	131.6957	146.7826	150.1304	162.3043
	(39.8126)	(40.8700)	(30.2194)	(31.8797)
Session 3	163.8261	172.4783	181.6087	186.9565
	(40.4111)	(39.2508)	(31.0933)	(32.4324)
Session 4	176.5652	184.5652	199.0435	205.5217
	(42.1111)	(38.3214)	(33.7457)	(33.7125)
Session 5	188.4783	195.9130	210.4348	214.5652
	(42.3007)	(39.0407)	(41.2463)	(34.3231)
Session 6	197.3478	201.8261	216.2609	225.8696
	(43.2725)	(36.9036)	(37.6916)	(33.8893)
Session 7	205.5217	212.7826	220.4348	231.8261
	(44.1978)	(42.8039)	(35.5564)	(34.3626)
Session 8	210.6087	212.3478	227.6957	241.6522
	(45.2526)	(40.3976)	(38.5739)	(37.1087)

Note: Performance was measured as the number of symbols correctly decoded.

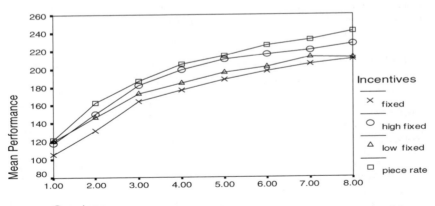

Fig. 1.   Mean Session Performances. *Note:* Performance was measured as the number of symbols correctly decoded.

Table 3.   Improvement Rates Between Successive Sessions for All Incentives.

	Fixed	Low Fixed	High Fixed	Piece Rate	F	p
Sessions 1 and 2	0.270	0.210	0.277	0.350	1.40	0.247
Sessions 2 and 3	0.290	0.196	0.225	0.160	2.47	0.067
Sessions 3 and 4	0.083	0.077	0.105	0.104	0.455	0.714
Sessions 4 and 5	0.074	0.068	0.053	0.046	0.599	0.618
Sessions 5 and 6	0.051	0.037	0.033	0.056	0.592	0.622
Sessions 6 and 7	0.044	0.051	0.025	0.029	0.991	0.401
Sessions 7 and 8	0.032	0.026	0.038	0.043	0.869	0.460

Note: p-Values are for two-tailed tests. Improvement rates were calculated as the proportionate increase across successive sessions. For example, for Sessions 1 and 2:

$$\text{Improvement rate} = \frac{\text{Session 2 performance} - \text{Session 1 performance}}{\text{Session 1 performance}}$$

for the four incentives. Improvement rates were calculated as the proportionate increase across successive sessions. For example, for Sessions 1 and 2:

$$\text{Improvement rate} = \frac{\text{Session 2 performance} - \text{Session 1 performance}}{\text{Session 1 performance}}$$

Table 3 indicates support for H1 for all cases except going from Session 2 to Session 3 where there is moderate support for a difference between the fixed incentive and the PB incentives ($F = 2.471, p = 0.067$). This result, and the mean differences presented in Table 4 indicate that improvements were greatest between Sessions 2 and 3 for the fixed incentive. For all other incentives, the greatest improvement was between Sessions 1 and 2 (Tables 5–7). These results provide support for

Table 4.   Paired Samples *t*-Tests Comparing Performances for Successive Sessions for the Fixed Incentive.

Pair	Mean Difference	Standard Deviation	t	p-Value
Session 2–Session 1	26.5652	27.0787	4.705	0.000
Session 3–Session 2	32.1304	14.1142	10.918	0.000
Session 4–Session 3	12.7391	12.8778	4.744	0.000
Session 5–Session 4	11.9130	13.7574	4.153	0.000
Session 6–Session 5	8.8696	11.7524	3.619	0.002
Session 7–Session6	8.1739	12.0591	3.251	0.004
Session8–Session7	5.0870	26.1115	0.934	0.360

Note: p-Values are for two-tailed tests. Performance was measured as the number of symbols correctly decoded.

Table 5. Paired Samples *t*-Tests Comparing Performances for Successive Sessions for the High Fixed Component Quota Incentive.

Pair	Mean Difference	Standard Deviation	*t*	*p*-Value
Session 2–Session 1	32.3043	18.6583	8.303	0.000
Session 3–Session 2	31.4783	17.9668	8.402	0.000
Session 4–Session 3	17.4348	18.9948	4.402	0.000
Session 5–Session 4	11.3913	13.3340	4.097	0.000
Session 6–Session5	5.8261	10.2853	2.717	0.007
Session 7–Session 6	4.1739	10.5815	1.892	0.036
Session 8–Session 7	7.2609	23.1658	1.503	0.074

Note: *p*-Values are for one-tailed tests.

H2a; performance improvements between successive sessions peak earlier with PB incentives than with fixed incentives.

Table 4 indicates consistently declining improvement between successive sessions for the fixed incentive. Statistically significant improvement persisted until Session 7 ($p < 0.00$). There was not a significant difference between Sessions 7 and 8 ($p > 0.35$). Tables 5–7 present the improvements between successive sessions for the PB incentives. These incentives did not have consistently declining improvements between successive sessions as with the fixed incentive, instead they had improvement surges at different times. The HF quota ($p < 0.10$) and the piece rate ($p < 0.05$) incentives had statistically significant improvements throughout the eight sessions. The LF quota incentive had significant improvement until Session 7 ($p < 0.05$). These results provide some support for H2b; performance improvements between successive sessions persist longer with PB incentives than with fixed incentives.

Table 6. Paired Samples *t*-Tests Comparing Performances for Successive Sessions for the Low Fixed Component Quota Incentive.

Pair	Mean Difference	Standard Deviation	*t*	*p*-Value
Session 2–Session 1	26.7391	18.6845	6.863	0.000
Session 3–Session 2	25.6957	9.3490	13.181	0.000
Session 4–Session 3	12.0870	12.3432	4.696	0.000
Session 5–Session 4	11.3478	15.0291	3.621	0.001
Session 6–Session 5	5.9130	14.9238	1.900	0.036
Session 7–Session 6	10.9565	11.9449	4.399	0.000
Session 8–Session 7	−0.4348	13.2933	−0.157	0.439

Note: *p*-Values are for one-tailed tests.

Table 7. Paired Samples *t*-Tests Comparing Performances for Successive Sessions for the Piece Rate Incentive.

Pair	Mean Difference	Standard Deviation	t	p-Value
Session 2–Session 1	40.6087	17.8752	10.895	0.000
Session 3–Session 2	24.6522	9.9572	11.874	0.000
Session 4–Session 3	18.5652	9.6899	9.189	0.000
Session 5–Session 4	9.0435	13.0296	3.329	0.002
Session 6–Session 5	11.3043	11.7568	4.611	0.000
Session 7–Session 6	5.9565	13.5562	2.107	0.024
Session 8–Session 7	9.8261	15.0625	3.129	0.003

Note: p-Values are for one-tailed tests.

A comparison of overall performance for the four incentives is shown in Table 8. Overall performance with the piece rate incentive was greater than the LF quota and fixed incentives ($p < 0.10$ and 0.05 respectively). Also, overall performance for the fixed incentive was less than with the HF incentive ($p < 0.10$) but no different from the LH incentive ($p > 0.35$). These results provide moderate

Table 8. Univariate Analysis of Variance with Overall (Total) Performance as the Dependent Variable and Incentive (Fixed, Low-Fixed Quota, High-Fixed Quota, or Piece Rate) as the Independent Variable.

Source	Sum of Squares	df	F	p
Model	580694.739	3	2.783	0.046
Intercept	202862880.391	1	2916.203	0.000
Incentive	580694.739	3	2.783	0.046
Error	6121636.870	88		
Total	209565212.000	92		
Corr. total	6702331.609	91		

Pair-wise Comparisons for Overall (Total) Performance with the Four Incentives

(I) Incentive	(J) Incentive	Mean Difference (J – I)	p
Fixed	High fixed	144.261	0.034
	Low fixed	67.565	0.194
	Piece-rate	211.217	0.004
High fixed	Low fixed	−76.696	0.164
	Piece-rate	66.957	0.196
Low fixed	Piece-rate	143.652	0.034

Note: p-Values are for one-tailed tests. Overall performance = The sum of performances over all the sessions.

Table 9. Univariate Analysis of Variance with Session 1 Performance as the Dependent Variable and Incentive (Fixed, Low-Fixed Quota, High-Fixed Quota, or Piece Rate) as the Independent Variable.

Source	Sum of Squares	df	F	p
Model	3913.478	3	2.167	0.098
Intercept	1241666.783	1	2062.346	0.000
Incentive	3913.478	3	2.167	0.098
Error	52981.739	88		
Total	1298562.000	92		
Corr. total	56895.217	91		

Note: $R^2 = 0.069$ (Adjusted $R^2 = 0.037$).

support for H3; overall performance is greater with a high fixed quota and piece rate incentives than with a low fixed quota incentive. Tables 9 and 10 indicate that there was no difference among the PB incentive's early session performances supporting H4.

Table 10. Univariate Analysis of Variance with Session 2 Performance as the Dependent Variable and Incentive (Fixed, Low-Fixed Quota, High-Fixed Quota, or Piece Rate) as the Independent Variable.

Source	Sum of Squares	df	F	p
Model	10951.946	3	2.816	0.044
Intercept	2007774.793	1	1548.934	0.000
Incentive	10951.946	3	2.816	0.044
Error	114068.261	88		
Total	2132795.000	92		
Corr. total	125020.207	91		

Pair-wise Comparisons for Session 2 Performance with the Four Incentives.

(I) Incentive	(J) Incentive	Mean Difference ($J - I$)	p
Fixed	High fixed	18.435	0.043
	Low fixed	15.087	0.079
	Piece-rate	30.609	0.003
High fixed	Low fixed	−3.348	0.377
	Piece-rate	12.174	0.128
Low fixed	Piece-rate	15.522	0.074

Note: p-Values are for one-tailed tests. $R^2 = 0.088$ (Adjusted $R^2 = 0.056$).

Differences among the PB incentives first occur in Session 4. F-tests for all the sessions indicated that there were significant differences in Sessions 4, 6, and 8 ($p < 0.05$). For these sessions the piece rate incentive outperformed the fixed incentive ($p < 0.05$, two-tailed) and the LF quota ($p < 0.10$ for Session 4; $p < 0.05$ for Sessions 6 and 8, all two-tailed) but was not significantly different from the HF quota incentive. The HF quota incentive outperformed the fixed incentive for Session 4 ($p < 0.05$, two-tailed) and Session 6 ($p < 0.10$, two-tailed) but was not significantly different from the LF quota incentive.

Low and high ability workers with quota incentives are expected to find their incentives relatively less fair than workers with a piece rate incentive. Low ability workers will not meet the quota and will thus be penalized. High ability workers will find that they are meeting the quota and are unable to earn more compensation by working harder. Workers with a piece rate incentive, however, have an incentive to work hard regardless of their ability. Subjects were asked in the post test questionnaire to respond using an 11-point scale (ranging from 0 to 10) indicating how fair they thought their incentive was. As expected, workers in the piece rate incentive thought their incentive was fairer than those in the quota incentives ($p < 0.04$, one-tailed test).

DISCUSSION AND CONCLUSION

The current study compared the effect of financial incentives on early performance, improvement, and overall performance for a new, simple, recurrent task. This extends the work of Bailey et al. (1998) that found no differences among the incentives with respect to improvement rates. They suggested that since their incentives did not reward improvements directly, workers with PB incentives chose to allocate their effort to improving initial performance rather than the more difficult task of improving subsequent performance. The current study confirms the finding of Bailey et al. (1998) but finds in fact that improvement continues after early performances gradually decreasing over time. Improvement persistence was greater for the high fixed component quota and the piece rate incentives than for the low fixed component quota and fixed incentives. Overall performance for the piece rate incentive was also greater than for the low fixed component quota incentive.

The results confirm the superiority of the high fixed component quota and piece rate incentives over the fixed incentive. However, there were strong indications that not all quota incentives are created equal. While the low fixed quota incentive outperformed the fixed incentive for Session 2 performance ($p < 0.079$, one-tailed test), overall performance was not different between the two incentives. There was also no difference between the two with respect to improvement persistence either.

Figure 1 paints the picture of a downward trend in performances for the quota incentives with respect to the piece rate and fixed incentives. This trend is particularly marked for the low fixed component quota incentive. This is consistent with the argument that the quota incentives initially provide motivation by providing a performance goal. However, as workers receive feedback on their performances in succeeding sessions, low ability workers to become de-motivated since they believe they will not be able to attain the goal that has been set for them. High ability workers also reduce effort exerted because they believe that they are already in line to achieve the goal without having to maximize their effort. This effect is more pronounced with the low fixed component quota incentive since failure to attain the goal will have a greater effect on their compensation than the high fixed component quota incentive.

The results of this study suggest implications for organizations when planning the productivity levels of its workers for new, simple tasks. The results suggest that significant performance improvements will occur gradually diminishing over time, whether or not PB incentives are used. However, improvements appear to peak more quickly and persist longer with PB incentives than a fixed incentive. Quota incentives appear to provide effective motivation to workers if they balance the positive effects of assigning goal with the risk to workers of not attaining the goals. Quota incentives with a 25% fixed component appear to be effective in motivating performance while those with a 400% fixed component do not. Future research is needed to identify what fixed component is optimal. While caution must be used in generalizing these results to management settings, the findings suggest that budget targets will be more effective when base salaries are a higher percent of total pay.

An interesting finding of the study was the effect all incentives had on performance over time. All four incentives had a diminishing effect on performance in succeeding sessions (Table 3). This is consistent with the classic article by Kohn (1993) on incentive plans which argues that "rewards succeed at securing one thing only: temporary compliance." Incentives alone appear to have limited effect on performance over time.

Studies investigating the effects of various incentives on performance should ideally be conducted within an actual organization. However, few organizations would permit the incentive manipulations necessary for conducting this study. Furthermore, performance within an organization may be affected by organization-specific factors that are not controllable by the experimenter. The current study was therefore conducted using a laboratory experiment. The generalizability of the results of this study will need to be tested using other tasks. While the study examines the effectiveness of incentives, it does not address the issue of incentive efficiency. Therefore, as is true of other studies of this nature, smaller or larger payments than were used in the study may not necessarily produce the same results.

REFERENCES

Ashton, R. H. (1990). Pressure and performance in accounting decision settings: Paradoxical effects of incentives, feedback, and justification. *Journal of Accounting Research, 28,* 148–180.

Bailey, C., Brown, L., & Cocco, A. (1998). The effects of monetary incentives on worker improvement and performance in an assembly task. *Journal of Management Accounting Research, 10,* 119–131.

Bandura, A., & Simon, K. M. (1977). The role of proximal intentions in self-regulation of refractory behavior. *Cognitive Therapy and Research, 1,* 177–193.

Berger, C., Cummings, L., & Heneman, H. (1975). Expectancy theory and operation conditioning predictions of performing under variable ratio and continuous schedules of enforcement. *Organizational Behavior and Human Performance, 14,* 227–240.

Bonner, S., Hastie, R., Sprinkle, G., & Young, S. (2000). A review of the effects of financial incentives on performance in laboratory tasks: Implications for management accounting. *Journal of Management Accounting Research, 12,* 19–64.

Bushhouse, F. E., Jr., Feeney, E. J., Dickinson, A. M., & O'Brien, R. M. (1982). Increased productivity in man-paced and machine-paced performance. In: R. M. O'Brien & A. M. Dickinson (Eds), *Industrial Behavior Modification.* New York: Pergamon Press.

Chow, C. W. (1983). The effects of job standard tightness and compensation incentive on performance: An exploration of the linkages. *The Accounting Review, 58,* 667–685.

Chow, C. W., Cooper, J., & Waller, J. (1988). Participative budgeting: Effects of a truth-inducing incentive and information asymmetry on slack and performance. *The Accounting Review* (January), 111–122.

Chung, K. H., & Vickery, W. D. (1976). Relative effectiveness and joint effects of three selected reinforcements in a repetitive task situation. *Organizational Behavior and Human Performance, 16,* 114–142.

Demski, J. S., & Feltham, G. A. (1978). Economic incentives in budgetary control systems. *The Accounting Review, 53,* 336–359.

Erez, M., Gopher, D., & Arzi, N. (1990). Effects of goal difficulty, self-set goals, and financial rewards on dual task performance. *Organizational Behavior and Human Decision Processes, 47,* 247–269.

Farr, J. L. (1976). Incentive schedules, productivity, and satisfaction in work groups. *Organizational Behavior and Human Performance, 7,* 159–170.

Gaetani, J. J., Hoxeng, D. D., & Austin, J. T. (1985). Engineering compensation systems: Effects of commissioned versus wage payment. *Journal of Organizational Behavior Management, 7,* 51–63.

Gershoni, H. (1971). Motivation and micro-method when improvement manual tasks. *Work Study and Management Services, 15,* 585–594.

Globerson, S., & Seidmann, A. (1988). The effects of imposed improvement curves on performance improvements. *IIE Transactions, 20,* 317–324.

Hilgard, E., & Bower, G. (1975). *Theories of improvement.* Englewood Cliffs, NJ: Prentice-Hall.

Huber, V. L. (1985). Comparison of monetary reinforcers and goal setting as improvement incentives. *Psychological Reports, 56*, 223–235.

Jorgenson, D., Dunnette, M. D., & Pritchard, R. D. (1973). Effects of the manipulation of a performance-reward contingency on behavior in a simulated work setting. *Journal of Applied Psychology, 57*, 271–280.

Kohn, A. (1993). Why incentive plans cannot work. *Harvard Business Review, 74*, 54.

Libby, R., & Lipe, M. G. (1992). Incentive effects and the cognitive processes involved in accounting judgments. *Journal of Accounting Research, 30*, 249–273.

Locke, E. A., & Latham, G. P. (1990). *Goal-setting and task performance*. Englewood Cliffs, NJ: Prentice-Hall.

Locke, E. A., Shaw, K., Saari, L., Latham, G., Feren, D. B., McCaleb, V. M., Shaw, K. N., & Denny, A. T. (1980). The relative effectiveness of four methods of motivating employee performance. In: K. D. Duncan, M. M. Gruneberg & D. Wallis (Eds), *Changes in Working Life* (pp. 363–388). New York, NY: Wiley.

McGraw, K. O. (1978). The detrimental effects of reward on performance: A literature review and a predictive model. In: M. R. Lepper & D. Greene (Eds), *The Hidden Costs of Reward* (pp. 33–60). Hillsdale, NJ: Lawrence-Erlbaum.

Nebeker, D. M., & Neuberger, B. M. (1985). Productivity improvement in a purchasing division: The impact of a performance contingent reward system. *Evaluation and Program Planning, 8*, 121–134.

Orphen, C. (1982). The effects of contingent and non-contingent rewards on employee satisfaction and performance. *The Journal of Psychology, 110*, 145–150.

Pritchard, R. D., & Curtis, M. I. (1973). The influence of goal setting and financial incentives on task performance. *Organizational Behavior and Human Performance, 10*, 175–183.

Ronen, J., & Livingstone, J. L. (1975). An expectancy theory approach to the motivational impacts of budgets. *Accounting Review* (October), 671–685.

Sprinkle, G. B. (2000). The effect of incentive contracts on learning and performance. *Accounting Review, 75*(3), 299–326.

Terborg, J. R., & Miller, H. E. (1978). Motivation, behavior and performance: A closer examination of goal setting and monetary incentives. *Journal of Applied Psychology, 63*, 29–39.

Young, S. M., & Lewis, B. (1995). Experimental incentive contracting research in management accounting. In: R. H. Ashton & A. H. Ashton (Eds), *Judgment and Decision Making Research in Accounting and Auditing* (pp. 55–75). New York, NY: Cambridge University Press.

Yukl, G., Wexley, K., & Seymore, J. (1972). Effectiveness of pay incentives under variable ratio and continuous reinforcement schedules. *Journal of Applied Psychology, 56*, 19–23.

EVALUATING PRODUCT MIX AND CAPITAL BUDGETING DECISIONS WITH AN ACTIVITY-BASED COSTING SYSTEM

Robert Kee

ABSTRACT

Product mix and the acquisition of the assets needed for their production are interdependent decisions. However, these decisions are frequently evaluated independently of each other and with conceptually different decision models. This article expands activity-based costing (ABC) to incorporate the cost of capital. The resulting model traces the cost of capital to products and thereby measures the economic value added (EVA) from their production. The discounted value of a product's EVA over its life is equivalent to its net present value (Hartman, 2000; Shrieves & Wachowicz, 2001). The discounted EVA of a product also equals the net present value of the assets used to manufacture the product. Consequently, evaluating products with an ABC model incorporating the cost of capital enables product mix and capital budgeting decisions to be evaluated simultaneously. The article also examines the role of ABC when product mix decisions are made at the product and portfolio levels of the firm's operations.

Advances in Management Accounting
Advances in Management Accounting, Volume 13, 77–98
ISSN: 1474-7871/doi:10.1016/S1474-7871(04)13004-9

The selection of long-term assets is one of the most crucial decisions affecting a firm's performance. Capital budgeting involves large expenditures of funds that determine, in part, the production opportunities available to the firm in the future. However, the financial implications of a capital budgeting decision are derived from the underlying economics of the products that a proposed asset will be used to produce. Conversely, the profitability of the firm's products is determined, in part, by the operational and financial attributes of the long-term assets acquired for their production. In effect, the economics of a product mix and the long-term assets acquired for its production are interrelated decisions. However, the analysis of product mix and capital budgeting opportunities is frequently performed as if the decisions were independent of each other. Furthermore, products are traditionally evaluated using accounting measures of profitability, while the assets used in their production are evaluated with discounted cash flow techniques. The evaluation of product mix and capital budgeting opportunities with conceptually different decision models can therefore result in incongruous decisions.

Balakrishnan and Sivaramakrishnan (1996) examined the usefulness of accounting profitability as a basis for product mix selection and the decision of how much capacity should be added to manufacture the products. When product demand is uniform and manufacturing capacity cannot be changed in the short run, the product mix and capacity decisions can be decomposed into a product-level problem. Products are evaluated based on their accounting profit and then sufficient capacity is acquired to enable the firm to manufacture the products. Under the conditions specified by Balakrishnan and Sivaramakrishnan (1996), accounting profitability provides sufficient information to assess the economic implications of product mix and capacity acquisition decisions simultaneously. However, when product demand is non-uniform and capacity cannot be changed in the short run, product mix and capacity decisions generally cannot be decomposed into a product-level problem. Instead, a product mix must be selected from an analysis of all feasible sets of products that can be manufactured with available capacity. Balakrishnan and Sivaramakrishnan (1996) refer to this as making product mix and capacity decisions at the portfolio level of a firm's operations. In their analysis, Balakrishnan and Sivaramakrishnan (1996) exclude the cost of capital and suppress the time value of money. However, financial theory requires discounting the cash flows of proposed assets at the cost of capital to determine their value.

The purpose of this article is to examine the relationship between product mix and capital budgeting decisions. Numeric examples are used to illustrate that accounting measures of profitability at both the product and portfolio levels of a firm's operations are insufficient, in some instances, for selecting a product mix that maximizes the discounted cash flows of the assets used in their production. The article examines how an activity-based costing (ABC) system can be modified to incorporate the cost of capital. The modified ABC model can be used to evaluate product mix and related capital budgeting decisions simultaneously. The article also examines conditions under which product mix and capital budgeting decisions must be made at the portfolio level of the firm's operations and the role that ABC plays in these types of decisions.

The remainder of the paper is organized as follows. The next section reviews studies comparing ABC and other cost systems. The section thereafter examines capital budgeting and how a modified ABC model can be used to evaluate proposed products, as well as the assets required for their production. A series of numerical examples then illustrate the application of the proposed ABC model under various assumptions about the nature of product demand. The final section presents the summary and conclusions of the paper.

STUDIES OF THE BENEFIT OF ACTIVITY-BASED COSTING RELATIVE TO OTHER COST SYSTEMS

ABC was developed to overcome the limitations of traditional cost systems. However, like any information system, the usefulness of ABC is dependent upon the economics of the information it provides. Early studies promoting ABC examined the significance of product cost measured with ABC relative to other cost systems (Cooper, 1988; Cooper & Kaplan, 1988). Equally important, early studies discussed the superiority of ABC, relative to alternative cost systems, for supporting operational and strategic decisions (Kaplan & Cooper, 1998; Turney, 1989). However, as noted by Dopuch (1993), a significant difference in the measurement of financial attributes with a new accounting system, relative to an existing system, is a necessary, but not a sufficient, condition for using a new system. That is, for ABC to be superior to other cost systems, ABC should lead to changes in decisions whose payoffs would be greater than the cost of its implementation (Lee, 2003).

Surveys of firms implementing ABC have examined the frequency of its adoption, how it is used in practice, and the satisfaction of users with ABC as an information system. Krumwiede (1998) and Shim and Stagliano (1997) found that a majority of firms in their surveys had either implemented, or were considering implementation of, ABC. Companies that had either not considered or considered and rejected ABC frequently cited cost benefit concerns as a reason for not implementing ABC (Shim & Stagliano, 1997). Malmi (1999), in a study of the use of ABC among Finnish firms, noted that early adoption of ABC was based upon factors, such as a firm's degree of competition and product diversity. Not surprisingly, these are the conditions under which differences in the measurement of cost objects with ABC and other cost systems would be the greatest.

In surveys of users of ABC, Swenson (1995), Shields (1995), and Foster and Swenson (1997) found that it is used for a variety of operational and strategic decisions, such as pricing, product mix, outsourcing, customer profit analysis, and product and process improvement. In the Swenson (1995) study, participants indicated that ABC was an improvement over their prior cost management systems. Similarly, in the Foster and Swenson (1997) study, managers indicated their firms' ABC efforts were moderate to very successful. Respondents in the Shields (1995) study reported, on average, a moderate level of success from using ABC, with 75% of respondents indicating that they had received a financial benefit from its use. The variation in the success among users of ABC was associated with the linkage of ABC to top management support, competitive strategies, performance evaluation and compensation, training, ownership by nonaccountants, and adequate resources (Shields, 1995). The frequency of ABC adoption and reported success by users suggests that firms have received an economic benefit from its implementation. However, success was measured differently across studies and respondents may have exhibited a self- selection bias.

Several studies have attempted to directly address the benefit of ABC by examining its association with a firm's financial performance. Ittner et al. (2002) examined the relationship between ABC usage and manufacturing performance. No significant association was found between the extensive use of ABC and a firm's return on assets. However, ABC was associated with improvements in quality and in cycle time (Ittner et al., 2002). In a similar study, Cagwin and Bouwman (2002) found a positive association between the use of ABC and return on investment (ROI) when ABC was used in conjunction with other management initiatives such as just in time and total quality management.[1] Cagwin and Bouwman (2002) note that ABC and improvement in ROI are associated when implemented in complex and diverse firms, in environments where cost are relatively important, and when there are a limited numbers of intra-company transactions to constrain benefits. Furthermore, enabling conditions, such as information technology sophistication, absence of excess capacity, and a competitive environment, affect the efficacy of ABC.

Kennedy and Affleck-Graves (2001), in a study of large UK companies, compared the financial performance of a sample of matched ABC and non-ABC firms. The difference in the holding period return over the three-year period, after the ABC firms had implemented ABC, was, on average, 27% higher than that of the non-ABC firms.[2] Other tests, such as an analysis of the cumulative abnormal return, wealth relatives, comparison to a market index, and accounting measures, supported the superior financial performance of the ABC relative to non-ABC firms. In the two years prior to ABC implementation, the financial performance of the ABC and non-ABC firms was not statistically significant. However, upon the implementation of ABC, the superior stock performance of the ABC firms, relative to the non-ABC firms, took about 18 months to manifest itself. Limitations of the Kennedy and Affleck-Graves (2001) study, such as, small sample size and the potential for factors not included in the study to be correlated with the use of ABC, restrict the generalizability of its conclusions.

The frequency of firms adopting and users' satisfaction with ABC and the results of studies examining the association of ABC and a firm's financial performance suggest that firms adopting ABC have received a financial benefit. However, as the Shields (1995), Ittner et al. (2002), and Cagwin and Bouwman (2002) studies indicate, firm-specific factors affect the benefits of ABC and not all firms may benefit from the adoption of ABC. Additional studies of the association between the adoption of ABC and financial performance, such as Kennedy and Affleck-Graves (2001), are needed to provide further evidence of the benefits of ABC as well as to provide greater specificity of the conditions under which firms receive a financial benefit from its implementation.[3]

CAPITAL BUDGETING, ECONOMIC VALUE ADDED, AND ACTIVITY-BASED COSTING

The acquisition of long-term assets involves economic issues that are unique to this type of decision. Capital budgeting commits substantial resources for lengthy periods of time. Investment decisions, once implemented, are frequently difficult and/or costly to reverse. Equally important, the purchases of long-term assets can significantly impact the firm's cost structure, along with the marketing and production opportunities available to the firm. Finally, capital budgeting decisions determine, in part, the competitive position of the firm's products. Accordingly, investment decisions are a major determinant of the firm's future operations and financial performance.

Financial theory prescribes the use of discounted cash flow techniques to evaluate capital investments. For example, the net present value (NPV) model discounts a project's cash flows at the firm's cost of capital to determine whether an asset's return is equal to or greater than the opportunity cost of invested funds. Conversely, the internal rate of return model computes the return that discounts an asset's cash flows to zero and then compares the calculated return with the firm's cost of capital. While financial theory specifies the use of discounted cash flow techniques to assess proposed capital projects, it provides little guidance for analysis of the products that a proposed asset will be used to create. With a few exceptions, capital assets do not generate cash flow, *per se*. Instead, they provide the capacity for manufacturing products that generate cash flows. In effect, evaluating a proposed asset involves an analysis of the cash flows of the products that an asset will be used to produce. Consequently, product mix and capital budgeting are interdependent decisions.

Product mix decisions are typically analyzed using accounting-based measures of their profitability. For example, Kaplan and Cooper (1998) provide an extended discussion of the role of ABC for product mix and pricing decisions. Swenson (1995) found that, for strategic decision-making, ABC was used most frequently for pricing and product mix decisions.[4] However, ABC, as well as traditional accounting systems, excludes the cost of capital in measuring the cost of the resources used to create a product. The opportunity cost of the funds used to produce a product is a cost the same as direct material, labor, and overhead. Consequently, only when a product has recovered the cost of all resources used in its production has it created value for the firm.

Stewart (1999) suggests that economic value added (EVA) should be used to measure the value created or destroyed from management decisions. Operationally, EVA is defined as an entity's operating profit after taxes less the cost of capital used to generate the profit. At the investment level of a firm's operations, a positive (negative) EVA indicates that, in that period, an asset will earn a return greater (less) than the cost of capital. When the EVA for each period of an investment's expected life is discounted to the asset's acquisition date, it is equivalent to the asset's NPV (Hartman, 2000; Shrieves & Wachowicz, 2001). Similarly, EVA can be used at the product level of a firm's operations. A product's EVA measures the economic value added or destroyed by manufacturing a proposed product. Since products are manufactured with an activity's assets, a product's EVA also reflects the economic income of the assets used in its production. Therefore, the discounted EVA of individual products also measures the NPV of the assets used in their production.

The relationship between EVA and NPV enables the economics of proposed products and the capital investments needed for their production to be analyzed with the same underlying conceptual models. Consequently, product mix and capital budgeting decisions, made with EVA and NPV, respectively, should lead to economically congruent decisions. Finally, EVA provides a metric for assessing the financial consequences of manufacturing proposed products that can be directly translated into the NPV of the proposed assets that will be used in their production. In effect, EVA provides a means of simultaneously evaluating the economics of product mix and capital investment decisions.

ABC is a model of a firm's cost structure that enables the cost of resources consumed by activities to be traced to the products that consume their services.

Relative to traditional cost systems, ABC represents a more accurate and detailed methodology for computing a product's cost. ABC also provides a powerful framework for measuring a product's EVA. This analysis may be accomplished using the principles of ABC to trace the opportunity cost of the firm's assets to activities and from activities to the products that use their services.

Incorporating the cost of capital into ABC provides a more comprehensive model of a firm's cost structure. For example, it aids a firm's management in understanding the cost of all of the resources consumed by an activity and the economic cost of their service. When the cost of capital used by an activity is traced to products, it provides a more general measure of the cost of producing the firm's products. Tracing the cost of capital from the activities to the products they are used to create allows ABC to expand from measuring a product's accounting profitability to measuring the economic value added or destroyed by the product. Consequently, managers are better able to understand the economics of their production processes and thereby make superior product mix decisions. Equally important, integrating the cost of capital into ABC can be used to stimulate efforts to reduce the quantity of capital and other resources employed by activities and/or the quantity of an activity's services used to produce a product. Either form of process improvement can reduce a product's cost and thereby increase its value added. Finally, the expansion of ABC permits it to be extended to the evaluation of the assets that will be used to manufacture the firm's products.

PRODUCT MIX AND CAPITAL BUDGETING DECISIONS

To illustrate the application of ABC incorporating the cost of capital to product mix and capital budgeting decisions, consider a firm evaluating the economic feasibility of manufacturing Products X and Y. Panel I of Table 1 lists the resource requirements for manufacturing Products X and Y. For example, three pounds of material, one labor hour, and two machine hours are required to produce a unit of Product X, while one and one half set-up hours and 15 purchase orders are needed to produce a batch of the product. Finally, 600 drawings from the engineering activity are used in product design. Products X and Y are new and will therefore require an investment in the assets of the activities used in their production. The costs of the assets required of each activity to manufacture Products X and Y are listed in Panels II and III, respectively. In Panels II and III, the cost driver for each activity is listed in parentheses. The investment in each activity was divided by its practical capacity and multiplied by the firm's opportunity cost funds of 10% to determine its capital driver rate. For example, the capital

Table 1. Investment, Cost, and Operating Data.

Panel 1: Products and Resource Requirements	Product X	Product Y
Direct material (Lbs @$5/Lb)	3 Lbs/Unit	2 Lbs/Unit
Direct labor (DLH @$15/DLH)	1 DLH/Unit	1 DLH/Unit
Assembly (MH)	2 MH/Unit	4 MH/Unit
Set-up (hours)	1.5 Hours/Batch	5 Hours/Batch
Purchasing (orders)	15 Orders/Batch	35 Orders/Batch
Engineering (drawings)	600 Drawings	600 Drawings
Batch size	1,000	1,000
Batches	250	200
Price	$55.00	$72.50
Expected annual demand (units)	250,000	200,000
Expected economic life of the product	3 Years	3 Years

Panel II: Invested Funds-Product X	Invested Funds*	Practical Capacity	Year 1 Capital Driver Rate**
Activity			
Assembly (MH)	$9,000,000	500,000	$1.80
Set-up (hours)	$300,000	375	$80.00
Purchasing (orders)	$75,000	3,750	$2.00
Engineering (drawings)	$900,000	600	$150.00
	$10,275,000		

*Useful life-three years
**Cost of capital is 10%.

Panel III: Invested funds-product Y			
Activity			
Assembly (MH)	$14,400,000	800,000	$1.80
Set-up (hours)	$800,000	1,000	$80.00
Purchasing (orders)	$140,000	7,000	$2.00
Engineering (drawings)	$900,000	600	$150.00
	$16,240,000		

*Useful life-three years
**Cost of capital is 10%.

Panel IV: Cost Driver Rates-Product X

Activity	Cash Expenditures	Depreciation Cost*	Operating Cost	Practical Capacity	Cost Driver Rates
Assembly (MH)	$1,000,000	$3,000,000	$4,000,000	500,000	$8
Set-up (hours)	$143,750	$100,000	$243,750	375	$650
Purchasing (orders)	$350,000	$25,000	$375,000	3,750	$100
Engineering (drawings)	$180,000	$300,000	$480,000	600	$800

Panel V: Cost driver rates-product Y

Activity					
Assembly (MH)	$1,600,000	$4,800,000	$6,400,000	800,000	$8
Set-up (hours)	$383,333	$266,667	$650,000	1,000	$650
Purchasing (orders)	$653,333	$46,667	$700,000	7,000	$100
Engineering (drawings)	$180,000	$300,000	$480,000	600	$800

*Straight-line depreciation is used

driver rate for the assembly activity is $1.80 per machine hour in Year 1, or
$9,000,000/500,000 machine hours *0.10.

Panel III identifies the investment for each activity needed to produce Product
Y. Products X and Y employ the same activities and assets in their production.
However, the capacity of the activities needed to produce Product Y is generally
more than that of Product X. It was assumed that the cost of the assets and their
capacity used by activities to create Product Y is proportional to the investment
and capacity of the activities used to manufacture Product X. Consequently, the
capital driver rates for the activities used to manufacture Product Y are the same
as those for Product X.

Panels IV and V list the operating costs of the activities used to manufacture
Products X and Y, respectively. The cash expenditures necessary to provide the
capacity required to manufacture Products X and Y are listed in the second column
of Panels IV and V, respectively. The annual depreciation expense for each
activity's assets was calculated using straight-line depreciation and an expected
useful life of three years. The cash expenditures and depreciation expense were
then added to determine each activity's operating cost. The resulting cost is divided
by an activity's practical capacity to determine its cost driver rate. For example,
the operating cost of the assembly activity for Product X of $4,000,000 per year is
divided by its practical capacity of 500,000 machine hours to derive a cost driver
rate of $8 per machine hour. The cost driver rates for the other activities in Panel
IV and those for activities used to produce Product Y in Panel V are computed in a
similar manner.

Case I: Uniform Product Demand

The initial illustration of ABC incorporating the cost of capital assumes that
the demand for Products X and Y is uniform and that capacity can initially be
acquired in the quantity needed. The capacity of the assets of each activity, except
assembly, is adjusted to the capacity needed to manufacture a given product or
set of products each period. For example, the capacity of the set-up, purchasing,
and engineering activities are used elsewhere in the firm's operations in periods
of excess capacity and additional resources are added to these activities in periods
when their capacity is insufficient. Conversely, the capacity of the assembly
activity is acquired in any quantity initially desired. However, once acquired, the
capacity of the assembly activity cannot be used elsewhere in the firm's operations
or augmented with additional resources. Balakrishnan and Sivaramakrishnan
(1996) refer to this type of capacity as a hard constraint that potentially limits the
firm's production opportunities.

The operating and capital costs of manufacturing Products X and Y are listed in Panel I of Table 2. Operating cost for material and labor is computed by multiplying the quantity of each input required to manufacture a unit of Product X and Product Y times their respective costs listed in Panel I of Table 1. Similarly, the operating cost of the assembly activity is the product of the machine hours used to create each product times the assembly activity's cost driver rate listed in Panel IV of Table 1. Set-up and purchasing are batch-level activities. Therefore, their costs are computed by multiplying the quantity of set-up hours and purchase orders required to manufacture a batch of Product X and Product Y times their respective cost driver rates. The last activity, engineering, is a product-level activity. Therefore, its operating cost is the product of the number of engineering drawings required for each product times the engineering activity's cost driver rate. The costs of direct material, labor, and assembly were added to determine total unit-level cost, while the costs of set-up and purchasing were summed to determine total batch-level cost. Total product-level cost is the cost of engineering.

There is no capital cost associated with material and labor. Therefore, the opportunity cost of these inputs for each product in Panel I is zero. Conversely, the assembly activity is comprised of capital assets. Therefore, its capital cost is computed by multiplying the quantity of machine hours needed to create Products X and Y times the assembly activity's capital driver rate. The opportunity cost of the set-up and purchasing activities is the product of the quantity of set-up and purchasing services needed to manufacture a batch of Product X and Product Y times their respective capital driver rates. Similarly, the capital cost for engineering is the number of drawings needed to design each product times the engineering activity's capital driver rate. Like operating cost, capital costs were summed to determine total unit- and batch-level capital costs. Total product-level capital cost is the opportunity cost of engineering for each product.

Panel II of Table 2 presents an income statement for manufacturing Products X and Y. The revenue of each product is determined by multiplying its annual demand and price listed in Panel I of Table 1. Similarly, unit- and batch-level costs are computed by multiplying the number of units and batches of each product listed in Panel I of Table 1 times their unit- and batch-level costs in Panel I of Table 2. Product-level cost is incurred if a product is produced and is independent of the number of units or batches produced. Therefore, product-level cost is expensed based on whether a product is produced. Unit-, batch-, and product-level costs are summed and subtracted from sales to determine operating income before taxes. The firm's tax rate of 20% is used to determine each product's tax expense and operating income after taxes.

To calculate the EVA of Products X and Y, the cost of capital consumed in their production is computed. Unit- and batch-level capital costs are computed

Table 2. Product EVA and NPV.

Panel I: Operating and Capital Costs

	Product X		Product Y	
	Operating Cost	Capital Cost-Yr 1	Operating Cost	Capital Cost-Yr 1
Direct material-unit level	$15.00	$0.00	$10.00	$0.00
Direct labor-unit level	$15.00	$0.00	$15.00	$0.00
Assembly-unit level	$16.00	$3.60	$32.00	$7.20
Total unit level	$46.00	$3.60	$57.00	$7.20
Set-up-batch level	$975.00	$120.00	$3,250.00	$400.00
Purchasing-batch level	$1,500.00	$30.00	$3,500.00	$70.00
Total batch level	$2,475.00	$150.00	$6,750.00	$470.00
Engineering-product level	$480,000.00	$90,000.00	$480,000.00	$90,000.00

Panel II: Product Operating Income and EVA in Year 1

	Product X	Product Y
Sales (units)	250,000	200,000
Revenue	$13,750,000	$14,500,000
Operating costs		
Unit-level	$11,500,000	$11,400,000
Batch-level	$618,750	$1,350,000
Product-level	$480,000	$480,000
Total cost	$12,598,750	$13,230,000
Operating income	$1,151,250	$1,270,000
Tax expense (20%)	$230,250	$254,000
Operating income after taxes	$921,000	$1,016,000
Capital cost (10%)		
Unit-level	$900,000	$1,440,000
Batch-level	$37,500	$94,000
Product-level	$90,000	$90,000
Total capital cost	$1,027,500	$1,624,000
EVA for year 1	$(106,500)	$(608,000)

Panel III: NPV

Product X	Year 1	Year 2	Year 3
Operating income after taxes	$921,000	$921,000	$921,000
Capital cost	$1,027,500	$685,000	$342,500
EVA	$(106,500)	$236,000	$578,500
Discounted EVA	$(96,818)	$195,041	$434,636
NPV	$532,859		
Product Y			
Operating income after taxes	$1,016,000	$1,016,000	$1,016,000
Capital cost	$1,624,000	$1,082,667	$541,333
EVA	$(608,000)	$(66,667)	$474,667
Discounted EVA	$(552,727)	$(55,096)	$356,624
NPV	$(251,200)		

by multiplying the annual demand and batches of each product times their respective unit- and batch-level capital driver rates listed in Panel I of Table 2. A product-level capital cost of $90,000 was expensed for each product. Unit-, batch-, and product-level capital costs are then summed and subtracted from operating income after taxes to determine the first year's EVA of each product.

In Panel III of Table 2, the EVA of Products X and Y, in Year 1 and subsequent periods, is computed. The operating income after taxes of each product remains constant since annual demand, price, and operating costs are uniform over each product's life. However, capital driver rates for each activity change due to the decline in the book value of each activity's assets, as each successive period's depreciation expense is taken. If the capacity of an activity's assets is unaffected by the passage of time, its capital driver rate declines monotonically over time. When straight-line depreciation is used, an activity's capital driver rate each period is given by the formula:

$$CDR_i = CDR_{i=1} \times \frac{N+1-i}{N} \tag{1}$$

where: CDR_i = capital driver rate in Period i, i = the period in which a capital driver rate is computed, $i = 1, \ldots, N$, $CDR_{i=1}$ = capital driver rate in Period 1, and N = the useful life of an activity's assets.

For example, the capital driver rate for the assembly activity is $1.80 per machine hour in Period 1. Therefore, its capital driver rates in Periods 2 and 3 would be $1.20 and $.60 per machine hour, respectively.

The capital costs in Years 2 and 3 in Panel III are computed similarly to those in Panel II, except that an activity's capital driver rate in Period 1 was multiplied times Eq. 1 with $i = 2$ and 3, respectively. The unit-, batch-, and product-level costs of capital are subtracted from operating income after taxes each period to determine each product's EVA in Periods 2 and 3. The EVA for each product is then discounted to the beginning of Period 1. As noted earlier, a cost object's discounted EVA equals its NPV. In Panel III, the NPV of Products X and Y and the investment in the assets necessary for their production are $532,859 and $-251,200, respectively.[5]

As indicated in Panel II of Table 2, the annual operating income, after taxes, for Products X and Y is expected to be $921,000 and $1,016,000, respectively. The profit margin, or operating income after taxes divided by revenue, for Products X and Y are 6.7% and 7.0%, respectively. Based on operating income after taxes or profit margin, Product Y appears to be the more profitable of the two products. If accounting income is used to evaluate which product to produce, then Product Y will be chosen. However, the discounted cash flows of the assets used to produce Product Y are negative. Therefore, the firm should conclude that the return on the assets used to manufacture Product Y is insufficient to justify purchasing the assets. Since Product X is less profitable than Product Y, a firm's management might erroneously drop Product X from further consideration. However, while Product X is the least profitable product, the discounted cash flows of the assets used in its production are positive.

Under the economic conditions of Case I, a product mix can be selected at the product level of the firm's operations. With uniform product demand and flexible capacity in Period 1, each product's marginal cost equals the cost of the resources used in its production, or its full cost. Furthermore, a product's marginal cost is unaffected by decisions made with respect to the firm's other products. Consequently, each product in Period 1 can be evaluated based on its profitability independently of other product and capacity considerations. Under Case I, the firm faces the same marketing and production opportunities each period. Therefore, the optimal product mix and capacity acquired for production in Period 1 are also optimal for each successive period.

A critical implication of product mix and capital budgeting decisions, illustrated in Table 2, is that products that maximize accounting measures of profitability will not necessarily maximize the discounted cash flows of the assets used in their production. This principle is true under the least stringent set of economic conditions, i.e. product demand is uniform and capacity, at the point of acquisition, is flexible. In Case I, a product's marginal cost, full cost, and long-run costs are equivalent. However, accounting-based measures of product costs exclude the opportunity cost of funds used in production. Consequently, accounting-based systems underestimate the marginal cost of a product, as well as that of the capacity used in production. This distortion may lead to the selection of products that use excessive capital resources, as well as lead to the acquisition of more capacity than is optimal. However, when the opportunity cost of funds is incorporated into a cost system, such as ABC, the resulting marginal cost reflects the incremental operating and capital costs of resources used to produce a product. Consequently, managers are able to evaluate whether a product's and a unit of capacity's marginal cost is less than or equal to the marginal revenue it generates.

Case II: Non-Uniform Product Demand

The second example of ABC incorporating the cost of capital is more restrictive and reflects more realistic conditions under which product mix and capital budgeting decisions are frequently made. The demand for prospective products is unlikely to be uniform, especially for those with a relatively short life cycle. Assume that the demand for Product X is 80,000, 240,000, and 125,000 units, respectively, while the demand for Product Y is 100,000, 250,000, and 100,000 units over their respective lives. The price of Product Y has also been changed from $72.50 to $76 per unit to enable one or more product mixes to have a positive NPV. All other cost and operating data are the same as in Case I.

The selection of a product mix when product demand is non-uniform and the capacity of one or more activities cannot be changed in the short run is more complicated than in Case I. With non-uniform product demand and fixed capacity for at least one activity, one or more production periods will incur unused capacity and/or unfilled product demand. In a period in which the firm has unused capacity, a product's marginal cost is no longer equal to its full cost. Conversely, in periods in which capacity is insufficient to meet product demand, producing a product incurs an opportunity cost from the other product(s) the firm must forego. In effect, the economics of producing a product are affected by the production of the firm's other products. Consequently, products cannot be evaluated based on their individual revenue and cost. Rather, products must be evaluated at the portfolio level of the firm's operations. Joint analysis of even a few products can involve evaluating a significant number of variables, such as production quantities, capacity, and products' marginal and opportunity costs. Therefore, to solve for the optimal product mix, the data for Products X and Y in Case II are formulated as a mixed integer programming model in Table 3.

The first equation in Table 3, or the objective function, reflects the goal of maximizing the discounted EVAs from the different mix of products that may be produced. The coefficient of the variable X_i, or the quantity of Product X produced in Period i, is the price of Product X less the unit-, and batch-level costs associated with manufacturing a unit of Product X. For example, the coefficient of Product X is its price of $55 minus the costs of the direct material, direct labor, set-up, and purchasing on a per-unit basis of $32.475, with the result multiplied by 1 minus the tax rate, or $18.02 per unit.[6] The coefficient for the variable, EX_i, or the use of engineering to design Product X in Period i, is the cost of engineering for Product X on an after-tax basis. The coefficients for Y_i and EY_i are computed the same as those for X_i and EX_i, respectively. The coefficient for C_i, or the quantity of machine hours acquired for the assembly activity in Period i, is the cost driver rate for the assembly activity on an after-tax basis. The coefficients for the remaining five terms are the costs of capital for X_i, Y_i, EX_i, EY_i, and C_i. For example, the coefficient for the sixth term is the capital cost of the set-up and purchasing activities needed to manufacture a unit of Product X_i times Eq. 1 for Period i. Similarly, the coefficient for the eighth term is the $90,000 in capital cost from engineering to design Product X in Period 1 times Eq. 1. The seventh and ninth terms in the objective function for Y_i and EY_i can be interpreted in a similar

Table 3.   Mixed Integer Programming Model.

Objective Function:

$$\text{Max}\, Z = \sum_{i=1}^{3}\left[\frac{18.02X_i}{(1+0.10)^i} + \frac{35.4Y_i}{(1+0.10)^i} - \frac{384,000\,EX_i}{(1+0.10)^i}\right.$$

$$-\frac{384,000\,EY_i}{(1+0.10)^i} - \frac{6.40C_i}{(1+0.10)^i} - \frac{(0.15(4-i)/3)X_i}{(1+0.10)^i}$$

$$-\frac{(0.47(4-i)/3)Y_i}{(1+0.10)^i} - \frac{(90,000(4-i)/3)EX_i}{(1+0.10)^i}$$

$$\left. -\frac{(90,000(4-i)/3)EY_i}{(1+0.10)^i} - \frac{(1.8(4-i)/3C_i}{(1+0.10)^i}\right]$$

Subject to

1. Demand for $X_{i=1}$	$1X_1$				$= 80{,}000$
2. Demand for $X_{i=2}$	$1X_2$				$= 240{,}000$
3. Demand for $X_{i=3}$	$1X_3$				$= 125{,}000$
4. Demand for $Y_{i=1}$		$1Y_1$			$= 100{,}000$
5. Demand for $Y_{i=2}$		$1Y_2$			$= 250{,}000$
6. Demand for $Y_{i=3}$		$1Y_3$			$= 100{,}000$
7. Assembly $C_{i=1}$	$2X_1$	$+4Y_1$		$-1C_1$	$= 0$
8. Assembly $C_{i=2}$	$2X_2$	$+4Y_2$		$-1C_2$	$= 0$
9. Assembly $C_{i=3}$	$2X_3$	$+4Y_3$		$-1C_3$	$= 0$
10. Assembly $C_{i=1,2}$				C_1-C_2	$= 0$
11. Assembly $C_{i=1,3}$				C_1-C_3	$= 0$
12. Engineering $X_{i=1}$	$1X_1$	$-80{,}000EX_1$			$= 0$
13. Engineering $X_{i=2}$	$1X_2$	$-240{,}000EX_2$			$= 0$
14. Engineering $X_{i=3}$	$1X_3$	$-125{,}000EX_3$			$= 0$
15. Engineering $Y_{i=1}$		$1Y_1$	$-100{,}000EY_1$		$= 0$
16. Engineering $Y_{i=2}$		$1Y_2$	$-250{,}000EY_2$		$= 0$
17. Engineering $Y_{i=3}$		$1Y_3$	$-100{,}000EY_3$		$= 0$

Note: Where: Z = NPV. X_i = units of Product X produced in Period i, $X_i \geq 0$, $i = 1, 2, 3$. Y_i = units of Product Y produced in Period i, $Y_i \geq 0$, $i = 1, 2, 3$. EX_i = engineering for Product X in Period i, $EX_i = 0$ or 1, $i = 1, 2, 3$. EY_i = engineering for Product Y in Period i, $EY_i = 0$ or 1, $i = 1, 2, 3$. C_i = quantity of machine hours acquired for the assembly activity in Period i, $i = 1, 2, 3$.

manner. The coefficient for the last term in the objective function is the capital driver rate for a unit of capacity in the assembly activity times Eq. 1. Finally, each term in the objective function is discounted to the beginning of Period 1.

The second part of the mixed integer programming model lists the constraints that reflect the production and marketing opportunities available to the firm. The first 6 constraints in Table 3 relate to the market demand for Products X and Y during each year of their lives. Constraints 7 through 9 capture the quantity of assembly hours, or C_i, required to manufacture Products X and Y in Period i. The inclusion of capacity as a variable in the objective function and in Constraints 7 through 9 enables the mixed integer programming model to identify the product mix and the quantity of capacity for the assembly activity that maximizes the discounted EVA simultaneously. Constraints 10 and 11 ensure that the quantity of capacity acquired is the same each period. The last six constraints determine the use of engineering to design Products X and Y in each year of their lives. The variables for engineering are restricted to binary values. Therefore, if Products X_i and Y_i are produced in Period i, EX_i and EY_i are assigned a value of 1; otherwise, they are assigned a value of 0.[7]

The optimal solution to the mixed integer model in Table 3 appears in Panel I of Table 4.[8] The optimal product mix consists of manufacturing 100,000 units of Y in Year 1, 200,000 units of X in Year 2, and 100,000 units of Y in year 3. The corresponding values for EX and EY are 1 for EX in Period 2 and 1 for EY in Years 1 and 3. Finally, the optimal quantity of capacity acquired for the assembly activity is 400,000 machine hours. Panel I of Table 4 contains an income statement for the optimal product mix. Annual sales, operating, and capital costs at the unit-, batch-, and product levels of the firm's operations are computed similarly to those in Panels II and III of Table 2. These computations result in a total operating income, after taxes, of $1,852,000 and a discounted value of each period's EVA of $78,530.

The mixed integer programming model in Table 3 was solved a second time with the cost of capital set to 0. A product's EVA, based on a cost of capital of 0, is equivalent to its accounting income after taxes. With a cost of capital of 0, the denominator for each term in the objective function in Table 3 equals 1, while the numerator of the last 5 terms is equal to 0.[9] Therefore, the objective function, based on maximizing accounting income, consists of the numerator for the first five terms in the objective function in Table 3. Changing the definition of cost in the objective function has no effect on the marketing and production constraints of the firm. Therefore, a mixed integer programming model, based on accounting income, will be the same as that in Table 3, except for the change in the objective function.

The optimal solution to the mixed integer programming model in Table 3, modified to reflect a cost of capital of 0, is given in Panel II of Table 4. The solution that maximizes accounting income produces 80,000, 0, and 125,000 units of Product X, respectively, and 100,000, 140,000, and 77,500 units of Product Y in Years 1, 2, and 3, respectively. The corresponding values of EX and EY are 1 in each period, except for Year 2, for EX. The capacity in the assembly activity that must be acquired to produce the optimal product mix is 560,000 machine hours. The accounting income of the product mix in Panel II of Table 4 is computed similarly to that of the product mix in Panel I of Table 4. The accounting income, after taxes, of the optimal product mix is $2,258,900. Even though the product mix in Panel II was selected based on accounting income, the firm's cost of capital

Table 4. Optimal Product Mix, Income, and NPV.

	Year 1	Year 2	Year 3
Panel I: Model solution based on discounted EVA			
Product *X*	0	200,000	0
Product *Y*	100,000	0	100,000
EX	0	1	0
EY	1	0	1
Assembly capacity acquired in MH	400,000	400,000	400,000
Sales	$7,600,000	$11,000,000	$7,600,000
Operating costs			
Unit-level	$5,700,000	$9,200,000	$5,700,000
Batch-level	$675,000	$495,000	$675,000
Product-level	$480,000	$480,000	$480,000
Operating income before taxes	$745,000	$825,000	$745,000
Operating income after taxes	$596,000	$660,000	$596,000
Capital costs			
Unit-level	$720,000	$480,000	$240,000
Batch-level	$47,000	$20,000	$15,667
Product-level	$90,000	$60,000	$30,000
EVA	$(261,000)	$100,000	$310,333
NPV	$78,530		
Panel II: Model solution based on accounting income			
Product *X*	80,000	0	125,000
Product *Y*	100,000	140,000	77,500
EX	1	0	1
EY	1	1	1
Assembly capacity acquired in MH	560,000	560,000	560,000
Sales	$12,000,000	$10,640,000	$12,765,000
Operating costs			
Unit-level	$9,380,000	$7,980,000	$10,167,500
Batch-level[a]	$873,000	$945,000	$835,875
Product-level	$960,000	$480,000	$960,000
Operating income before taxes	$787,000	$1,235,000	$801,625
Operating income after taxes	629,600	988,000	641,300
Capital costs			
Unit-level	$1,008,000	$672,000	$336,000
Batch-level[a]	$59,000	$43,867	$18,470
Product-level	$180,000	$60,000	$60,000
EVA	$(617,400)	$212,133	$226,830
NPV	$(215,535)		

[a] The number of batches for Product *Y* in Period 3 was rounded up to 78 to compute batch-level cost.

remains 10%. Therefore, the EVA of the optimal product mix in Panel II is computed the same as that in Panels II and III of Table 2. The discounted EVAs of the optimal product mix are −$215,535.

The product mixes listed in Panels I and II of Table 4 maximize the discounted EVA and accounting income, respectively. As illustrated, these objectives lead to different product mixes, levels of capacity for the assembly activity, accounting income, and NPVs. The differences in accounting income and NPVs, in Panels I and II, respectively, demonstrate that the selection of a product mix based on operating income after taxes, even at the portfolio level of the firm's operations, may not lead to the selection of a product mix that maximizes the NPV of the assets used in their production. The accounting measure of profitability fails to incorporate the opportunity cost of funds into an activity's and product's cost. Therefore, accounting-based measures of income will underestimate the marginal cost of performing an activity, as well as the cost of manufacturing a product. Using accounting income to evaluate products may also lead to the selection of products and related production capacity whose marginal cost exceeds their marginal revenue.

The marketing and production structure of Case II creates an environment in which the marginal and opportunity costs of a product can be affected by the firm's other products. Consequently, a product mix must be evaluated based on joint analysis of the firm's products. In Case II, the role of ABC is dramatically different than in Case I. In Case I, ABC incorporating the cost of capital is useful for measuring the economic income for evaluating which products are sufficiently profitable to produce. Conversely, in Case II, ABC measures both the cost of the operating and capital resources used to perform an activity's service. The cost of each activity's service, the quantity of its service used by a product, each activity's practical capacity, and the production and marketing opportunities of the firm can be modeled to reflect the interdependencies of a product mix decision. Thus, ABC provides the level of cost granularity and the causal relationship necessary for developing a model reflecting the interactions among the physical and economic attributes of products.

SUMMARY AND CONCLUSIONS

Product mix and capital budgeting are among the most important decisions affecting a firm's financial performance. However, these decisions are typically evaluated independently of each other and are analyzed with conceptually different economic models. Balakrishnan and Sivaramakrishnan (1996) demonstrate that, when a product's demand is uniform and capacity cannot be changed in the short run, an optimal product mix can be selected by an analysis of individual products using accounting measures of profitability. However, when product demand is non-uniform, product mix and capacity decisions must be made at the portfolio level of the firm's operations.

In this article, ABC is expanded to incorporate the cost of capital and used to evaluate product mix and capital budgeting decisions. Like Balakrishnan and Sivaramakrishnan (1996), this article demonstrates that, when product demand is uniform and the capacity of one or more activities cannot be changed in the short run, product mix and capital budgeting decisions can be evaluated at the product level of the firm's operations. Similarly, when product demand is non-uniform, a product mix must be selected from an analysis of all potential product combinations. However, the product mix that maximizes accounting profitability is not necessarily the same as the product mix that maximizes the discounted cash flows of the assets used in its production. Consequently, accounting measures of profitability are insufficient for evaluating proposed products and the capacity required for their production at both the product and the portfolio levels of the firm's operations.

An ABC model incorporating the cost of capital is more expensive to develop and use than other cost systems. However, it provides a more comprehensive model of the economics of performing production-related activities and that of the products they are used to produce. Consequently, an ABC model, based on the cost of operating and capital resources, provides a means of measuring a product's economic income, as well as the NPV of the assets that are used in its production. Consequently, it enables managers to integrate product mix and capital budgeting decisions. The benefits of ABC are often firm- specific (Cagwin & Bouwman, 2002). Therefore, firms must consider how the proposed ABC model would change their product mix and capital budgeting decisions and the payoffs relative to the increased cost of implementing an ABC model that incorporates the cost of capital.

NOTES

1. Similar to Ittner et al. (2002), Cagwin and Bouwman (2002) did not find a positive association between ABC and an improvement in a firm's financial performance. However, as noted by Cagwin and Bouwman (2002), firms that use ABC extensively also frequently implement other management initiatives.

2. The improvement in financial performance of ABC relative to non-ABC firms was statistically significant at the 5% level (Kennedy & Affleck-Graves, 2001). A positive stock market reaction to firms adopting ABC measures whether the benefits of ABC exceed the cost of its implementation. Assuming market efficiency, if decisions made

with ABC add value to the firm, then the market would be expected to demonstrate a positive association with the adoption of ABC. Conversely, a negative or non-reaction of the market, with respect to firms adopting ABC, would indicate a negative and non-benefit, respectively. There are several problems associated with an events study of firms implementing ABC. See Kennedy and Affleck-Graves (2001) for an extended discussion of these issues.

3. In Lee's (2003) taxonomy of cost systems research, Ittner et al. (2002), Cagwin and Bouwman (2002), and Kennedy and Affleck-Graves (2001), research would be classified as general-state studies. These cost accounting studies deal directly with ABC as a "better" cost system in a general context.

4. Marketing textbooks discuss the role of accounting profitability in establishing product prices. For example, Kotler and Armstrong (2004) note that many firms use current profit maximization as a pricing goal. Also, Solomon and Stuart (2003) discuss how a firm's profit objectives are met through pricing to achieve a target level of profit growth or desired net profit margin.

5. The annual cash flow for the assets used to produce Product X totals $4,346,000. Total cash flow is the sum of operating income after taxes, of $921,000, plus the depreciation expense of $3,425,000. The NPV for an initial cash outlay of $10,275,000, with annual cash inflows of $4,346,000 for 3 years at a cost of capital of 10%, is $532,859. Similar analysis of the operating income after taxes and depreciation expense for Product Y leads to an NPV of −$251,200.

6. In Panel I of Table 2, the cost of material and labor to produce a unit of Product X is $30. Conversely, the cost of set-up and purchasing to create a batch of 1,000 units of Product X is $2,475, or $2.475 on a per- unit basis. Therefore, the cost of material, labor, set-up, and purchasing to produce a unit of Product X equals $32.475.

7. Each product is redesigned each period to incorporate new and improved features.

8. The computational time required to solve a mixed integer program model may be substantially more than a comparable linear programming model. However, computation time can be reduced by the manner in which a problem is formulated or structured. The mixed integer model, illustrated in Table 3, was simplified by combining the cost of consumable and capital resources for the variables X_i, Y_i, EX_i, EY_i, and C_i and includes batch-related cost for the set-up and purchasing activities in unit-level costs. These adjustments significantly reduced the number of variables in the objective function, as well as the number of constraints. For an extended discussion of mixed integer programming, see Ignizio and Cavalier (1994) and Wolsey (1998).

9. The coefficients for the last 5 terms in the objective function of Table 3 are the cost of capital for X_i, Y_i, EX_i, EY_i, and C_i. Consequently, when the cost of capital is 0, the coefficients for these terms are also 0.

REFERENCES

Balakrishnan, R., & Sivaramakrishnan, K. (1996). Is assigning capacity costs to individual products necessary for capacity planning? *Accounting Horizons, 10*(September), 1–11.

Cagwin, D., & Bouwman, M. (2002). The association between activity-based costing and improvement in financial performance. *Management Accounting Research, 13*, 1–39.

Cooper, R. (1988). The rise of activity-based costing-part one: What is an activity-based cost system? *Journal of Cost Management* (Summer), 45–53.

Cooper, R., & Kaplan, R. (1988). Measure costs right: Make the right decisions. *Harvard Business Review*, *66*(September–October), 96–103.

Dopuch, N. (1993). A perspective on cost drivers. *Accounting Review*, *68*, 615–620.

Foster, G., & Swenson, D. (1997). Measuring the success of activity-based cost management and its determinants. *Journal of Management Accounting Research*, *9*(Fall), 111–141.

Hartman, J. (2000). On the equivalence of net present value and market value added as measures of a project's economic worth. *Engineering Economist*, *45*, 158–165.

Ignizio, J., & Cavalier, T. (1994). *Linear programming*. Englewood Cliffs, NJ: Prentice-Hall.

Ittner, C., Lanen, W., & Larcker, D. (2002). The association between activity-based costing and manufacturing performance. *Journal of Accounting Research*, *40*, 711–726.

Kaplan, R., & Cooper, R. (1998). *Cost & effect: Using integrated cost systems to drive profitability and performance*. Boston, MA: Harvard Business School Press.

Kennedy, T., & Affleck-Graves, J. (2001). The impact of activity-based costing techniques on firm performance. *Journal of Management Accounting Research*, *13*, 19–45.

Kotler, P., & Armstrong, G. (2004). *Principles of marketing* (10th ed.). Upper Saddle, NJ: Prentice-Hall.

Krumwiede, K. (1998). ABC: Why it's tried and how it succeeds. *Management Accounting*, *79*(April), 32–38.

Lee, J. (2003). Cost system research perspectives. *Advances in Management Accounting*, *11*, 39–57.

Malmi, T. (1999). Activity-based costing diffusion across organizations: An exploratory empirical analysis of Finnish firms. *Accounting, Organizations and Society*, *24*, 649–672.

Shields, M. (1995). An empirical analysis of firms' implementation experiences with activity-based costing. *Journal of Management Accounting Research*, *7*(Fall), 148–166.

Shim, E., & Stagliano, A. (1997). A survey of U.S. manufacturers on implementation of ABC. *Journal of Cost Management*, *11*(March–April), 39–41.

Shrieves, R., & Wachowicz, J. (2001). Free cash flow (FCF), economic value added (EVA), and net present value (NPV): A reconciliation of variations of discounted-cash-flow (DCF) valuation. *Engineering Economist*, *46*, 33–51.

Solomon, M., & Stuart, E. (2003). *Marketing: Real people, real choices* (3rd ed.) Upper Saddle, NJ: Prentice-Hall.

Stewart, G. (1999). *The quest for value: A guide for senior managers*. New York, NY: Harper Business.

Swenson, D. (1995). The benefits of activity-based cost management to the manufacturing industry. *Journal of Management Accounting Research*, *7*(Fall), 167–180.

Turney, P. (1989). Using activity-based costing to achieve manufacturing excellence. *Journal of Cost Management* (Summer), 23–31.

Wolsey, L. (1998). *Integer programming*. New York, NY: Wiley.

PERFORMANCE-BASED ORGANIZATIONS (PBOs) – THE TALE OF TWO PERFORMANCE-BASED ORGANIZATIONS

Valerie J. Richardson

ABSTRACT

In 1998 and 1999, the Office of Student Financial Assistance of the Department of Education and the Patent and Trademark Office of the Department of Commerce, were designated as Performance-Based Organizations (PBOs), respectively. This paper examines the transformation progress of the agencies, as they attempt to convert to high-performing organizations by utilizing and establishing new and more flexible systems of performance-oriented business practices and processes.

The paper compares and contrasts the different approaches and tools used to improve management and organizational performance, as well as concentrate on human resources, procurement, budget, customer service, and internal controls. The document explores whether or not these agencies have improved their performance as a result of these flexibilities and examines the organizational and cultural challenges encountered as the agencies move from a restrictive and bureaucratic system, to a more liberal system of management and internal controls.

The Performance-Based Organizations (PBOs) concept is to have federal agencies focus on the customer, deliver high quality products, and devise

Advances in Management Accounting
Advances in Management Accounting, Volume 13, 99–142
© 2004 Published by Elsevier Ltd.
ISSN: 1474-7871/doi:10.1016/S1474-7871(04)13005-0

more efficient operations. Therefore, the paper further examines whether or not the PBO legislation has been effective in changing the performance of federal organizations by granting administrative and managerial flexibilities aligned with corporate (agency) strategies, performance, and pay.

The 1990s were a period in which the federal government of the United States experimented with a myriad of new laws and initiatives designed to dramatically improve the manner and methods of governing and administering public programs. As the federal government searched for a means of improving government performance and service delivery, the National Partnership for Reinventing Government (NPR) created an initiative that would eliminate or alter, for "businesslike" organizations, the traditional federal procurement and personnel administrative procedures that have long been viewed as obstacles for attaining enhanced performance.

For the last half of the century (1880s to 1929) the central themes of the American public administration was businesslike management and the science of administration (Gawthrop, 1998). Therefore, the concept of operating in a businesslike manner was not new to public agencies upon its introduction in the 1990s. The objective of the NPR initiative was to create PBOs within the federal government that would operate in a businesslike fashion similar to private sector organizations. Federal agencies (with current operations similar to the private sector) were the initial candidates for PBOs. Each agency being considered had common characteristics: measurable mission statements, revenues generated as a result of fee-for-service activities, performance measurement systems in place or under development, and an external customer focus. Unlike a traditional federal agency, the objective of the NPR initiative was to have a PBO that would be committed to clear objectives, have specific measurable goals, establish customer service standards, and define specific targets for enhancing organizational performance.

Conversion to a performance-based organization would give these unique agencies the autonomy necessary to operate in a more businesslike and results-oriented fashion, by granting certain administrative and procedural flexibilities that address these barriers. Three federal agencies have received this designation over the last five years, and have become known as performance-based organizations (PBOs), to operate under a five-year plan for overhauling operations. It has been a little more than three years since the first PBO was established.

In 1998, the Office of Student Financial Assistance Programs (OSFAP), an agency of the Department of Education, became the first performance-based organization. In 1999 the conversion of the United States Patent and Trademark Office (USPTO) took place, which is an agency of the Department of Commerce, and then the Air Traffic Service division followed in 2000. Once functional, it will be known as the Air Traffic Organization (ATO) of the Federal Aviation Administration (FAA). This paper examines the progress of two of the three PBOs, the OSFAP and the USPTO.

The paper assesses progress made since the enactment, and the challenges and triumphs encountered as each engaged in innovative and trailblazing methods of transforming their agencies into high-performing organizations. Specifically, these new PBOs were to be held accountable for performance objectives that included: improving customer satisfaction; providing high-quality, cost-effective services; enhancing the ability to respond to the rapid rate of technological change; implementing a common, open, integrated system for product and service delivery; and providing complete, accurate, and timely information to ensure program integrity (Department of Education, Office of Student Financial Assistance Programs, 1998).

This paper compares and contrasts the different approaches and tools used by each agency to improve management and organizational performance, based upon data provided from each agency via one-on-one interviews and surveys conducted. It also concentrates on the key areas of management that were expected to provide benefits from the PBO status, including human resources, procurement, budget and financial management, customer service, and internal controls.

For federal organizations operating as fee-for-service agencies, four major barriers were consistently identified as having a restraining impact upon their ability to provide services and products, which meet the needs and demands of the public user. The barriers include: (1) pay-for-performance, and recruitment and retention practices; (2) budgetary and financial practices; (3) contract and acquisition practices; and (4) accountability.

The paper explores whether or not these agencies have improved their performance as a result of these flexibilities. It also examines the organizational and cultural challenges encountered as the agencies moved from a restrictive and bureaucratic system into a more performance-oriented system of organizational management and internal controls.

The paper further explores and examines whether or not the PBO legislation has been effective in changing the performance of federal organizations, by granting administrative and managerial flexibilities aligned with corporate (agency) performance and pay. The PBO philosophy rests on the concept of having federal agencies focus on the customer, deliver high-quality products, and devise more efficient operations.

AGENCY BACKGROUNDS

Office of Student Financial Assistance Programs (OSFAP)

The legislation that established OSFAP as a PBO was the Reauthorization Act of the Higher Education Act of 1998 (P.L. 105-244). Once a part of the Office of Higher Education within the United States Department of Education, OSFAP became the United States' first performance-based organization by way of the 1998 Reauthorization Act. OSFAP is charged with administering the student financial assistance programs for the United States, such as Pell Grants, Perkins Loans, Stafford Loans, PLUS Loans, Federal Supplemental Educational Opportunity Grants, and work-study assistance. OSFAP is the largest source of student aid in America. OSFAP assists 8.7 million American students attending institutions of higher learning by providing more than $67 billion[1] in financial aid and works with over 4,000 lenders (Department of Education, Office of Student Financial Assistance Programs, 2000). With approximately 1,100 employees and 500 contractors, OSFAP's budget authority for fiscal year 2002 was $13,286,000,000.[2]

Unlike, the USPTO, which had its human resource, procurement, Chief Financial Officer (CFO), Chief Information Officer (CIO), and finance and accounting office practices already in place, OSFAP was required to staff and design offices and procedures from the beginning. The OSFAP offices of Human Resources, Procurement, CFO, CIO, Finance, and Accounting and Procurement were each created to support the PBO once it was operating independently from the Department of Education. The uniqueness of OSFAP is that along with creating resource support and information technology offices, it was also required to establish other offices such as Analysis, Ombudsman, and Communications.

United States Patent and Trademark Office (USPTO)

The United States Patent and Trademark Office (USPTO) is an agency of the United States Department of Commerce, which gained its PBO status under the American Inventors Protection Act of 1999, Title VI, Subtitle G (P.L. 106-113). Conversion from a traditional and bureaucratic agency to a performance-based agency was introduced as a part of a larger piece of legislation that focused on the agency's adjusting patent and trademark fees. The legislation further presented the agency with the ability to publish patent applications 18 months after filing, with certain exceptions, and broadened the circumstances under which a patent could be reexamined (35 USC 3, Officers & Employees – Reauthorization Act of 1998). Finally, it established a forum for the agency to consult with Public Advisory

Committees, for both the Patent and Trademark organizations. In addition, the legislation also reestablished the USPTO as an agency within the Department of Commerce.

The USPTO, which was established in 1790, is one of the few agencies within the government whose existence is clearly stated in the U.S. Constitution (Article I, Section 8, Clause 3). Fully-fee funded since 1993 from the sale of products and services, the USPTO had $1,151,832,000[3] in budgetary resources in fiscal year 2002.

The mission of the USPTO, as stated in the Fiscal Year 2000 U.S. PTO Performance and Accountability Report, is fairly straightforward. It states: The PTO promotes industrial and technological progress in the United States and strengthens the national economy by:

- Administering the laws relating to patents and trademarks.
- Advising the Secretary of Commerce, the President of the United States, and the administration on patent, trademark, and copyright protection.
- Advising the Secretary of Commerce, the President of the United States, and the Administration on the trade-related aspects of intellectual property.

The following statistics in the Budget of the United States Government for fiscal year 2004 indicates there were 333,688 patent inventions filed (received) and 260,245 disposed (issued) in fiscal year 2002. The Trademark Organization received 258,873 applications filed (classes) and there were 133,225 trademark registrations issued, including 164,457 classes in fiscal year 2002. The USPTO, which has approximately 6,593 employees, predicts 360,884 patent applications and 290,000 trademark applications to be filed in fiscal year 2004. The USPTO customers range from everyday individuals seeking patent grants or trademark registrations, to large corporations, foreign countries, and other U.S. government agencies.

MAJOR PERFORMANCE BARRIERS

In 1992, in a groundbreaking book, *Reinventing Government*, authors David Osborne and Ted Gaebler promote a "revolt against bureaucratic malaise." Osborne and Gaebler recognized and stated that "the hierarchal, centralized bureaucracies designed in the 1930s and 1940s simply did not function well in the rapidly changing, information-rich, knowledge-intensive society and economy of the 1990s" (Osborne & Gaebler, 1992). It was during this time of revolutionary thinking that all levels of government began to look for a means to break down the bureaucratic barriers that have (for decades) prevented managers from administering public programs effectively and efficiently. Today's program results have given cause to revisit outdated laws and regulations (designed to apply to a world that no longer exists) that govern human capital, procurement, budgeting, and management and internal control processes. The need for government reform has led to a worldwide search for better systems for delivering products and services to the public. Kettl offers "governments have used management reform to reshape the role of the state and its relationship with citizens" (Kettl, 2000). The search for "how public agencies oversee, manage and guide" (Barzelay, 2001) their organizations has initiated rich debates that challenge the *status quo* of government operations (2001).

The Code of Federal Regulations (CFR), Title 5, provides the guidance and regulations that cover all aspects of federal government personnel administration such as pay, recruitment, retention, hiring, classification, examinations, and security investigations.

Over the last three decades many problems (real and perceived) within the civil service system still surface as impediments for public administrators' effectiveness. Robert D. Behn offers that in many public sector organizations there are "ambiguities, contradictions, and inadequacies in the current systems of accountability for finances, fairness, and performance" (Behn, 2000). Those wishing to transform government, validate that well-trenched inconsistencies and deficiencies in the civil service system continue to frustrate public administrators.

Unfortunately, these limitations are not constrained to the civil service system, as rigid bureaucratic budgetary and procurement practices have proven to be equally limiting. While these impediments continue to be identified by many public administrators, for those in business-like public entities, these barriers are especially troublesome. Four major barriers that continue to surface in these organizations, as obstacles to meeting customer demand are:

(1) Pay-for-performance, recruitment, and retention practices.
(2) Budgetary and financial practices.
(3) Contract and acquisition practices.
(4) Accountability.

PAY-FOR-PERFORMANCE, RECRUITMENT, AND RETENTION

To examine how, and if, the status as a PBO has provided any relief from traditional human capital bureaucratic practices, representatives from each PBO were asked eight human resource and ten performance management system questions, shown in Figs 1 and 2.

HUMAN RESOURCES	5 Major Change	4 Somewhat Moderate Change	3 Moderate Change	2 Minor Change	1 No Change
1. How would you rate your current human resource processes/systems as compared to the processes/systems in place prior to PBO status?	O	O	O	O	O
2. How would you rate human resource flexibilities as compared to the flexibility available prior to PBO status?	O	O	O	O	O

	YES	NO
3. Do you think there has been a significant change in how the agency, as a whole, regards its human resource services and systems?	O	O
4. Are your rewards systems linked to agency performance?	O	O
5. Has your compensation systems changed as a result of PBO status?	O	O
6. Has being a PBO allowed you to operate more like a private sector human resource office?	O	O
7. What has been the most positive result of PBO status in the area of human resources?		
8. What has been the most negative result of PBO status in the area of human resources?		

Fig. 1. Human Resources – Interviewer's Guide Questions.

Recruitment and Retention

Agency representatives responded to these questions by sharing their individual perspectives of life as a PBO. A major challenge in the human capital management area was that neither the USPTO, nor the OSFAP, received relief from Title 5. U.S. Code-Title 5-Government Organization and Employees, which is the United States statute that defines how government agencies are organized and how employees are treated. It covers such things as employment and retention, employee performance, pay and allowances, attendance and leave, labor management and employee relations, insurance and annuities, access to criminal history record information, and other miscellaneous areas pertaining to personnel flexibilities. For the USPTO, this presented a real challenge, as the biggest issue was, and continues to be, the recruitment and retention of examiners to examine the hundreds of thousands of applications that are submitted to the agency each year. To keep pace with the

PERFORMANCE MANAGEMENT SYSTEM	5 Major Change	4 Somewhat Moderate Change	3 Moderate Change	2 Minor Change	1 No Change
1. How would you rate measurable services now that your agency is a PBO?	O	O	O	O	O
2. How would you rate the level of managers' focus on results-oriented performance since PBO status?	O	O	O	O	O
3. How would you rate the overall (all employees) agency's focus on results-oriented management and performance?	O	O	O	O	O
4. How would you rate the level of managers' focus on inputs and outputs since PBO status?	O	O	O	O	O
5. How would you rate your agency's interaction (e.g., more dialogue) with your external customers as a result of PBO status?	O	O	O	O	O
6. How would you rate the contents of performance reporting documents as a result of PBO status?	O	O	O	O	O
7. How would you rate the level of change in overall customer satisfaction that has (or has not) been achieved as a result of PBO status?	O	O	O	O	O
8. How would you rate levels of improvement in the quality of the agency's outputs that have been achieved as a result of PBO status?	O	O	O	O	O
	YES	NO			
9. Has a pay-for-performance method of compensation been linked to the pay of any of the employees other than the Director, CEO position?	O	O			
10. Has your agency created any new performance measures, goals or objectives as a result of being designated a PBO?	O	O			

Fig. 2. Performance Management System – Interviewer's Guide Questions.

demand for services at the USPTO, it is critical for the agency to have the ability to recruit and retain employees. Relief from Title 5 would have provided some of the autonomy the agency required to meet this challenge.

The Director of the Human Resource Office at the OSFAP (C. Thomas, personal communication, May 25, 2001) came to the agency after PBO status had been enacted. Therefore, Thomas had no real basis of comparison of how the human resources department operated prior to legislation, as compared to how it currently operates. The advantage for Thomas was that he brought no preconceived beliefs of how the department should or should not have operated. According to the former Chief of Staff at OSFAP (K. Cane, personal communication, June 5, 2001), the agency made a conscious decision to recruit human resource professionals who did not necessarily have governmental backgrounds. The approach for recruiting senior executives for this position was to attract a manager who would bring a fresh non-governmental perspective to the role of Human Resource Director. It was also to attract one who would have an awareness of private-sector experiences that could lend themselves to incorporation as best practices from private sector organizations within OSFAP.

Pay-for-Performance

Coming from the private sector, the present Director (Thomas) has free reign to be creative and innovative as he creates a human resource system that will meet the needs of a performance-oriented, non-traditional federal organization. Even though the Director of the Office of Human Resources at OSFAP has not been privy to the prior activities of the agency, he stated that there have been major changes in OSFAP's human resource practices. Thomas stated that the OSFAP human resource practices, processes, and procedures differ from those previously experienced by OSFAP employees, while a part of the Department of Education's Office of Higher Education. For example, OSFAP's award systems are different, as every employee's performance is based on overall agency-stated objectives; this is not the case at the Department of Education. Similarly, OSFAP has its award systems linked to the agency's overall performance, but the U.S. Department of Education does not. Other differences are that OSFAP employees are rated based on a pass/fail and a 360° performance evaluation system. The pay of the OSFAP general managers is aligned to specific performance measures that are, in turn, linked to a percentage of their pay. Thereby, the Director felt that there had been a significant change in how the agency, as a whole, regarded its human resource services and practices.

In response to a survey given to Senior Executive Service (SES) members in August 1999, one of the respondents stated "the issue of how federal employees will be compensated for their work in future years is one of the most important matters to be addressed in the next century. A new compensation system that rewards contribution and serves as an incentive to productivity is required" (U.S. Office of Personnel Management, 1999).

Brown and Armstrong (2000) argue that "the tides of interest in performance pay plans have more to do with social, political and economic fashions than with any scientific evidence on effectiveness of pay-for-performance systems." Brown and Armstrong's (2000) questioning of the value of these systems differ very little from the results of resent studies of pay-for-performance compensation, implemented as demonstration projects, within the federal sector. Amazingly, while pay-for-performance systems have been around since the industrial revolution (2000), organizations still struggle with implementing pay-for-performance systems and conducting meaningful assessments of how those systems improve organizational performance.

Ceilings for the amount of rewards, types and frequency of awards are important tools for managers to use as vehicles for driving higher performance, which are lacking in the public sector. The ability to provide incentives and rewards to motivate employees to achieve and maintain the desire to perform at organizational set standards is a challenge for most managers, and especially difficult for public administrators due to limited vehicles for employee rewards. In the public sector, managers rarely align performance with pay.

OSFAP has worked to motivate and reward employees through their pay-for-performance system. The OSFAP Performance representative (T. Oliveto, personal communication, May 22, 2001) stated that OSFAP has a pay-for-performance method of compensation linked to the pay of the Chief Operating Officer, five general managers, and 25 technical specialists. Employees have the opportunity to receive up to two weeks of their base pay as an award through the OSFAP Performance Excellence Program, as long as the agency achieves its overall goals for the performance year. In 2001, the employees received 97% of their base pay as an award, due to the success of the agency reaching 97% of its targeted performance.

Comparable pay for employees with the skills required to provide quality services is vital if the agency is to keep pace with customer demand. When asked whether or not the agency's compensation systems had changed as a result of PBO status, OSFAP's answer was "no"; specifically because the agency was not given flexibilities that are inherent in Title 5.

The USPTO did not create any new measures, goals, or objectives as a result of PBO conversion. Although, they are now using the balanced scorecard (BSC) or family of measures approach for measuring performance, this is a system that was being put into place, prior to the enactment of the legislation. Currently, the USPTO has not incorporated the achievement of agency mission and goals into non-management employee performance plans, nor have they implemented any pay-for-performance compensation systems. When asked whether or not the USPTO had encountered any challenges with unions as a result of linking pay with performance, the answer was "no." However, this was because, at that point, no attempt had been made to do so.

Pay-at-Risk for Executives

The Under Secretary of Commerce for Intellectual Property and Director of the USPTO is appointed by, and serves at the pleasure of the President. The

Commissioners of the subsidiary organizations (Patent and Trademark) are appointed by the Secretary of Commerce and are required to have performance contracts with the Secretary. While, the majority of senior and upper management have some form of a performance agreement, at this point, bonuses are not tied to the performance plans of administrative executives (e.g. Comptroller, HR Director, Procurement Officer, etc.).

At the USPTO, new guidelines for those employees in the SES are being examined to ensure all SES employees' performance plans are linked to the agency's performance plan. While it is yet to be determined if all SES employees' performance plans are directly linked to agency plans, it was noted that executives could always be decertified as a SES for non-performance and the bonuses of SES employees are "at risk," as the amount of the their bonuses are directly tied to the performance of the agency. At-risk pay is defined as the employee's salary is not fully guaranteed, because it is based on meeting pre-established performance standards.

Internal Human Resources Operations

When asked whether or not being a PBO had allowed his department at the OSFAP to operate more like a private sector human resource office, C. Thomas, Human Resource Director, OSFAP, said that he felt it had not. Thomas' reasoning was that there is limited flexibility, because what they must accomplish is budget driven. Given that there is no precedence or historical spending pattern for the amount of funding required to support the office, his department has not been able to justify the true cost of operating the office. Inadequate funding for the department has had a negative impact on recruitment for his immediate office, as well as the agency. Subsequently, the Director has been hampered in getting his staff up to a level that can adequately support the PBO. Hiring freezes imposed during the first year of the G. W. Bush Administration and a departmental moratorium slowed the progress of OSFAP, as well as placed an enormous strain on the current staff to meet the demands of an agency in transformation.

During the interview with the Director, USPTO Human Resource Office, (S. Rose, personal communication, May 24, 2001) Rose expressed that her department had been able to operate more like a private sector human resource office. Rose felt the PTO was able to implement immediate changes that were introduced via Day-One and Day-Two Initiatives and believed that the quality of life for employees at the USPTO had been enhanced. The agency immediately abolished the need for sign-in/sign-out time and attendance sheets, implemented mid-day flexible hours, and changed the manner in which employees could request leave from only one-hour increments to 1/2 hour or 1/4 hour increments. Employees were allowed to work six days in any two-week pay period, in any form, as long as the maximum of 80 hours are worked during the time period. For example, an employee can meet this requirement within six to seven days by working 12 hours per day for six days and one additional eight hour day. While occurring after PBO implementation, these innovative initiatives required no approval from the Office of Personnel Management, prior to implementation.

Peters and Savoie (2001) argue many "individuals involved in change give the appearance of change while, in fact, are moving very slowly or even standing still." Peters and Savoie further offer that "it is often stated that civil servants favor the *status quo*," thus, supporting Thomas' assertion that on occasion, there has been employee resistance, as well as challenges by some that believe they can do it better. He believed this was true because being the first PBO in government has drawn close scrutiny from Congress. Thomas added that although the internal results at OSFAP have been quick and they are meeting and exceeding expectations, the agency is only half way through the five-year PBO period; therefore it may be too soon to determine its true performance.

The early success of OSFAP supports Peters and Savoie's argument that "while civil servants can change and do change, it is still not at all clear what works, what does not work, and which changes offers the most promise to strengthen the government's policy advisory capacity and its ability to deliver services" (2001).

When asked what had been the most positive result of having PBO status, Thomas of OSFAP stated that they are able to look at programs, projects, and services that will actually help employees grow and develop. When asked what was the most negative result of PBO status in the area of human resources, Thomas stated that blazing a trail would always cause individuals to question what you do.

The interview with the Director of Human Resources at the USPTO (S. Rose, personal communication, May 24, 2001) proved to be the most candid. Identical human resource questions were asked of the USPTO Director. The question of how she would rate the amount of change in current human resource processes and systems, as compared to the processes and systems in place prior to PBO status was addressed as major. Rose stated that the Office of Human Resources immediately found itself in a position of having to justify its existence under the new legislation. As a support organization within the USPTO, they were now in the position of serving at the pleasure of the two major organizations for who they provided services (Patent and Trademark). Therefore, the Office was faced with reexamining and reassessing the services they were providing to their clients. Rose stated that this was a major wake-up call for her department.

Mixed Benefits in Human Resources Practices

Rose felt that the negative result of the PBO conversion was the fact that the USPTO did not get freedom from Title 5. Thus, fundamentally, the processes and procedures in the Human Resource Office did not change. The Director stated that the agency is still trying to figure out "what is a PBO?" While, the agency is still in the transformational phase, the most positive result was viewed as the ability to totally stretch their wings towards being more creative in how they provide human resource services.

BUDGETARY AND FINANCIAL PRACTICES

Budgetary Practices

Many practitioners in the public sector view the budgetary processes in the federal sector as restrictive; particularly, because of how the budget is formulated. In simple terms, federal budgets are formulated based upon the projected workload and resources that will be necessary to do the work. While fee-for-service organizations are diligent about developing accurate workload projections and customer demand, these numbers, as in any budget, are estimates. The difficulty in the public sector is that once Congress has appropriated the budget, budgets can rarely be adjusted easily or quickly, or without negative implications upon the agency requesting the change.

The Office of Management and Budget (OMB) Circular A-11 – Preparation, Submission, and Execution of the Budget sets the standards for what information is to be included in the budgets of federal entities. Budgets are prepared in the disaggregate, but are rolled up into one overall budget for the U.S. Government. The lower down in the organizational structure an agency is located; the less of a final word an agency has with regards to the content of its budget request and how it will be submitted in its final form to the OMB.

As with resources, entities are required to include budget projections for anticipated workloads and the number of personnel necessary to meet workload projections two years into the future. For fee-for-service agencies, developing projections that hold true in the out years are a difficult task, as the demand for services are based upon a number of unforeseen variables. Accurate out-year projections are extremely difficult as the level of demand for services are directly in the control of the paying customers of these agencies; therefore, when there are shifts in the economy, the workload of a fee-for-service agency can increase or decrease based upon the level of services or products being requested. Due to the fact that agencies are tied to budget restrictions and caps, when there is a dramatic shift in demand, fee-for-service agencies are challenged to adjust to demand, agencies do not have the agility necessary to respond. It is on these occasions that budgetary barriers have a more significant impact upon the performance of these types of agencies.

One of the biggest complaints of fee-for-service agencies is the lack of control over their specific budgets. Without autonomy from the parent-level departments, public administrators with limited budget control in sub-agencies, like the USPTO and OSFAP, are placed at a severe disadvantage for meeting their organizational missions, goals, and customer demand. To ascertain if any changes in budgetary practices occurred, the eight questions in Fig. 3 were asked of OSFAP and USPTO representatives.

The USPTO Deputy Chief Financial Officer and Comptroller (S. Weisman) felt that there had been major changes in the budget processes at the agency as

BUDGETARY SYSTEMS	5 Major Change	4 Somewhat Moderate Change	3 Moderate Change	2 Minor Change	1 No Change
1. How would you rate your current budget processes as compared to the processes prior to PBO status?	O	O	O	O	O
2. How would you rate budgetary flexibilities as compared to the flexibilities prior to PBO status?	O	O	O	O	O
3. How would you rate planning processes as compared to planning processes prior to PBO status?	O	O	O	O	O
4. How would you compare budgetary Congressional Hearing questions?	O	O	O	O	O
5. How would you rate the current use of resources as compared to prior PBO status?	O	O	O	O	O
	YES	NO			
6. Do you think there has been any significant change in how the agency, as a whole, regards its resources now that it is a PBO?	O	O			
7. What has been the most positive result or change as a result of having PBO status?					
8. What has been the most negative result or change as a result of having PTO status?					

Fig. 3.   Budgetary Practices – Interviewer's Guide Questions.

a result of PBO status and Weisman hopes that the independence gained through PBO legislation remains. When asked how she rated budgetary flexibilities, as compared to the flexibilities prior to PBO status, Weisman felt that there had been no change. The agency is still bound. Weisman stated that although there is still a way to go, there have been moderate changes in the way the agency plans, such as having a business plan strategy.

Weisman indicated that questions asked at Congressional hearings are beginning to change, however, Lynch (OSFAP) ranked the amount of change in this area as no change. When asked whether or not she felt that there had been any significant change in how the agency regards its resources, Weisman's response was no. However, according to Weisman, the USPTO does have budgetary independence from the Department of Commerce, which has been a positive. The agency is now allowed to submit its budget document directly to the Office of Management and Budget, and has the ability to stand alone.

One OSFAP employee feels their effectiveness is placed in jeopardy as budgetary appropriations have remained flat and there has not been enough money to support the hiring of additional staff. The representative for the OSFAP Administration stated that the agency is trying to mirror the private sector; however, it has been difficult, because the department consistently steps in when they are on the edge of real change. He likened it to being in a football game by stating, "every time we get ready to score a victory, a grenade is tossed in by the U.S. Department of Education to stop the play."

Financial Practices

New emphasis on financial practices in the federal government have been evolving over the last decade, primarily due to the enactment of the Chief Financial Officers' Act of 1990. This Act, which requires agencies to have a Chief Financial Officer and produce annual financial statements, forever changed how agencies approached financial management. The impact of this change; however was not necessarily changing how agencies operated, but rather issued in a new set of requirements, such as advanced automated systems and employees with competencies capture and monitor the financial data necessary for financial reporting.

As PBOs (USPTO and OSFAP) emulating best practices of "private-sector" organizations, budgetary and financial practices would need to change significantly. Seven questions (Fig. 4) were asked to examine whether or not there have been financial management changes since PBO designation.

The major difference between the OSFAP and the USPTO is that the USPTO's support offices (Finance, Procurement, Corporate Planning, Chief Information

FINANCE	5 Major Change	4 Somewhat Moderate Change	3 Moderate Change	2 Minor Change	1 No Change
1. How would you rate your current financial system/procedures as compared to the systems/procedures in place prior to PBO status?	O	O	O	O	O
2. How would you rate the impact of flexibilities available under PBO status as compared to those available prior to PBO status?	O	O	O	O	O
3. How would you rate your relationship with vendors since PBO status?	O	O	O	O	O
4. How would you rate the accuracy of your reporting documents since PBO status?	O	O	O	O	O
5. How would you rate the integrity of the financial data since PBO status?	O	O	O	O	O
6. What has been the most positive result of PBO status in the area of finance?					
7. What has been the most negative result of PBO status in the area of finance?					

Fig. 4. Financial Practices – Interviewer's Guide Questions.

Officer, and Human Resources) were already in place. To ascertain changes in financial practices the seven questions in the table above were asked of OSFAP and USPTO representatives. At the OSFAP, support offices had to be created. Thereby, the Director of Financial Management Systems/Requirements and Testing Division and Acting Chief of Staff, had no basis for comparison for pre/post operations in this area at the agency.

The Financial Director (P. Stonner, personal communication, May 21, 2001) stated that a notable challenge for the agency had been the fact, that there was no CFO within the agency prior to PBO legislation. Consistent education of the staff to culturally understand the role of a CFO has been a priority. Stonner states that the importance of the CFO role, in building an organization with strong financial systems, processes, and practices, is key to the agency's overall performance.

In a well-structured plan to develop a strong financial foundation for OSFAP, one of the CFO's most significant efforts has been to deploy a comprehensive financial management system which will allow OSFAP to significantly improve the integrity of its financial data by integrating its financial systems. It must also include better reconciliation between varying financial reports, as well as significantly reduce fraud and abuse of loan programs.

At the USPTO, the Finance office has been in place for decades; therefore the agency was spared the challenge of creating a new office with new roles and systems. The agency instituted the position of Chief Financial Officer as a result of the Chief Financial Officers' Act legislation of 1990 and has had a Comptroller in place for nearly a decade. Therefore, USPTO employees were culturally acclimated to operating in this environment. Recognized as progressive in its approach to financial management, the USPTO had little to change in this area when it was converted to a PBO and is still required to follow the mandates of the Chief Financial Officers' Act of 1990. The Director of Finance (M. Picard, personal communication, May 22, 2001) stated that the PBO legislation did not provide for any flexibility in the areas of finance and accounting.

Picard stated that one of the most positive aspects of being a PBO (for her office) has been how they now view their internal operations. Picard's office now pays closer attention to the cost of their operations, in comparison to the major organizations they support within the USTPO. Picard stated that fortunately for the USPTO, their financial and accounting procedures and systems were far ahead of most agencies and no major adjustments were needed. She stated that unit cost accounting, which was already in place, and the manner in which the office approaches resource management continues to be like the private sector and is business oriented. Picard emphasized that her office does ensure that the cost of how they perform their specific operations and how they account for overall agency performance levels and the related uses of resources, are optimized.

Internal Controls

The key to operating as a "businesslike" enterprise is the ability to manage and control internal systems. With the full autonomy to develop new and innovative administrative and procedural systems, comes the responsibility of establishing solid and sound internal controls. Therefore, the four questions in Fig. 5 were asked of the USPTO and OSFAP representatives to determine whether or not internal control practices were created, enhanced, or eliminated, as a result of PBO designation.

Both agencies reported that they had instituted additional or new internal controls as a result of being a PBO, although the USPTO did not mention specific elimination of any major non-value added internal controls. However, the OSFAP stated that they eliminated the use of time and attendance sign-in/sign-out sheets

INTERNAL CONTROLS	YES	NO
1. Has your agency put in additional or new internal controls as a result of being a PBO?	O	O
2. Has your agency eliminated any non-value added internal controls as a result of being a PBO?	O	O
3. Has your agency adopted or adapted any private sector internal control systems or methodologies as a result of being a PBO?	O	O
4. Please provide some examples of your internal controls systems.		

Fig. 5.   Internal Control Practices – Interviewer's Guide Questions.

and reengineered many aspects of operations based upon best practices from the private sector. The OSFAP has made significant advances in approximately 26 different projects since September 1999.

Responsible for one of the agency's three major goals of reducing unit cost, the former CFO (J. Lynch, personal communication, May 25, 2001) at OSFAP stated that the agency put new and additional internal controls in place as a result of being a PBO. One of the major goals within the former CFO's organization was to achieve a clean audit of OSFAP's financial books. OSFAP recently implemented a new financial management system to address internal control issues. Additionally, travel cards, purchase cards, and other internal controls were put into place to eliminate fraud, waste, and abuse. Lynch said the agency also eliminated any non-value added internal controls as a result of being a PBO, such as exception-based attendance reporting for employees. Other non-value added steps in their travel process were eliminated. The agency now has re-engineering processes and has taken, extensively from the private sector, much of what is included in its modernization blueprint. OSFAP is engaged in a significant effort to modernize its agency and developed a modernization blueprint that establishes a framework for making positive and results-oriented changes within the agency. The modernization blueprint can be viewed at (www.ed.gov/offices/OSFAP).

CONTRACT AND ACQUISITION PRACTICES

The Federal Acquisition Regulations System is established for the codification and publication of uniform policies and procedures, for acquisition by all executive agencies. The Federal Acquisition Regulations System consists of the Federal Acquisition Regulation (FAR) Manual, which is the primary document used by federal agencies to conduct the acquisition of all products and services. This 54-chapter, 1,000 plus page document does not include internal agency guidance. Thus, the procurement of products and services has long been viewed as arduous, heavily time laden, and burdensome. Agencies that need to address the needs of paying customers on demand and must have the ability to acquire products and services such as computers, consultants, or contractors to improve or augment its processes, need an acquisition process that is straightforward, swift, and effective.

There were six questions (Fig. 6) asked of the Procurement Officer (M. Anastasia, personal communication, May 22, 2001) at the USPTO and within the Acquisition and Contract Performance Office (N. Taylor, personal

PROCUREMENT SYSTEMS	5 Major Change	4 Somewhat Moderate Change	3 Moderate Change	2 Minor Change	1 No Change
1. How would you rate your current procurement processes as compared to the processes prior to PBO status?	O	O	O	O	O
2. How would you rate procurement flexibilities as compared to the flexibilities available prior to PBO status?	O	O	O	O	O
3. Do you think there has been a significant change in how the agency as a whole regards its procurement of products and services as compared to prior to PBO status?	O	O	O	O	O
	YES	NO			
4. Has being a PBO allowed you to operate more like a private sector procurement office?	O	O			
5. What has been the most positive result of PBO status in the area of procurement?					
6. What has been the most negative result of PBO status in the area of procurement?					

Fig. 6. Contract and Acquisition Practices – Interviewer's Guide Questions.

communication, May 21, 2001) at the OSFAP. Surprisingly, what was revealed during this examination of acquisition processes is that the authority to scale down the size and complexity of the FAR is available for all public agencies, and has been available for some time.

The USPTO procurement officer ranked the amount of change in current procurement processes in comparison to the previous process as major. Anastasia felt that the most significant change was how the office approaches its acquisition of products and services and believes that the office is much more inventive in how it approaches its work. Anastasia stated that his employees exhibit more risk taking attributes now, than ever before, and the most significant change for his department has been the reduction of the FAR Manual. The FAR is the mandatory guidance used by all federal agencies, and Anastasia's office has been able to reduce the manual from hundreds of pages down to 70. However, Anastasia pointed out that the ability to reduce the FAR was not directly related to the USPTO's PBO status. Anastasia stated that any agency can do this and commented that the ability to reduce this overwhelming and cumbersome manual has always been available; however, the department did not act upon it until recently, which was a direct result of being a PBO. The Procurement Officer felt that the manner in which the office and its employees view its work has changed significantly and he contributes this to the USPTO's conversion to a PBO.

The Acquisition and Contract Officer (N. Taylor) from the OSFAP rated the procurement flexibilities available to the agency as a PBO, as limited. Taylor rated current procurement processes as compared to the processes prior to PBO status, as moderately changed. When Taylor was asked whether or not she thought there had been a significant change in how the agency regarded its procurement of products and services, as compared to prior to PBO status, Taylor stated that there had been major changes. Taylor went on to say that the agency is still required to follow the FAR; therefore, PBO status did not allow the OSFAP to operate more like a private sector procurement office. OSFAP's acquisition efforts are still tightly linked to the Department of Education. The negative result of PBO status has been the friction between the Department and OSFAP. Nevertheless, Taylor felt that the concept of PBOs is great; however, suggested that it would work better if there were more flexibility in the use of the FAR. Taylor said that with more flexibility, OSFAP would be able to operate better, as a private sector acquisition office. Nevertheless, Taylor would recommend PBO status to other agencies because she believes: (1) services to the public would be much better; (2) taxpayers would get more from government workers; and (3) services would be better if agencies were actually stand-alone (autonomous) organizations, similar to the United States Postal Service.

ACCOUNTABILITY

The performance-based organization concept, and the subsequent passage of the Government Performance and Results Act of 1993, "sent clear signals that the private sector's corporate culture-with its emphasis on accountability to stakeholders (stockholders), customer satisfaction, performance measurement, strategic planning, and downsizing tactics-is to be the template for a twenty-first century government" (Gawthrop, 1998).

The essence of performance-based management is accountability for performance. Advocates for performance and accountability in government are asking to see the results of resources invested in public sector organizations. Interviewees from both PBOs discussed problems of role delineation as serious impediments to clear role of responsibilities or accountability between the parent department and the PBOs during transformation. J. Christopher Mihm, Acting Associate Director, Federal Management and Workforce Issues General Government Division, General Accounting Office, in his testimony before the Subcommittee on Government Management Information, and Technology-Committee on Government Reform and Oversight House of Representatives states the "lack of clarity concerning the respective roles and responsibilities of agencies and departments affects accountability for results" (GAO/T-GGD-97-151). USPTO and OSFAP are challenged to align employee performance with organizational goals and their mission as PBOs, the inability to do this effectively impacts clarity of accountability. Three questions (Fig. 7) were posed

ACCOUNTABILITY	YES	NO
1. Has your agency changed its employee rating system to align with the agency's mission and performance goals?	O	O
2. Has your agency implemented any new employee reward systems to align with the achievement of the agency's mission and goals?	O	O
3. Has your agency implemented any new systems of consequence for employees that do not achieve the mission or goals?	O	O

Fig. 7. Accountability Practices – Interviewer's Guide Questions.

to representatives of each organization to examine how this issue is being approached.

Representatives (B. Bokong & K. Strohecker) from the two major programs (Patent and Trademark) of the USPTO felt that there has been a somewhat moderate to major change in accountability within their agency, as a result of being a PBO. The Trademark representative (K. Strohecker, personal communication, May 22, 2001) stated that there is recognition to do more to link a manager's performance with rewards. Additionally, for the first time, there is a performance contract (in writing) that has served to instill a good structure within the agency for focusing on performance. Both representatives agreed that there was no real change in the support the agency receives from top management.

Accountability within the agency has not changed at the line level within the agency, as the non-management employee's rating system has not been aligned with the agency's mission and performance goals. Conversely, the USPTO has a system of consequence for senior employees who do not achieve the mission or goals, as the performance bonuses of the Commissioners can be reduced for nonperformance.

As a result of the PBO status, the level of improvement has made great strides in the quality of the agency's output. A primary improvement has been that OSFAP is more web-enabled, making their services more accessible to their partners, banks, and projected 8.7 million students. Students can file financial assistance applications on-line and school partners can download specific information from the website. Additionally, there is a lot more information and better communication for anyone visiting their website.

The USPTO implemented a Day-One and Day-Two Initiative as a catalyst for quick change to ignite the overall focus of the agency's performance on results-oriented management and performance. In speaking with the Administrator (M. Lee, personal communication, May 22, 2001) and former Deputy Administrator (C. Kern, personal communication, May 22, 2001) for Quality Management at the USPTO, they agreed that there had been moderate change in measurable services now that the agency is a PBO. The reason for ranking the amount of change as moderate in this category is because the agency has always measured its services. Additionally, a manager's focus on results-oriented performance was rated moderate for the same reason. Focusing on measuring services and the importance of USPTO managers focusing on quality and delivery was always the management style of the leadership. Therefore, no significant change was expected. What did change was aligning the performance plans of the Senior Executive Service and the Senior Patent Examiner with the achievement of the agency's measurable performance. The agency also developed a Memorandum of Understanding (MOU) with the United States Department of Commerce (DOC) to document the relationship with the agency under the auspices of PBO legislation, which serves to sustain its focus.

Customer Satisfaction

When questioned of how would she rank the agency's focus on external customers, the former OSFAP Chief of Staff, Cane lamented "that is our focus!" She rated the overall performance, efficiency, and effectiveness at OSFAP as outstanding. Cane stated that management's empowerment at OSFAP has changed from the top down, through middle management. When asked to rank the amount of change in empowerment among non-management employees, Cane felt there had been major change. Cane stated that all employees more than realize what the agency is working toward and they are all more focused on customers. Cane felt that the employee's accountability for the agency's overall performance is an evolutionary process. While there are performance scorecards for teams, individual development plans are not currently in place.

The level of a USPTO manager's focus on inputs and outputs and the agency's interaction with external customers has not changed since PBO conversion. Quality representatives (M. Lee & C. Kern) stated that because the agency has always had a keen focus on its inputs, outputs, and customers, no genuine change was noted as a result of becoming a performance-based organization. However, there were minor changes in their reporting documents.

Lee and Kern stated that the USPTO experienced a somewhat moderate difference, in the level of change, in overall customer satisfaction as a result of their conversion to a PBO. Customer satisfaction had improved significantly agency wide, so Lee and Kern felt the level of change had also been major. The recent 3.74 customer satisfaction score placed the agency high among other government agencies in the area of customer satisfaction. While higher in the Patent Organization, than in Trademark's, the reaction time to feedback data received pertaining to customer satisfaction is much faster than was previous reported.

There has been a major difference in the level of improvements, in the quality of the agency's outputs. Both organizations (Patent and Trademark) have award systems for productivity. As stated earlier, the Trademark Organization has experienced a significant increase in the timeliness of the examination of trademark applications. One of the drivers is thought to be the amount of performance awards that are available to employees for production. Major changes were implemented in the area of how USPTO employees are rewarded for enhanced performance. For example, in the Trademark Organization of the agency, they now offer examiners up to $10,000 in bonus pay every six months for lowering the cycle time of processing applications.

Performance Management

Oliveto from OSFAP's Performance Office was asked 10 questions pertaining to the performance management system at the agency. When asked how Oliveto would rate measurable services now that the agency is a PBO, he stated that there had been a major change. Oliveto contributes this change to an environment that stresses the importance of talking with their customers. He felt that there had also been a major change in the level of managers' focus on results-oriented performance since PBO status. To keep this focus centered, there is bi-weekly reporting and an annual report of performance that is developed and distributed.

Oliveto rated the overall agency's emphasis on results-oriented management and performance, and their managers' focus on inputs and outputs since PBO status, as moderately changed. The agency has created new performance measures and goals or objectives to measure unit costs, employee satisfaction, call center service, and receipt of clean financial audits to insure program and fiscal integrity.

When asked, Oliveto rated the amount of change in the agency's interaction with their external customers as major and commented that their customers have noticed significant improvements, as indicated in their recent American Customer Satisfaction Index (ACSI) score. The monitoring of performance is organized around customer segments and there is a task force of 50 frontline supervisors and managers who are dedicated to feeding customer input and feedback to the Chief Operating Officer (COO) of the agency. Oliveto felt that there is significant dialogue with OSFAP customers through focus group sessions and customer and employee conferences. As a natural extension of this increased interaction, there has been a major change in the content of performance reporting documents. Every quarter, a report is published with the financial section of the report now available via the web. These reports, of what has been accomplished, are provided to OSFAP partners, customers, stakeholders, and Congress.

The Patent representative (B. Bokong, personal communication, June 6, 2001) ranked the amount of focus on external customers as changing moderately, because the agency has always had a keen focus on its external customers. The Trademark representative (K. Strohecker) stated that its PBO status gave its organization cause to recognize the need to approach their customers more. Both representatives were asked how they rated the agency's overall performance, efficiency, and effectiveness since the enactment of the PBO legislation. Bokong felt there had been no change, while Strohecker stated that their organization has begun to rethink its goals and initiatives and find a means to achieve them, as a result of becoming a PBO.

When asked how each would rate management's empowerment, both representatives agreed that there had been minor changes. When asked how they would rank the amount of empowerment of the average employee at the USPTO, Bokong stated that she had noticed minor changes, and Strohecker stated she had noticed moderate change. In addition, their employees did have more flexible work schedules, which translated into feelings of a better quality of work life on the job. Both representatives generally agreed that there was no change in the employee's accountability for the agency's overall performance, as the agency is still working to get a direct linkage among employee's performance plans and the goals and mission of the agency.

Bokong and Strohecker were asked what they considered the most positive result or change at the agency that has taken place as a result of having PBO status. Strohecker stated that the new status got the agency to re-examine its structure and establish performance contracts that align with the work and efforts of the agency, and did not believe that this discussion (of how the agency is approaching how it does its work) would have taken place otherwise. Bokong responded to this question by stating that there is more accountability within the agency, especially among the executive team, managers, and down to the first line managers; whereby, each are now held accountable for specific performance goals and objectives through the use of performance scorecards.

The former Chief of Staff (K. Cane, personal communication, June 5, 2001) of OSFAP ranked the amount of change in accountability at the OSFAP as major. Cane stated that the business of the agency is much clearer, much more focused and all employees understand what the agency is trying to achieve. The agency has three very concise and basic measures: (1) Customer Satisfaction; (2) Unit Cost; and (3) Employee Satisfaction. Cane stated there has been no change in the amount of change in top-level support, as OSFAP has always received outstanding top-level support from the Secretary of Education.

OVERALL FINDINGS

OSFAP's former Chief of Staff's response to what had been the most positive result or change as a result of having PBO status was that they (OSFAP) are changing government forever. Cane went on to say that they are taking care of the customers more; employees more, and more people are attending school now than ever before. When asked what was the most negative result or change as a result of having PBO status, Cane stated that it is the constant request for information on how they are progressing. While, a small negative, they would rather focus more time on doing their work, than discussing it.

The former CFO (J. R. Lynch, personal communication, May 25, 2001) of OSFAP was in agreement with many of the comments made by the former Chief of Staff. Lynch said that the agency is very much focused on its three goals and declared that OSFAP was ranked as the best in government when it comes to employee satisfaction. The latest Gallup Workplace Management (GWM) scores for OSFAP's employee satisfaction (3.5) beat the average of government agencies (3.4) and is 0.1 behind private financial businesses at (3.6). In a statement by the former COO of OSFAP to the Chairman and members of the Subcommittee hearing the fiscal year 2002 request for the OSFAP budget, the COO said "customer satisfaction at OSFAP – as measured on the 100-point American Customer Satisfaction Index (ACSI), which is one of Wall Street's leading indicators of success, rose. In comparison to other private and public organizations using ACSI to measure customer satisfaction, banks average 68 and the industry average is 74 – OSFAP scored a respectable 69 out of 100. This score was just one point under the score for all private financial services organizations."

Cane felt that top-level support had not changed and Lynch supported her assertion that OSFAP top-level support is good. Lynch agreed that there has been a major change in both the agency's focus on external customers and in the empowerment of management and employees of OSFAP. When asked what had been the most negative result or change at the agency as a result of having PBO status, Lynch stated the Department of Education's inability to accept the change that is occurring at OSFAP.

When asked about the negative aspects of being a PBO, Patent representative (Bokong) said the high expectations that external stakeholders held of how the agency would operate under the new legislation, were immense. Many were expecting great things to take place immediately. Conversely, not all the flexibilities were granted and change did not take place quickly.

The final question under the general management category was whether or not any of the interviewees would recommend PBO status or its concepts of managing be extended to other agencies within the government that may meet basic PBO criteria. Patent representative Bokong believed that in concept-yes, the focus of managing for results and accountability would help any agency manage better.

For the USPTO, the agency had new responsibilities, while operating in an old structure, so some felt the PBO concept has been misleading. Trademark representative (Strohecker) felt that government is inherently not structured to operate as a private sector organization; therefore, to expect that a government agency can operate as efficiently as a private sector organization, is unrealistic.

Strohecker stated that no real authority was bestowed, and doubts that any federal agency can ever really operated as a business.

When the same general category questions were asked of Weisman (Comptroller and Deputy Chief Financial Officer at the USPTO) she felt there was a major change in accountability at the USPTO, principally because the expectations are greater for those who manage the agency. Wesiman viewed top-level support as having moderately changed since conversion to the PBO. Weisman further stated that the USPTO did not get much flexibility as a PBO and was not removed totally from administrative restrictions that were needed to perform as one. The negative aspect is that the agency essentially did not get to be a PBO per its conceptual provisions; nevertheless, expectations were high. The agency faced many expectations with limited flexibilities. Weisman stated that while there is a memorandum of understanding between the USPTO and USDOC that is helpful; however, that document can change with each Administration.

METHODOLOGY

There are currently three performance-based organizations: the Office of Student Financial Assistance Program (OSFAP), the United States Patent and Trademark Office (USPTO), and the Air Traffic Division, also known as the Air Traffic Organization (ATO); however, I elected to only assess OSFAP and USPTO, as ATO is not yet operational. The initial objective was to conduct agency wide surveys of all employees at both agencies to gather information on the progress of PBOs in the United States. USPTO and OSFAP were each contacted to gain permission from their respective officials to conduct the interviews with employees. Based upon conversations with point-of-contact representatives, the anticipated return rate would be too low to yield any significant results. Therefore, the 65-question survey instrument (see Appendix 1) was not pre-tested; however, it was used as an interview guide to conduct one-on-one interviews with key representatives in core areas afforded PBO flexibilities.

At the USPTO, senior management representatives from the following offices were interviewed: Human Resources, Office of the Controller, Quality Management, Public Affairs, Finance, Procurement, Trademark Organization, and Patent Organization. Senior manager representatives from the offices of Finance, Acquisition and Contracts, Administration, Human Resources, Performance Management, former Chief Financial Officer, and the former Chief of Staff of the OSFAP were interviewed. Overall there were 17 individuals interviewed to gather progress information for this paper. There were 10 from the USPTO and seven from the OSFAP. All interviewees were federal career senior managers with only a few serving in excepted positions. Years of service within the organization ranged from less than two years to more than 28 years of service.

The 65-question interview guide contained 31 Likert-Scale questions measuring no change ranked at (1) one to a major change ranked at (5) in a specific category. There were 21 yes or no questions; and 13 open-ended questions. The guide was divided into nine major categories: general, budgetary, finance, procurement, human resources, internal controls, performance measurement systems, accountability, and overall management.

SUMMARY

"We're going to dramatically change the way many agencies provide their services . . . PBOs would be run by chief executives who sign contracts and will be personally accountable for delivering results . . . Their pay and job security will be tied directly to performance"[4] (Gore, 1996). In a speech on creating performance-based organizations he stated that "numerous state, local, and foreign governments have implemented similar performance-based models to improve services and reduce costs for the last 15 years, thus, suggested there was enough evidence to warrant applying these models to federal agencies meeting specific criteria" (Department of Education, Office of Student Financial Assistance Program, 1998).

Legislation for both agencies did concisely state such general statements pertaining to the officers and employees; appointment and duties; salary and performance agreements; and removal, training, and national security position clauses, as well as discussion of the adoption of existing labor agreements and transition provisions (35 USC 3, Officers & Employees – Reauthorization Act of 1998). PBO legislation focuses on four major categories: leadership, procurement flexibility, management and personnel flexibility, and accountability for results. Therefore, let us examine each one separately.

(1) *Leadership*: Generally, a PBO is to be led by a chief operating office (COO) with a strong background in information technology and management, who is employed through a performance-based contract and reports directly to a cabinet Secretary. COO, Theresa S. Shaw, is currently leading OSFAP. The USPTO is being led by the Under Secretary of Commerce for Intellectual Property and Director of the United States Patent and Trademark Office, James E. Rogan. The USPTO was recently under the leadership of Director, Q. Todd Dickinson who was appointed under the Clinton Administration. Both individuals did (and do) have performance-based contracts with the respective Secretaries, and both may receive a bonus in an amount of up

to, but not in excess of, 50% of his or her annual rate of basic pay, based upon an evaluation by the Secretary. Annual performance agreements are to incorporate measurable organizational and individual goals in key operational areas, as delineated in an annual performance plan agreed to by the COO and the Secretary.

(2) *Procurement Flexibility*: PBOs are to have increased flexibility in procurement, with an emphasis on performance-based contracting. Both interviewees in this area stated that very little flexibilities were granted as they are still bound by the Federal Acquisition Regulation (FAR) Manual. The USPTO was able to significantly decrease the size of the regulation, while the OSFAP still utilizes the complete regulation as its dominant guidance. OSFAP and USPTO representatives stated that their offices have become more inventive in their approach to work and have implemented some creative methods for acquiring goods and services.

(3) *Management and Personnel Flexibility*: PBOs were to have new flexibility in personnel management, including hiring and evaluating senior managers, and recruiting technical personnel. This area appeared to be the most disappointing for both agencies, as neither received the flexibilities needed to recruit or retain employees. Title 5, which is the statutory law that provides guidance to federal agencies on personnel issues, was not waived; therefore both agencies have continued to struggle to recruit the amount and caliber of employees necessary to adequately achieve their performance goals.

(4) *Accountability for Results*: COO and employees of PBOs were to have specific, measurable performance goals, ensuring accountability for defined results. With a new focus on results, both agencies have restructured themselves to ensure that the most senior managers are held accountable for performance goals that are measurable and achieve results; however, neither has cascaded methods to measure accountability throughout their agencies. Employees lower than the first-line supervisor currently do not have performance-based employee performance plans. However, OSFAP employees do receive group performance awards based on the achievement or non-achievement of the agency reaching its predefined performance goals.

In the areas of budgeting and acquisition, both agencies' strict ties with parent agencies (U.S. Department of Education and U.S. Department of Commerce) have remained and have presented, on occasion, contentious rather than collaborative relationships. None of the individuals interviewed felt their agency had received sufficient exemptions from federal rules that would allow them to improve agency performance. More so at OSFAP, than at USPTO, procurement efforts have often been stymied due to the parent agency's insistence that the PBO utilize the Department, rather than giving the agency the necessary freedoms to pursue cheaper, faster, and better services unimpeded. The USPTO stated that one of the positive aspects of the PBO status was the ability to present their budget document to OMB, rather than to the Department. However, both agencies have encountered some resistance to the submission of fiscal year budget documents directly to the Office of Management and Budget rather than via the parent agencies, even though this is a provision written into the legislation.[5] Understanding that because the revenue of the PBOs are included in the overall budgets of the parent agencies, it is reasonable to expect that the parent agencies would want to be aware of what is contained in, and requested by, their PBO via their budget documents. As the steward of the overall funds appropriated by Congress for each sub-agency or bureau, parent agencies are held ultimately accountable for all expenditures requested and received; thus their stake in this process is significant.

The majority of those interviewed, while not overly thrilled with the fact that flexibilities envisioned were not flexibilities received, most were optimistic that, with time, their respective agencies would make noteworthy progress. All were in agreement that the concept of managing for results is necessary for a better government; however, some expressed concern that their progress has stalled because they have not truly been granted full administrative and management flexibilities nor have they been given the full autonomy necessary to operate unimpeded. Although, all of the interviewees expressed some disappointment in the reality of being a PBO versus expectations, by and large the perspectives of the interviewees appeared to have not been influenced by the years of experience in the traditional federal environment or by their new experiences operating within a uncharted performance-based environment.

In an interview with the representative (J. Barnard, personal communication, May 25, 2001) from the Office of Administration at OSFAP, Barnard stated that the actual PBO legislation is short and sweet with little substantive language to allow the agency to independently flourish as a true performance-based organization. Policy and budgetary decisions are still directed by the U.S. Department of Education. The lack of clear lines of responsibilities have hindered the agency in setting administrative policies and procedures, meet self-imposed standards, deliver quality products, or be efficient.

The PBO concept was modeled after the British Next Steps Initiative. The Next Step initiative was designed to improve the use of services, employee work environments and conditions, and the return (via products and services) on taxes paid by the citizens. Although successfully emulated (in concept) by many countries around the world, in the testimony by J. C. Mihm, he presents three primary difficulties experienced by the British government: (1) lack of clarity in the relationship between agencies and their parent departments; (2) uncertainty concerning who is accountable for performance; and (3) difficulties in developing and setting performance goals (GAO/T-GGD-97-151). As with the British Next Steps Initiative, one primary obstacle to the effectiveness of OSFAP, as perceived by Barnard, is the tenuous parent/sub-department relationships between OSFAP and the U.S. Department of Education. Barnard stated that OSFAP has no control and still depends on the U.S. Department of Education to accomplish many things they are capable of doing for themselves. What often takes place is that the priorities of the U.S. Department of Education become the priorities of OSFAP. On occasion OSFAP has had to rely on administrative services and support from the U.S. Department of Education. There are times when OSFAP can do or procure services better, cheaper, and faster than the services received from the U.S. Department of Education. Barnard stated that OSFAP is not sure where the U.S. Department of Education is going; however, OSFAP is forced to come along. OSFAP would like a Memorandum of Understanding with the U.S. Department of Education to delineate roles for each in the areas of human resources, contracts, and financial management operations.

Barnard stated that the U.S. Department of Education is currently controlling policy on student aid, financial systems, information technology, and their budget. Hampered by the lack of U.S. Department of Education policies that are of value, OSFAP would like to issue their own policies, but have been unable to so. U.S. Department of Education polices developed in 1980–1982 currently dictate guidance. Barnard stated that these policies are in dire need of upgrading and modernization and are just too old to be effective in today's environment. Barnard added that there are no guidelines or procedures because they were discarded under the Clinton Administration under an initiative to reduce the number of federal regulations. What remained, as a result of the elimination of those documents, are outdated regulations and policies without the replacement of new ones. Barnard went on to say that the Department has hidden behind general guidelines versus real policies.

Barnard felt that the transition to a performance-based organization has been a slow and painful process, and added that there is a feeling that the new Administration may be trying to reel OSFAP back into the Department. Under the new Administration, the agency has had to address questions of whether or not they are necessary or feasible. The U.S. Department of Education has had concerns of efficiency and the duplication of efforts (i.e. CIO, CFO, HR Acquisition, etc). The Administration appointed a team to assess these concerns and at the time of the interview, OSFAP was awaiting the results of this assessment and action plan. Barnard stated that internally, OSFAP is conducting some "soul-searching" activities to get ideas and feedback on issues, and consequently, and will take the necessary steps to improve the Office.

Barnard stated that although it was only 80–90% staffed, OSFAP's employees are efficient, timely, and worthy of the trust of their external customers. OSFAP employees are empowered, which came naturally. Barnard further stated that the culture of the organization is important, and thereby it is essential to have all employees have a good indication of what OSFAP does, be aware of the three major goals, and build around a culture to work as a team.

Both Patent and Trademark representatives (Bokong & Strohecker) stated that internal and external expectations for the USPTO's becoming a PBO were high. Flexibilities included in the initial legislative language were all but missing from the legislation passed. Both agencies (USPTO and OSFAP) stated that there is very little reference to performance-based organizations in their respective legislations. Thus, there is no definitive guideline for establishing roles and responsibilities between the parent agency and the PBO. Further, there is no clear guidance as to how the agencies are to operate in this new environment. One interviewee stated that there is no template for how the agency should operate; therefore, expectations could not be established, which have been present and unrealistic.

It was observed in both agencies that being designated a PBO carries with it great responsibility, as operating in such an environment has never been attempted in the United States at the federal level. There are no templates, rules, policies, regulations, or standards for operating and managing performance-based organizations; therefore, the path is uncharted. Issues such as bureaucratic culture weigh heavy on those attempting to change the face of government. Max Weber (1864–1920) states, "once it is fully established, bureaucracy is among those social structures which are the hardest to destroy. Bureaucracy is the means of carrying 'community action' over into rationally ordered 'societal action.' Therefore, as an instrument for 'societalizing' relations of power, bureaucracy has been and is a power instrument of the first order-for the one who controls the bureaucratic apparatus" (Yarwood, 1987). The results of the interviews rarely differed from Weber's theory, as many felt changing the organizational, employee, and parent organization's mental maps were the most difficult. One interviewee simply stated that they were trying to operate in a new environment within an old environment mentality. Strohecker stated the majority of employees have worked within the traditional bureaucratic environment for decades (especially at the USPTO), so how they work and what they believe about how they should approach their work, is not something that could be altered overnight. The uniqueness of OSFAP is that the majority of their top managers do not have prior governmental experience and thereby were able to enter their positions unencumbered by bureaucratic mind maps. Given the concept that "organizational cultures are structurally complex" (Schein, 1985), it came as no surprise, that for both agencies, it has been an uphill battle to maintain the energy of a few individuals who dare to think and work differently.

There have been challenges and triumphs in both agencies. Each have used different approaches to meet the challenges and realize triumphs, such as deploying integrated financial management systems, reducing a cumbersome federal regulation manual, improving the quality of life for employees, eliminating non-value added tasks and policies, and establishing internal controls that decrease waste and inefficiencies. In some cases, both agencies were very similar in their processes. One reason was the fact that the USPTO used OSFAP as a model for best practices and as a vehicle for taking advantage of lessons learned. In each of the major categories (budgetary systems, finance, procurement systems, and human resources) examined in both agencies, each has realized measurable improvements and senior managers are being held accountable via bonus/pay-at-risk reward systems.

CONCLUSION

In concept, federal government executives of performance-based organizations, were suppose to be given broad exemptions from federal procurement and personnel rules, in exchange for tough performance standards. The idea was that some federal programs would be able to perform better if they were allowed to run like private companies (GovernmentExecutive.com, 2000). The agencies of OSFAP, USPTO, and ATO are three such agencies testing this concept and blazing the trail for other federal agencies to join their ranks.

The objective of model legislation developed by the National Partnership for Reinventing Government was to allow federal agencies to reinvent themselves and their procedures to become results-driven organizations and deliver the best possible services.

PBO legislation is designed on a five-year period and both agencies assessed have not reached the halfway mark; therefore, it may be too soon to ascertain a clear and true picture of the results of this initiative. Challenges of how to achieve results with limited flexibilities and high expectations may be conquered as time goes on. The former Chief of Staff at OSFAP articulated it perfectly by stating "what is taking place is the natural evolution of transformation. There will be competing visions that will create natural tension among individuals involved in the transformation. One has to be prepared to expect that what individuals know, and what they know to do, will surface within an agency during transformation."

Equally challenging has been the requirement to continue to use old and obsolete regulations that must be applied in the absence of modernized regulations, which meet the needs of progressive and innovative agencies attempting to break free of regulations that currently no longer make sense in their performance-oriented environment. To achieve true success, these agencies must be allowed to operate unimpeded and knock down the well-entrenched walls of inflexibility.

The results of this assessment revealed that all interviewees were in agreement that "managing for results" is not only necessary, but also vital in the public sector. As stewards for administering public programs and the resources that fund those programs, being a performance-based organization brings a focus on achievements and measuring those achievements to the forefront, which was not previously done. The importance of improving customer satisfaction, providing high quality and cost effective services, and enhancing information technology has been highlighted and addressed very impressively in both agencies. Customer satisfaction levels have increased, systems to measure the costs of doing business are measured by unit cost accounting methodologies, and web-based access to products and services have eased and allowed for more and more individuals to do business with each agency, despite limited flexibilities and resources.

Through discussions with representatives of both PBOs, it appears no government entity can realistically be expected to improve performance, whether performance-based or traditional, if they are bound to overly restrictive, inflexible, or standardized rules and regulations. As individualistic and as unique as human beings, private, public, or non-profit organizations cannot, and should not, be expected to operate under identical administrative and management procedures. Each has unique, explicit, and idiosyncratic needs, customers, and stakeholders.

In conclusion, converting traditional federal agencies to performance-based organizations has had a positive impact (however, early the assessment), as these agencies are genuinely committed to "managing for results" and affecting change in government. Only time will reveal whether or not the performance-based initiative was a success. However, in the interim, these agencies are writing the pages of history and will continue to provide models of success and lessons learned for governments and private and non-profit organizations around the globe.

Since the time of this research (May 2000) and now (June 2003), there has been a change in the Administration. With that, there has been a significant change in the level of support from the current Administration for PBOs and subsequently, a change in leadership and momentum, especially at OSFAP. However, status as a PBO and the internal philosophy of how these agencies operate never appeared to be an issue for these two unique organizations; thereby, the impact of the present lack of support, only stalls progress-not prevents it.

NOTES

1. Budget of the United States Government, Fiscal Year 2004.
2. Budget of the United States Government, Fiscal Year 2004.
3. Budget of the United States Government, Fiscal Year 2004.
4. Creating the Government's first performance-based organization to modernize student aid delivery, Vice President Al Gore, National Press Club, March 4, 1996.

REFERENCES

35 USC 3, Officers & Employees – Reauthorization Act of 1998.
American Inventors Protection Act of 1999, § Subtitle G, Title IV, U.S.C. (1999).
Barzelay, M. (2001). *The new public management: Improving research and policy dialogue*. Berkeley: University of California Press.
Behn, R. D. (2000). *Rethinking democratic accountability*. Washington, DC: Brookings Institution.
Brown, D., & Armstrong, M. (2000). *Paying for contribution: Real performance-related pay strategies*. London: Kogan Page Business Books.
Code of Federal Regulations, Title 5, Volume 1, [Revised as of 1/1/02].
Daily Briefing (2000, December 8). *Government Executive.Com*.
Department of Education Office of Student Financial Aid (1998). *Creating the Government's first performance-based organization to modernize student aid delivery*. http://www.ed.gov/offices/OPE/PPI/Reauthor/pbo1016.html.
Department of Education, Office of Student Financial Assistance Programs Fiscal Year 2001 Performance Plan, Fiscal Year 2000 3rd Quarter Progress Report.
Gawthrop, L. C. (1998). *Public service and democracy*. Chappaqua: Seven Bridges Press, LLC.
Kettl, D. (2000). *The global public management revolution: A report on the transformation of governance*. Washington, DC: Brookings Institution.
Osborne, D., & Gaebler, T. (1992). *Reinventing government – How the entrepreneurial spirit is transforming the public sector, from the Schoolhouse to Statehouse, City Hall to the Pentagon*. Massachusetts: Addison-Wesley.
Peters, G., & Savoie, D. (2001). *Governance in the twenty-first century: Revitalizing the public sector*. Montreal: McGill-Queens University Press.
Reauthorization of the Higher Education Act of 1998, Part D, § 141, Title 35, U.S.C., 1998.
Schein, E. H. (1985). *Organizational culture and leadership*. San Francisco: Jossey-Bass Publishers.
United States Patent and Trademark Office (2000). A new organization for a new millennium, performance and accountability report, fiscal year 2000, 47.
U.S. Office of Personnel Management Survey of the Senior Executive Service, August 1999.
Yarwood, D. L. (1987). *Public administration politics and the people*. New York: Longman.

APPENDIX A

European Institute for Advanced Studies in Management Performance
Measurement and Management Control Performance-Based Organization
Assessment.
 Prerequisites for becoming a PBO were that agencies:

* Have a clear mission, measurable services, and a performance measurement
  system in place or in development.
* Generally focus on external, not internal, customers.
* Have a clear line of accountability to an agency head that has policy
  accountability for the functions.
* Have top-level support to transfer a function into a PBO.
* Have predictable sources of funding.

	5 Major Change	4 Somewhat Moderate Change	3 Moderate Change	2 Minor Change	1 No Change
General					
1. How would you rate accountability now that your agency is a PBO?	o	o	o	o	o
2. How would you rate top-level support?	o	o	o	o	o
3. How would you rate the agency's focus on external customers?	o	o	o	o	o
4. How would you rate the agency's overall performance, efficiency, and effectiveness?	o	o	o	o	o
5. How would you rate management's empowerment?	o	o	o	o	o
6. How would you rate employee's empowerment?	o	o	o	o	o
7. How would you rate employee's accountability for your agency's overall performance?	o	o	o	o	o

	5 Major Change	4 Somewhat Moderate Change	3 Moderate Change	2 Minor Change	1 No Change
8. What has been the most positive result or change as a result of having PBO status?					
9. What has been the most negative result or change as a result of having PBO status?					
10. Would you recommend that PBO status or concepts of PBO be implemented government wide?					

Optional Information:
Name: _____Title: _____
Agency/Office: _____

	5 Major Change	4 Somewhat Moderate Change	3 Moderate Change	2 Minor Change	1 No Change
Budgetary systems					
1. How would you rate your current budget processes as compared to the processes prior to PBO status?	o	o	o	o	o
2. How would you rate budgetary flexibilities as compared to the flexibilities prior to PBO status?	o	o	o	o	o
3. How would you rate planning processes as compared to planning processes prior to PBO status?	o	o	o	o	o

	5 Major Change	4 Somewhat Moderate Change	3 Moderate Change	2 Minor Change	1 No Change
4. How would you compare budgetary Congressional Hearing questions?	o	o	o	o	o
5. How would you rate the current use of resources as compared to prior PBO status?	o	o	o	o	o

	YES	NO			
6. Do you think there has been any significant change in how the agency, as a whole, regards its resources now that it is a PBO?	o	o			
7. What has been the most positive result or change as a result of having PBO status?					
8. What has been the most negative result or change as a result of having PTO status?					

Finance

	5	4	3	2	1
1. How would you rate your current financial system/procedures as compared to the systems/procedures in place prior to PBO status?	o	o	o	o	o
2. How would you rate the impact of flexibilities available under PBO status as compared to those available prior to PBO status?	o	o	o	o	o
3. How would you rate your relationship with vendors since PBO status?	o	o	o	o	o

	5 Major Change	4 Somewhat Moderate Change	3 Moderate Change	2 Minor Change	1 No Change
4. How would you rate the accuracy of your reporting documents since PBO status?	o	o	o	o	o
5. How would you rate the integrity of the financial data since PBO status?	o	o	o	o	o
6. What has been the most positive result of PBO status in the area of finance?					
7. What has been the most negative result of PBO status in the area of finance?					

Procurement systems

	5 Major Change	4 Somewhat Moderate Change	3 Moderate Change	2 Minor Change	1 No Change
1. How would you rate your current procurement processes as compared to the processes prior to PBO status?	o	o	o	o	o
2. How would you rate procurement flexibilities as compared to the flexibilities available prior to PBO status?	o	o	o	o	o
3. Do you think there has been a significant change in how the agency as a whole regards its procurement of products and services as compared to prior to PBO status?	o	o	o	o	o

	YES	NO
4. Has being a PBO allowed you to operate more like a private sector procurement office?	o	o

	5 Major Change	4 Somewhat Moderate Change	3 Moderate Change	2 Minor Change	1 No Change
5. What has been the most positive result of PBO status in the area of procurement?					
6. What has been the most negative result of PBO status in the area of procurement?					

Human resources

	5 Major Change	4 Somewhat Moderate Change	3 Moderate Change	2 Minor Change	1 No Change
1. How would you rate your current human resource processes/systems as compared to the processes/systems in place prior to PBO status?	o	o	o	o	o
2. How would you rate human resource flexibilities as compared to the flexibility available prior to PBO status?	o	o	o	o	o

	YES	NO
3. Do you think there has been a significant change in how the agency, as a whole, regards its human resource services and systems?	o	o
4. Are your rewards systems linked to agency performance?	o	o
5. Has your compensation systems changed as a result of PBO status?	o	o
6. Has being a PBO allowed you to operate more like a private sector human resource office?	o	o

	5 Major Change	4 Somewhat Moderate Change	3 Moderate Change	2 Minor Change	1 No Change
7. What has been the most positive result of PBO status in the area of human resources?					
8. What has been the most negative result of PBO status in the area of human resources?					

Internal controls	YES	NO
1. Has your agency put in additional or new internal controls as a result of being a PBO?	○	○
2. Has your agency eliminated any non-value added internal controls as a result of being a PBO?	○	○
3. Has your agency adopted or adapted any private sector internal control systems or methodologies as a result of being a PBO?	○	○
4. Please provide some examples of your internal controls systems.		

Performance management system

1. How would you rate measurable services now that your agency is a PBO?	○	○	○	○	○
2. How would you rate the level of managers' focus on results-oriented performance since PBO status?	○	○	○	○	○

	5 Major Change	4 Somewhat Moderate Change	3 Moderate Change	2 Minor Change	1 No Change
3. How would you rate the overall (all employees) agency's focus on results-oriented management and performance?	o	o	o	o	o
4. How would you rate the level of managers' focus on inputs and outputs since PBO status?	o	o	o	o	o
5. How would you rate your agency's interaction (e.g. more dialogue) with your external customers as a result of PBO status?	o	o	o	o	o
6. How would you rate the contents of performance reporting documents as a result of PBO status?	o	o	o	o	o
7. How would you rate the level of change in overall customer satisfaction that has (or has not) been achieved as a result of PBO status?	o	o	o	o	o
8. How would you rate levels of improvement in the quality of the agency's outputs that have been achieved as a result of PBO status?	o	o	o	o	o

	YES	NO
9. Has a pay-for-performance method of compensation been linked to the pay of any of the employees other than the Director, CEO position?	o	o

	5 Major Change	4 Somewhat Moderate Change	3 Moderate Change	2 Minor Change	1 No Change
10. Has your agency created any new performance measures, goals or objectives as a result of being designated a PBO?	o	o			

Accountability	YES	NO
1. Has your agency changed its employee rating system to align with the agency's mission and performance goals?	o	o
2. Has your agency implemented any new employee reward systems to align with the achievement of the agency's mission and goals?	o	o
3. Has your agency implemented any new systems of consequence for employees that do not achieve the mission or goals?	o	o
4. Has your agency incorporated the achievement of agency mission and goals into employee performance plans?	o	o
5. Has your agency implemented any pay-for-performance systems as a result of becoming a PBO?	o	o
6. Has your agency encountered any challenges with unions as a result of linking pay with performance?	o	o

	5 Major Change	4 Somewhat Moderate Change	3 Moderate Change	2 Minor Change	1 No Change
Overall management					
1. What level of change has taken place in overall management at your agency as a result of being a PBO?	o	o	o	o	o

	YES	NO
2. Did your agency experience any significant management changes (i.e. retirement, reassignment, resignation) as a result of changes in operational management due to the result of acquiring PBO status?	o	o
3. Has your agency had to eliminate any positions as a result of converting to a PBO?	o	o
4. Do you feel that PBO status has been a positive tool for achieving the mission and goals of your agency?	o	o
5. Do you feel that PBO status has granted you the flexibilities that you envisioned they would prior to implementation?	o	o
6. What was your greatest challenge in converting your previous management systems from traditional bureaucratic methodologies to operating under the status and flexibilities of a PBO?		

A NOMOLOGICAL FRAMEWORK OF BUDGETARY PARTICIPATION AND PERFORMANCE: A STRUCTURAL EQUATION ANALYSIS APPROACH

Jeffrey J. Quirin, David O'Bryan and David P. Donnelly

ABSTRACT

This study extends Quirin et al. (2000) by incorporating equity theory (Adams, 1965) into a theoretical model of budgetary participation and performance. The study develops and tests a nomological framework of budgetary participation that includes two organizational constructs, budgetary participation and budget-based compensation, and three individual characteristics, perception of equity, organizational commitment, and employee performance. Measures of these constructs were gathered from a sample of 98 employees in 15 organizations.

In accordance with the proposed theory and hypotheses, results reveal that budgetary participation is associated with increased use of budget-based compensation as well as higher levels of perception of equity and organizational commitment. Budget-based compensation and perception of equity, in turn, are also associated with increased levels of organizational commitment, while elevated commitment was related to higher performance. The results provide further insight into the beneficial aspects of budgetary participation. Specifically, the results indicate that budgetary participation

Advances in Management Accounting
Advances in Management Accounting, Volume 13, 143–165
ISSN: 1474-7871/doi:10.1016/S1474-7871(04)13006-2

is positively associated with perception of equity, which in turn increases organizational commitment and, ultimately, employee performance.

INTRODUCTION

The budget is a commonly used managerial accounting tool that serves two primary functions. First, budgets provide a means for planning and coordination, which primarily includes resource allocation. Second, budgets serve as a benchmark for performance evaluation. Budgetary participation is the extent to which subordinates have influence on, and are involved in, setting the budget (Brownell,1982b).

A large body of accounting research has investigated the relationship between budgetary participation and employee performance. In fact, few questions in accounting research have generated more controversy (Murray, 1990). Despite this vast quantity of literature, the evidence remains mixed. Numerous studies have shown participation to have a strong positive effect on job performance (e.g. Argyris, 1952; Becker & Green, 1962; Kren, 1990; Nouri & Parker, 1998), while others report that the relationship is positive but not overwhelmingly strong (Brownell, 1982a; Dunk, 1989; Greenberg et al., 1994; Merchant, 1981). Still others report a negative relationship between the two (Bryan & Locke, 1967; Mia, 1988; Stedry, 1960).

Based on a review of 47 studies on budgetary participation, Shields and Shields (1998) recommend that future research recognize that budgetary participation does not exist in isolation but rather is a key part of a broader system. They suggest that this recognition should lead to expanding the scope of investigation in this area by including other variables, such as budget-based compensation. They also recommend that *nomological frameworks* be developed to include additional variables that intervene between budgetary participation and dependent variables.

Quirin et al. (2000) develop and test a theoretical model which includes constructs pertaining to two weaknesses identified by Shields and Shields (1998). Specifically, budget-based compensation and organizational commitment were included as intervening variables between budgetary participation and performance. The empirical results supported their proposed theoretical model.

Recent research suggests that the perceived fairness of the budget process may also impact the relation between budgetary participation and performance (Libby, 1999; Libby, 2001; Lindquist, 1995; Wentzel, 2002). Equity theory (Adams, 1965) incorporates the concept of perceived fairness and extends it by recognizing that individuals assess the fairness of their outcomes by comparing them to the outcomes of referent others. This study extends Quirin et al. (2000) by incorporating equity theory into a proposed nomological framework of budgetary participation and performance.

Using a cross-organizational design and a structural equation analysis technique, results of the main analysis support the study's proposed nomological model and the two main hypotheses derived from equity theory. Budgetary participation is positively associated with the equity theory construct, perception of equity, which in turn is positively associated with organizational commitment. Thus, this study provides additional insight into the beneficial aspects of budgetary participation.

The remainder of this paper is organized into four sections. The first section presents the theoretical development, while the second section discusses the research method including data collection and measurement information. In the third section, empirical results are presented. The final section concludes with a summary, discussion, and limitations.

THEORETICAL DEVELOPMENT

The full theoretical model appears in Fig. 1. To develop the model, the links examined in prior literature are discussed first, followed by a presentation of the two hypotheses derived from equity theory.

Participation and Budget-Based Compensation

The information gathered by management during the budgetary participation process is used for at least two purposes (Shields & Young, 1993). First, information supplied by subordinates can improve the overall efficiency of resource allocation among the operating units. Second, the information from participation can be used to design more effective budget-based incentive systems that can be used to increase motivation. One would therefore expect that when budgetary participation is used more extensively, managers possess an evaluation style which makes greater use of incentives that reward performance based on meeting or exceeding the budget (i.e. budget-based compensation). Studies by Shields and Young (1993) and Quirin et al. (2000) report preliminary evidence supporting this relationship.

Participation and Organizational Commitment

The concept of organizational commitment has received a great deal of empirical study both as a consequence and an antecedent of other work-related variables

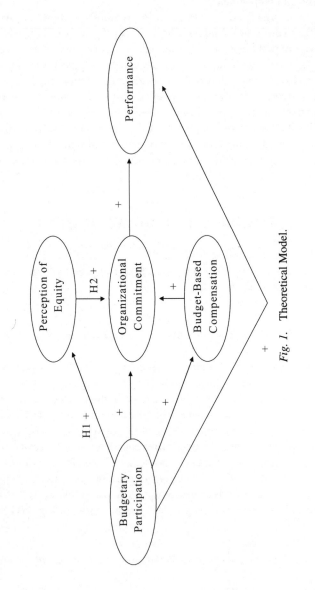

Fig. 1. Theoretical Model.

of interest. In theory, committed employees should work harder, remain with the organization, and contribute more effectively to an organization (Mowday et al., 1979). Mowday et al. (1982) suggest that gaining a greater understanding of the processes related to organizational commitment has implications not only for employees and organizations, but also for society as a whole. Society tends to benefit from employee's organizational commitment in terms of lower rates of job movement and perhaps higher national work productivity and/or quality.

Two common approaches have evolved in the commitment research: behavioral and attitudinal (Brown, 1996). In the behavioral approach, a person attains a state or position of commitment as a result of engaging in committing behaviors. Engaging in these behaviors makes it costly to subsequently reverse a position or disengage from some line of activity. Thus, to act is to commit oneself (Salancik, 1977). According to the attitudinal approach, commitment develops as a result of some common work experiences, perceptions of the organization, and personal characteristics. These factors lead to positive feelings about the organization which in turn becomes commitment (Mowday et al., 1982).

Hanson (1966) argued that members of an organization associate themselves more closely with and become better acquainted with budget goals if they are involved in the creation of the budget. Furthermore, participation allows employees to become better acquainted with organizational goals. Organizational commitment is developed from work experiences and individual perceptions according to the attitudinal view of commitment. Since organizational commitment involves the belief in and acceptance of organizational goals and values, an employee's work experiences through budgetary participation could lead to increased levels of organizational commitment. Nouri and Parker (1998) and Quirin et al. (2000) found evidence to support this relationship.

Participation and Performance

A large body of accounting research has investigated the relationship between budgetary participation and employee performance (Murray, 1990). Despite the vast quantity of literature, the evidence remains somewhat mixed. While a few studies report a negative relationship between the two (Brownell, 1983; Bryan & Locke, 1967; Stedry, 1960), substantially more literature has shown participation to have a positive effect on job performance (e.g. Brownell, 1982a; Dunk, 1989; Merchant, 1981; Mia, 1988; Nouri & Parker, 1998). Based on a meta-analysis of 40 studies, Greenberg et al. (1994) conclude that there is a positive relationship between participation and employee performance, but that the extent of this relation should be considered between medium and small.

Budget-Based Compensation and Organizational Commitment

Given the mixed nature of results on the relationship between the use of budget-based numbers for evaluation purposes (managerial evaluative style) and performance, an intervening variable could be the cause of this inconsistency in the literature. This study proposes that an individual's level of organizational commitment is directly affected by his/her manager's evaluation style, and that the resulting level of commitment affects the employee's performance. Specifically, budget-based compensation, a construct which measures how heavily a manager relies upon budget-based information for pay and promotion decisions, is expected to affect an individual's level of organizational commitment, which in turn will affect that individual's performance.

Once again, the attitudinal approach to organizational commitment asserts that work experiences and perceptions of the organization form the employee's ultimate commitment level. Having a compensation system that rewards employees for meeting budget-based goals allows employees to set compensation and/or promotion-related goals for themselves which are congruent with organizational-wide goals. It is more likely that an employee will believe in and accept organizational goals (become committed) if these goals are congruent with their own. It is predicted that this is more likely under budget-based compensation circumstances.

An additional rationale which suggests a linkage between budget-based compensation and commitment centers around the employee's perception of his/her own contribution to the organization. Morris and Steers (1980) suggest that as employees become more aware of their own contribution to the organization, the heightened awareness enhances ego involvement and thereby increases their attitudinal commitment. Managers utilizing budget-based compensation schemes often discuss with employees how meeting budget-based goals not only affects their individual status (e.g. raise or promotion), but also how meeting individual budget targets affects the company as a whole. Thus, it is predicted that budget-based compensation supplies the employee with better knowledge of his/her individual contribution to the organization and this knowledge thereby affects commitment. Evidence supporting this relationship was found in Quirin et al. (2000).

Organizational Commitment and Performance

A primary objective of industrial behavioral research is to identify the determinants of employee performance. More specifically, determining ways of increasing performance could have significant implications from a practical standpoint.

Numerous studies have viewed organizational commitment as an antecedent to various organizational constructs including performance (Randall, 1990). Work by Mowday et al. (1974) suggested that highly committed employees do perform better than less committed ones, as highly committed employees by definition are willing to exert greater effort on the job. Ferris (1981) found that the performance exhibited by junior-level professional accountants was in-part affected by their level of organizational commitment. Similarly, in a study of the determinants of auditor performance, Ferris and Larcker (1983) indicated that an auditor's rated performance was primarily a function of motivation and organizational commitment. In a study of multiple organizations, Quirin et al. (2001) reported that employees exhibiting higher levels of organizational commitment do indeed perform at higher levels. The results of Randall's (1990) meta-analysis revealed that organizational commitment has a positive relationship with employee performance, but that this relationship is small.

Participation and Perception of Equity

Perception of equity has been linked to a variety of important behaviors including dissatisfaction, reduced effort, and willingness to leave the organization (Mowday, 1987). Perception of equity refers to whether an employee believes that the ratio of his/her organizational inputs relative to the outcomes received from the organization is equal to that of referent others. If an employee's perceived input-to-outcome ratio is equal to that of either an internally-based standard or comparison other (e.g. peer), a sense of fairness or equity results (Adams, 1965). Adams (1965) also distinguishes between compensation/pay equity and effort/workload equity.

The process of establishing fair and equitable budgetary processes is one of the more important activities carried out by organizations, especially if employee compensation is linked in some way to the budgetary goals. Allowing an employee to participate in the budget-setting process provides him/her with a sense of input into the setting of goals to be achieved. In addition, a participating employee is more likely to feel that he/she possesses a higher degree of control over his/her work-related activities as well as workload.[1] Several studies have found that the perceived fairness of the budgetary process is important in determining employee attitudes and behaviors (Folger & Konovsky, 1989; Libby, 1999; Magner & Johnson, 1995). Furthermore, if pay is linked to the accomplishment of budget goals, the employee who is allowed to participate in the establishment of budgetary goals is more likely to perceive that their resulting compensation is equitable.

It is hypothesized that this input into the setting of goals and the feeling of control over work-related activities and workload will increase an individual's perception of both effort/workload equity and compensation/pay equity. Specifically, budgetary participation will increase an employee's perceptions of equity because the budgetary process and outcomes will be perceived to be fairer and more equitable. That is, when compared to other employees who are not involved in setting budget-related standards, the participating employee feels that he/she has more control over, and input into, the goals to be achieved as well as the effort needed to attain those goals. This leads to the following hypothesis stated in the alternative form:

H1. There is a positive relationship between budgetary participation and perception of equity.

Perception of Equity and Organizational Commitment

Empirical evidence suggests that an individual's level of pay satisfaction has a positive impact on organizational commitment (Balfour & Wechsler, 1996). In a study of antecedents and outcomes of organizational commitment in the public sector, it was determined that employees who were more satisfied with their salary were more likely to possess higher levels of organizational commitment. A similar study taking place in a university setting examined the effects of a restructuring of job classifications (Lowe & Vodanovich, 1995). It was found that distributive justice (outcome fairness) factors as a result of a restructuring played an important role in employees' resulting levels of organizational commitment. Thus, it appears organizational commitment can be modeled as a function of both pay and outcome equities.

Given that employees can perceive an inequity with respect to pay and workload (effort), it is important to not only distinguish between the two, but also to understand the relationship between the two (Adams, 1965). Furthermore, since research exists which supports the notion of multiple comparisons (internal and external) for the purposes of forming equity perceptions (Hills, 1980), for measurement purposes it is useful to effectively capture an employee's reference point for forming such perceptions. Results from Quirin et al. (2001) suggest that organizational commitment is affected by both pay and workload-related equities across a number of referents.

In light of the previous findings, which indicate that perception of equity and distributive justice factors play antecedent roles in organizational commitment contexts, the following hypothesis can be formed:

H2. There is a positive relationship between perception of equity and organizational commitment.

RESEARCH METHOD

Data Collection

Data were collected using a survey questionnaire sent to a total of 240 managers from a cross-section of 15 large U.S. companies. Companies were selected based upon the number of their employees who were graduates of a large, Midwestern public university. The sample of companies represented a variety of industries. Some of the companies represented in the sample include AT&T, Boeing, Conoco, General Electric, IBM, Payless Shoe Source, Phillips Petroleum, Sprint, and Wal-Mart. Employees who received surveys were randomly selected from an alumni database at the university. Sixteen employees from each of the 15 companies were sent questionnaires. Respondents possessed degrees from a variety of functional areas including accounting, finance, marketing, and production operations.

A survey instrument package was distributed directly to each potential respondent and returned via mail. Accompanying each questionnaire was a cover letter containing an explanation of the research as well as instructions for completing the survey. A self-addressed, stamped envelope was also included.

Of the 240 surveys distributed, respondents returned a total of 98 usable surveys for a response rate of 41%. The average respondent was 39 years old, had 16 years of work experience, and supervised 29 employees. Males outnumbered females in the sample by a ratio of two to one.[2]

Measures

The variables measured in the questionnaire include perception of equity, budgetary participation, budget-based compensation, organizational commitment, and job performance. All measures were drawn from prior literature. A copy of each research instrument is reported in the Appendix, and descriptive statistics for all measures are reported in Table 1.

A number of studies have utilized a survey instrument to measure an individual's perceptions of pay or workload equity in a field study setting (i.e. Berkowitz et al., 1987; Greenberg, 1989; Hills, 1980; Quirin et al., 2001; Wicker & Bushweiler, 1970). Although most of these instruments stem from

Table 1. Descriptive Statistics.

Variable	Mean	Standard Deviation	Potential Range	Observed Range	Cronbach Alpha
Budgetary participation	21.05	10.52	6–42	6–41	0.94
Perception of equity	46.79	11.15	10–70	18–70	0.94
Budget-based compensation	13.96	6.16	4–28	4–26	0.87
Organizational commitment	47.13	8.99	9–63	23–63	0.91
Performance	48.23	7.17	9–63	20–63	0.86

the original equity theory work of Adams (1965), only one survey instrument was designed to measure both pay and workload perceptions across a number of internal as well as external referents. Possible referent "others" for the purposes of pay and workload comparisons include others within the organization at the same level, other employees within the organization at lower levels, a supervisor within the organization, other employees doing similar types of work in other organizations, and an internal standard based upon a verbal agreement with the employer at the time of hiring (Goodman, 1974; Hills, 1980; Sweeney, 1990).

The Quirin et al. (2001) ten-item, two-part perception-of-equity instrument was used in the current study. Five items relate to the pay equity construct, while the remaining five relate to workload equity. Items in the Quirin et al (2001) instrument were developed from a review of prior literature in the equity theory area (i.e. Berkowitz et al., 1987; Greenberg, 1989; Hills, 1980; Wicker & Bushweiler,). The items were constructed on a seven-point Likert-type scale anchored by (1) strongly disagree and (7) strongly agree. Questions were written so that a response of (7) indicates a high perception of equity. The Cronbach alpha for the ten-item measure in the current study was 0.94, while the reliability alphas for the individual pay and workload portions of the survey were 0.89 and 0.92 respectively. For hypotheses testing purposes, a summed total for the entire ten-item instrument was used.[3]

Milani's (1975) six-item scale was used to measure budgetary participation. The instrument attempted to assess the respondent's involvement in and influence on the budget process. The instrument was written in a seven-point Likert-type format ranging from (1) very little to (7) very much. Satisfactory reliability and validity have been reported for the scale by prior researchers (e.g. Mia, 1988; Nouri & Parker, 1998). In the current study, the Cronbach alpha was 0.94.

Budget-based compensation was measured using a four-item instrument developed by Searfoss (1976). The instrument asks respondents whether their compensation and promotion is related to their budget performance. The items were designed on a seven-point Likert-type scale anchored by (1) strongly disagree and (7) strongly agree. The instrument's reliability and validity have been acceptable in prior research (e.g. Nouri & Parker, 1996). In the current study, the Cronbach alpha was 0.87.

Mowday et al.'s (1979) nine-item short-form instrument was used to measure organizational commitment. The instrument was written in a seven-point Likert-type format ranging from (1) strongly disagree to (7) strongly agree. A response of (7) indicates a high level of organizational commitment. Prior studies report acceptable levels of reliability and validity for the nine-item scale (e.g. Blau, 1987; Nouri & Parker, 1998). In this study, the Cronbach alpha was 0.91.

Performance was measured using Mahoney et al.'s (1963, 1965) multi-dimensional nine-item scale. Respondents were asked to evaluate their individual performance with regard to eight performance dimensions, such as planning, coordinating, supervising, and staffing. Respondents were then asked to rate their overall effectiveness in the final question. The instrument was constructed using a seven-point Likert-type scale ranging from (1) well below average to (7) well above average. The instrument's reliability and validity have been deemed appropriate in a host of prior studies including the accounting-related work of Brownell and Dunk (1991), Dunk (1989), and Brownell (1982a, b). The Cronbach alpha for the current study was 0.86.

Structural Equation Modeling

Structural equation analysis was used to evaluate the proposed hypotheses. An advantage of structural equation analysis is that it provides an efficient technique for estimating interrelated dependence relationships, such as those proposed in this study. Structural equation analysis, rather than moderated regression analysis (MRA) or ANOVA, was also used because the theoretical model presented in this study is viewed as a budgetary participation nomological framework. That is, the current study expands the scope of traditional investigation by including additional variables that intervene between participation and key dependent variables such as organizational commitment and performance. Use of structural equation modeling for testing of such frameworks as well as contingency-based hypotheses, like those contained in this study, has been suggested as the statistical method of choice in recent literature (Hartmann & Moers, 1999; Shields & Shields, 1998).

The structural equation model used in the analysis corresponds to the model in Fig. 1. In Fig. 1, each link between the variables has a path coefficient that measures the impact of the antecedent variable in explaining the variance in the outcome variable. For example, the path coefficient for the link between budgetary participation and organizational commitment indicates the increase in organizational commitment, measured in standard deviations, associated with a one standard deviation increase in budgetary participation.

EMPIRICAL RESULTS

Overall Model Fit

The goal of structural equation modeling is to evaluate whether associations proposed in theory, or in prior research, fit the present data set. Evidence of proper fit is provided by the chi-square statistic and various other fit indices. However, measures of proper fit can be problematic. For example, the potential exists with small sample sizes for the chi-square statistic to indicate a close fit when in fact there is none. In that the sample size used in this study is relatively small ($n = 98$), multiple measures of overall model fit are reported. This lends some assurance that the measures of fit produced are not spurious.

The Normed Fit Index (NFI) was proposed by Bentler and Bonett (1980) as an alternative to the chi-square test. Values of this index range from 0 to 1, with values over 0.9 indicating a good fit. This index may be viewed as the percentage of observed-measure covariation explained by a given model. The disadvantage of the NFI is that it can underestimate goodness-of-fit in small samples. A variation of the NFI is the Non-Normed Fit Index (NNFI) which was also proposed by Bentler and Bonett (1980). This measure has been shown to better reflect model fit at all sample sizes. As with the NFI, values exceeding 0.9 indicate a relatively good fit. However, the NNFI may assume values below 0 and above 1. Bentler's (1990) revised normed comparative fit index (CFI) is based upon the Bentler and Bonett (1980) NFI but with a correction for sample-size dependency. CFI values always lie between 0 and 1, with values over 0.9 indicating a relatively good fit (Bentler, 1990). Finally, the adjusted goodness of fit index (AGFI), devised by Joreskog and Sorbom (1984), is an additional fit index that ranges from 0 to 1, with values above 0.9 indicating acceptable fit.

Figurative depictions of the results of the structural equation analysis are presented in Fig. 2. With adjusted GFI, NFI, NNFI, and CFI values approaching 1.0 in all instances and RMSEA of 0.0332, the theoretical model appears to possess an extremely good fit.[4] Discussions of each structurally-derived path coefficient for the purposes of hypothesis testing follow.

Table 2 reports the correlation matrix for the variables. Table 3 presents tabular results of the structural equation analysis including a listing of each hypothesis and its corresponding path coefficient. Consistent with the high model fit indices, results in Table 3 indicate that the relationships suggested by prior literature were

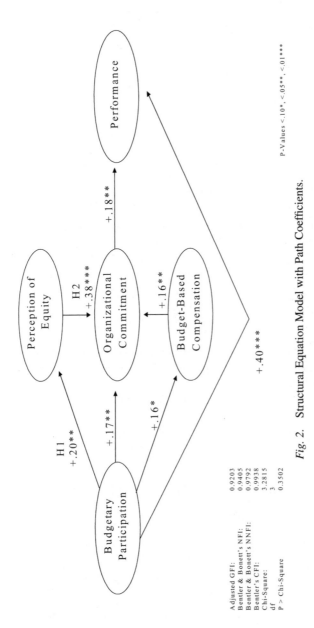

Fig. 2. Structural Equation Model with Path Coefficients.

Adjusted GFI: 0.9203
Bentler & Bonett's NFI: 0.9405
Bentler & Bonett's NNFI: 0.9792
Bentler's CFI: 0.9938
Chi-Square: 3.2815
df 3
P > Chi-Square 0.3502

P-Values < .10*, < .05**, < .01***

Table 2. Correlation Matrix.

	Budgetary Participation	Perception of Equity	Budget-Based Compensation	Organizational Commitment	Performance
Budgetary participation	1.000				
Perception of equity	0.199*	1.000			
Budget-based compensation	0.162	0.154	1.000		
Organizational commitment	0.266**	0.431**	0.244*	1.000	
Performance	0.451**	0.251**	0.188*	0.284**	1.000

Note: $n = 98$
One tailed significance.
*$p < 0.05$.
**$p < 0.01$.

all significant. This suggests that budgetary participation is positively associated with the use of budget-based compensation plans, and that employees allowed to participate possess higher levels of organizational commitment and performance. Furthermore, employers who have budget-based compensation plans possess employees with higher levels of organizational commitment and this increased commitment leads to improved performance.

Tests of Hypotheses

Hypothesis 1 states that there is a positive relation between budgetary participation and an individual employee's perception of equity. The appropriate path coefficient between participation and equity is 0.199 and is significant at the $p < 0.033$ level. This implies that employees who participate more in the budget setting process generally possess higher perceptions of equity.

Hypothesis 2 proposes that perception of equity acts as an antecedent to organizational commitment. The path coefficient related to this hypothesis is 0.376 and is significant at the $p < 0.001$ level. Given the size of the path

Table 3. Structural Equation Modeling Results.

Dependent Variable	Independent Variable	Associated Hypothesis	Path Coefficient	t-Value	p-Value
Perception of equity	Budgetary participation	H1	0.199	1.87	0.033
Budget-based compensation	Budgetary participation	H2	0.162	1.51	0.068
Organizational commitment	Budgetary participation	H3	0.166	1.69	0.048
	Perception of equity	H5	0.376	3.88	0.001
	Budget-based compensation	H6	0.161	1.67	0.049
Performance	Budgetary participation	H4	0.404	4.10	0.001
	Organizational commitment	H7	0.176	1.79	0.040

Note: $n = 98$.

coefficient and the resulting level of significance for the path, the results do indeed indicate a very strong antecedent effect.

Additional Analysis

In aggregate, the results of the main analysis are very supportive of the proposed theoretical model. One advantage of structural equation analysis is that the relative magnitude of the underlying effects can be assessed by decomposing the total relationships into direct, indirect, and spurious components. Table 4 provides information regarding the decomposition of the relationships in the proposed theoretical model.

As shown in Table 4, four of the relationships have indirect effects associated with them. The indirect effect of budgetary participation on organizational commitment is 0.100. This effect can be calculated by adding the indirect effects of budgetary participation on organizational commitment through both perception of equity and budget-based compensation $(0.199 \times 0.376) + (0.162 \times 0.161)$. This result implies that a substantial portion of the 0.266 correlation between budgetary participation and organizational commitment is indirect in nature. Thus, the effects of participation on commitment rely upon both the perception of equity and budget-based compensation constructs.

Table 4. Decomposition of Observed Correlations.

Combination of Variables	Observed Correlation	=	Direct Effect	+	Indirect Effect	+	Spurious Effect
BP-PE	0.199		0.199		–		–
BP-BC	0.162		0.162		–		–
BP-OC	0.266		0.166		0.100		–
BP-P	0.451		0.404		0.047		–
PE-OC	0.431		0.376		–		0.055
PE-P	0.251		0.113		0.066		0.072
BC-OC	0.244		0.161		–		0.083
BC-P	0.188		0.081		0.028		0.079
OC-P	0.284		0.176		–		0.108

Note: BP = Budgetary Participation; PE = Perception of Equity; BC = Budget-Based Compensation; OC = Organizational Commitment; P = Performance.
Solutions to indirect effect calculations: BP-OC = (BP → PE × PE → OC) + (BP → BC × BC → OC) = $(0.199 \times 0.376) + (0.162 \times 0.161) = 0.100$; BP-P = (BP → PE × PE → OC × OC → P) + (BP → BC × BC → OC × OC → P) + (BP → OC × OC → P) = $(0.199 \times 0.376 \times 0.176) + (0.162 \times 0.161 \times 0.176) + (0.166 \times 0.176) = 0.047$; PE-P = PE → OC × OC → P = $0.376 \times 0.176 = 0.066$; BC-P = BC → OC × OC → P = $0.161 \times 0.176 = 0.028$.

The indirect effect of budgetary participation on performance can be calculated in a similar manner (see Table 4 footer for calculation). Only a small portion (0.047) of the correlation between the two variables can be attributed to indirect effects. Thus, the correlation between budgetary participation and performance is largely a function of the 0.404 direct effect.

Additional indirect effect computations between both perception of equity and budget-based compensation on performance were also calculated in Table 4. These resulting indirect effects are insignificant.

DISCUSSION

Quirin et al. (2000) develop and test a theoretical model that includes constructs pertaining to two weaknesses identified by Shields and Shields (1998). Specifically, budget-based compensation and organizational commitment were included as intervening variables between budgetary participation and performance. The empirical results supported their proposed theoretical model.

This study extends Quirin et al. (2000) by incorporating equity theory into a proposed nomological framework of budgetary participation and performance. Equity theory (Adams, 1965) incorporates the concept of perceived fairness and extends it by recognizing that individuals assess the fairness of their outcomes by comparing them to the outcomes of referent others. Recent research suggests that the perceived fairness of the budget process may impact the relation between budgetary participation and performance (Libby, 1999; Libby, 2001; Lindquist, 1995; Wentzel, 2002).

Using a cross-organizational design and a structural equation modeling technique, the results of this study indicate that perception of equity is an important intervening variable in the relation between budgetary participation and performance. Specifically, budgetary participation increases perception of equity, and higher levels of perception of equity lead to increases in organizational commitment. Collectively, these results suggest that perception of equity is an important consequence of budgetary participation. As such, equity theory appears to yield additional insights into the budgetary participation framework.

This study has several practical and empirical implications. First, in the model proposed in this study a manager has the greatest control over budgetary participation and budget-based compensation. In contrast, the manager has less direct control over perception of equity and organizational commitment. Results of this study suggest that careful attention to the design and implementation of the budgetary participation process and the budget-based compensation system can lead to increases in perception of equity and organizational commitment. In turn, these elevated perception of equity and organizational commitment levels result in higher performance.

Second, prior research has linked perception of equity and organizational commitment to numerous other beneficial organizational constructs, such as higher job satisfaction and lower turnover. This study reveals that budgetary participation and budget-based compensation are means by which managers can enhance employees' perceptions of equity and organizational commitment. While not directly examined in this study, by incorporating budgetary participation programs and budget-based compensation schemes managers can reasonably expect other positive effects (e.g. increased job satisfaction, lower turnover) to result in addition to increased performance.

Finally, from an empirical standpoint, future budgetary participation studies might also find the perception of equity construct a useful measure of the substance of the participation process. Argyris (1952) suggests that supervisors often solicit subordinate opinions during the budgeting process but have predetermined that the subordinate will have little influence on the budget. This concept is referred to as "pseudo-participation" (Hopwood, 1976). It is possible that the subordinate's perception of the actual substance of his/her participation could manifest itself in the equity measure. Thus, controlling for pseudo-participation by including a perception of equity measure in future budgetary participation studies does seem logical.

The findings of this survey are subject to several limitations. First, survey studies are by nature subject to both lack of control limitations and potential bias associated with self-reporting. Problems of omitted and uncontrolled intervening or moderating variables may also exist. Second, several studies have criticized self-reported measures of performance (like those used in this study) as unreliable due to leniency bias (e.g. Parker et al., 1959). Moreover, Briers and Hirst (1990) suggest that self-report measures of performance also allow the respondent to make his/her own judgments about the benchmarks used to evaluate performance and the time period over which performance is evaluated. Although other studies have indicated that leniency bias is inconsequential unless the bias is systematically related to an independent variable (Chenhall & Brownwell, 1988; Kren, 1992), the extent to which this study's results are affected by self-report biases is unknown. Third, the nomological framework presented in this study includes only the consequences of budgetary participation. Antecedents to participation such as task interdependence and information asymmetry were not theorized and consequently uninvestigated. As a result, the conditions under which managers should or should not utilize budgetary participation were not addressed herein. Finally, in interpreting the results of this study, causality must be considered. Although alternative methodologies, such as experiments, may be able to provide more information about causality, their ability to model complex organizational behavior may be limited. With respect to this study, a laboratory experiment may be able to yield more causality than a survey approach, but simulating constructs such as perception of equity and organizational commitment in a laboratory setting would be difficult.

NOTES

1. However, as Libby (1999) points out, this is true provided the employee does not view the process as pseudo-participative. Pseudo-participation occurs when the employee is asked to participate in the budget process but determines that her/his input is ignored.

2. A sensitivity analysis was performed to ascertain whether demographic variables contained significant relations with the variables of interest. Three correlations were significant. Age and organizational commitment were positively correlated, as were number of years of experience and organizational commitment. The correlation between gender and budgetary participation was also significant with males possessing higher levels of participation.

3. The structural equation model was also estimated using the summed total for the five items measuring pay equity and then with only the five items measuring workload equity. The results were qualitatively similar to those reported in the main analysis section of the study.

4. For comparative purposes, fit indices for the independence or null model are as follows: adjusted GFI = 0.6747, Bentler and Bonett's NFI = 0.00, Bentler and Bonett's NNFI = 0.00, Bentler's CFI = 0.00, Chi-square (p-value) = 48.064 (<0.01).

ACKNOWLEDGMENT

Jeffrey J. Quirin wishes to acknowledge financial assistance provided by Grant Thornton, LLP.

REFERENCES

Adams, J. (1965). Injustice in social exchange. In: L. Berkowitz (Ed.), *Advances in Experimental Social Psychology* (pp. 267–299). New York: Academic Press.

Argyris, C. (1952). *The impact of budgets on people*. Controllership Foundation.

Balfour, D., & Wechsler, B. (1996). Organizational commitment: Antecedents and outcomes in public organizations. *Public Productivity and Management Review, 19*, 256–277.

Becker, S., & Green, D. (1962). Budgeting and employee behavior. *Journal of Business* (October), 392–402.

Bentler, P. (1990). Comparative fit indices in structural models. *Psychological Bulletin, 107*, 238–246.

Bentler, P., & Bonett, D. (1980). Significance tests and goodness of fit in the analysis of covariance structures. *Psychological Bulletin, 88,* 588–606.

Berkowitz, L., Fraser, C., Treasure, F., & Cochran, S. (1987). Pay, equity, job gratifications, and comparisons in pay satisfaction. *Journal of Applied Psychology, 72,* 544–551.

Blau, G. (1987). Using a person-environment fit model to predict job involvement and organizational commitment. *Journal of Vocational Behavior, 30,* 240–257.

Briers, M., & Hirst, M. (1990). The role of budgetary information in performance evaluation. *Accounting, Organizations and Society, 15,* 373–398.

Brown, R. (1996). Organizational commitment: Clarifying the concept and simplifying the existing construct typology. *Journal of Vocational Behavior, 49,* 230–251.

Brownell, P. (1982a). The role of accounting data in performance evaluation, budgetary participation, and organizational effectiveness. *Journal of Accounting Research* (Spring), 12–27.

Brownell, P. (1982b). Participation in the budgeting process: When it works and when it doesn't. *Journal of Accounting Literature, 1,* 124–153.

Brownell, P. (1983). Leadership style, budgetary participation and managerial behavior. *Accounting, Organizations and Society, 8,* 307–321.

Brownell, P., & Dunk, A. (1991). Task uncertainty and its interaction with budgetary participation and budget emphasis: Some methodological issues and empirical investigation. *Accounting, Organizations and Society, 16,* 693–703.

Bryan, J., & Locke, E. (1967). Goal setting as a means of increasing motivation. *Journal of Applied Psychology* (June), 274–277.

Chenhall, R., & Brownwell, P. (1988). The effect of participative budgeting on job satisfaction and performance: Role ambiguity as an intervening variable. *Accounting, Organizations and Society, 13,* 225–233.

Dunk, A. (1989). Budget emphasis, budgetary participation, and managerial performance: A note. *Accounting, Organizations and Society, 14,* 321–324.

Ferris, K. (1981). Organizational commitment and performance in a professional accounting firm. *Accounting, Organizations and Society, 6,* 317–325.

Ferris, K., & Larcker, D. (1983). Explanatory variables of auditor performance in a large public accounting firm. *Accounting, Organizations and Society, 8,* 1–11.

Folger, R., & Konovsky, M. (1989). Effects of procedural and distributive justice on reactions to pay decisions. *Academy of Management Journal, 1,* 115–130.

Goodman, P. (1974). An examination of referents used in evaluation of pay. *Organizational Behavior and Human Performance, 12,* 170–195.

Greenberg, J. (1989). Cognitive reevaluation of outcomes in response to underpayment inequity. *Academy of Management Journal, 32,* 174–184.

Greenberg, P., Greenberg, R., & Nouri, H. (1994). Participative budgeting: A meta-analytic examination of methodological moderators. *Journal of Accounting Literature, 13,* 117–141.

Hanson, E. (1966). The budgetary control function. *The Accounting Review* (April), 239–243.

Hartmann, F., & Moers, F. (1999). Testing contingency hypotheses in budgetary research: An evaluation of the use of moderated regression analysis. *Accounting, Organizations and Society, 24,* 291–315.

Hills, F. (1980). The relevant other in pay comparisons. *Industrial Relations, 19,* 345–351.

Hopwood, A. (1976). *Accounting and human behavior.* Englewood Cliffs, NJ: Prentice-Hall.

Joreskog, K., & Sorbom, D. (1984). *LISREL – VI users guide* (4th ed.). Mooresville, IN: Scientific Software.

Kren, L. (1990). Performance in a budget-based control system: An extended expectancy theory model approach. *Journal of Management Accounting Research, 2,* 100–112.

Kren, L. (1992). Budgetary participation and managerial performance: The impact of information and environmental volatility. *The Accounting Review, 67*, 511–526.

Libby, T. (1999). The influence of voice and explanation on performance in a participative budgeting setting. *Accounting, Organizations and Society, 24*, 125–137.

Libby, T. (2001). Referent cognitions and budgetary fairness: A research note. *Journal of Management Accounting Research, 13*, 91–105.

Lindquist, T. (1995). Fairness as an antecedent to participative budgeting: Examining the effects of distributive justice, procedural justice and referent cognitions on satisfaction and performance. *Journal of Management Accounting Research, 7*, 122–147.

Lowe, R., & Vodanovich, S. (1995). A field study of distributive justice and procedural justice as predictors of satisfaction and organizational commitment. *Journal of Business and Psychology, 10*, 99–114.

Magner, N., & Johnson, G. (1995). Municipal officials' reactions to justice in budgetary resource allocation. *Public Administrative Quarterly, 18*, 439–456.

Mahoney, T., Jerdee, T., & Carroll, S. (1963). *Development of managerial performance: A research approach*. Cincinnati, OH: South-western.

Mahoney, T., Jerdee, T., & Carroll, S. (1965). The jobs of management. *Industrial Relations, 4*, 97–110.

Mia, L. (1988). Managerial attitude, motivation, and the effectiveness of budget participation. *Accounting, Organizations and Society, 13*, 465–475.

Milani, K. (1975). The relationship of participation in budget-setting to industrial supervisor performance and attitudes: A field study. *The Accounting Review, 50*, 274–284.

Merchant, K. (1981). The design of the corporate budgeting system: Influences on managerial behavior and performance. *The Accounting Review, 56*, 813–829.

Morris, J., & Steers, R. (1980). Structural influences on organizational commitment. *Journal of Vocational Behavior, 17*, 50–57.

Mowday, R. (1987). Equity theory predictions of behavior in organizations. In: R. Steers & L. Porter (Eds), *Motivation and Work Behavior*. New York: McGraw-Hill.

Mowday, R., Porter, L., & Dubin, R. (1974). Unit performance, situational factors and employee attitudes in spatially separated work units. *Organizational Behavior and Human Performance, 11*, 231–248.

Mowday, R., Porter, L., & Steers, R. (1982). *Organizational linkages*. New York: Academic Press.

Mowday, R., Steers, R., & Porter, L. (1979). The measurement of organizational commitment. *Journal of Vocational Behavior, 14*, 224–247.

Murray, D. (1990). The performance effects of participative budgeting: An integration of intervening and moderating variables. *Behavioral Research in Accounting, 2*, 104–123.

Nouri, H., & Parker, R. (1996). The interactive effect of budget-based compensation, organizational commitment, and job involvement on managers' propensities to create budgetary slack. *Advances in Accounting, 14*, 209–222.

Nouri, H., & Parker, R. (1998). The relationship between budget participation and job performance: The roles of budget adequacy and organizational commitment. *Accounting, Organizations and Society, 23*, 467–483.

Parker, J., Taylor, E., Barrett, R., & Martens, L. (1959). Rating scale content: Relationship between supervisory and self-ratings. *Personnel Psychology, 12*, 49–63.

Quirin, J., Donnelly, D., & O'Bryan, D. (2000). Consequences of participative budgeting: The roles of budget-based compensation, organizational commitment, and managerial performance. *Advances in Management Accounting, 9*, 127–143.

Quirin, J., Donnelly, D., & O'Bryan, D. (2001). Antecedents of organizational commitment: The role of perception of equity. *Advances in Accounting Behavioral Research, 4*, 261–280.

Randall, D. (1990). The consequences of organizational commitment: Methodological investigation. *Journal of Organizational Behavior, 11*, 361–378.

Salancik, G. (1977). Commitment and the control of organizational behavior and belief. In: B. Staw & G. Salancik (Eds), *New Directions in Organizational Behavior* (pp. 1–95). Chicago: St. Clair Press.

Searfoss, G. (1976). Some behavioral aspects of budgeting for control: An empirical study. *Accounting, Organizations and Society, 4*, 375–385.

Shields, J. F., & Shields, M. D. (1998). Antecedents of participative budgeting. *Accounting, Organizations and Society, 23*, 49–76.

Shields, M., & Young, S. (1993). Antecedents and consequences of participative budgeting: Evidence on the effects of asymmetrical information. *Journal of Management Accounting Research, 5*, 265–280.

Stedry, A. (1960). *Budget control and cost behavior.* Englewood Cliffs, NJ: Prentice-Hall.

Sweeney, P. (1990). Distributive justice and pay satisfaction: A field test of an equity theory prediction. *Journal of Business and Psychology, 4*, 329–341.

Wentzel, K. (2002). The influence of fairness perceptions and goal commitment on managers' performance in a budget setting. *Behavioral Research in Accounting, 14*, 247–271.

Wicker, A., & Bushweiler, G. (1970). Perceived fairness and pleasantness of social exchange situations: Two factorial studies of inequity. *Journal of Personality and Social Psychology, 15*, 63–75.

APPENDIX

Survey Instruments

Perception of Equity (Quirin et al., 2001)
Current study Cronbach alpha = 0.94

1 = strongly disagree   7 = strongly agree

(A) I feel my pay is equitable when compared to:
   (1) Others in this company at my job level.
   (2) What other employers are paying for the type of work I am asked to do.
   (3) What others below me in the company are being paid.
   (4) What my supervisor is paid.
   (5) What the company told me I would be paid.

(B) I feel my workload is equitable when compared to:
   (1) Others in this company at my job level.
   (2) What other employers are asking employees at my job level to do.
   (3) What the company told me I would do when I accepted this position.
   (4) What others below me in the company are asked to do.
   (5) What my supervisor is asked to do.

Budgetary Participation (Milani, 1975)
Current study Cronbach alpha = 0.94
1 = very little   7 = very much

(1) The portion of the budget I am involved in setting.
(2) The amount of reasoning provided to me by a superior when the budget is revised.
(3) The frequency of budget-related discussion with superiors initiated by me.
(4) The amount of influence I feel I have on the final budget.
(5) The importance of my contribution to the budget.
(6) The frequency of budget-related discussions initiated by my superior when budgets are being set.

Budget-Based Compensation (Searfoss, 1976)
Current study Cronbach alpha = 0.87
1 = strongly disagree   7 = strongly agree

(1) Budget variances have been mentioned by my superior as factors in his/her consideration of me for promotion.
(2) Budget variances in my department have been mentioned by my superior as factors in considering me for pay raises.
(3) Pay increases are closely tied into budget performance.
(4) Budget performance is an important factor in getting a promotion.

Organizational Commitment (Mowday et al., 1979)
Current study Cronbach alpha = 0.91
1 = strongly disagree   7 = strongly agree

(1) I am willing to put in a great deal of effort beyond that normally expected in order to help this organization be successful.
(2) I talk up this organization to my friends as a great organization to work for.
(3) I would accept almost any type of job assignment in order to keep working for this organization.
(4) I found that my values and the organization's values are very similar.
(5) I am proud to tell others that I am a part of this organization.
(6) This organization really inspires the very best in me in the way of job performance.
(7) I am extremely glad that I chose this organization to work for over others I was considering at the time I joined.
(8) For me this is the best of all possible organizations for which to work.
(9) I really care about the fate of this organization.

Performance (Mahoney et al., 1963, 1965)
Current study Cronbach alpha = 0.86
1 = well below average   7 = well above average

(1) My performance with regards to planning (i.e. determining goals and policies, budgeting, preparing agendas).
(2) My performance with regards to investigating (i.e. collecting and preparing information, financial reports, inventorying).
(3) My performance with regards to coordinating (i.e. exchanging information with others, arranging meetings, advising others).
(4) My performance with regards to evaluating (i.e. assessment of employee performance, product and financial report inspection).
(5) My performance with regards to supervising (i.e. directing, leading, counseling and training subordinates).
(6) My performance with regards to staffing (i.e. college recruiting, employment interviewing, promoting employees).
(7) My performance with regards to negotiating (i.e. purchasing, selling, advertising, dealing with sales representatives).
(8) My performance with regards to representing (i.e. advancing general organizational interests).
(9) My overall performance.

DOES ORGANIZATION-MANDATED BUDGETARY INVOLVEMENT ENHANCE MANAGERS' BUDGETARY COMMUNICATION WITH THEIR SUPERVISOR?

Laura Francis-Gladney, Harold T. Little,
Nace R. Magner and Robert B. Welker

ABSTRACT

Large organizations typically mandate that managers attend budget meetings and exchange budget reports with their immediate supervisor and budget staff. We explored whether such organization-mandated budgetary involvement is related to managers' budgetary communication with their supervisor in terms of budgetary participation, budgetary explanation, and budgetary feedback. Questionnaire data from 148 managers employed by 94 different companies were analyzed with regression. Mandatory budget meetings with supervisor had a positive relationship with all three forms of budgetary communication with supervisor, and mandatory budget reports from supervisor had a positive relationship with budgetary explanation from supervisor. Mandatory budget meetings with budget staff had a positive relationship with both budgetary participation with supervisor and budgetary feedback from supervisor. Mandatory budget reports from budget staff had

Advances in Management Accounting
Advances in Management Accounting, Volume 13, 167–182
© 2004 Published by Elsevier Ltd.
ISSN: 1474-7871/doi:10.1016/S1474-7871(04)13007-4

a negative relationship with all three forms of budgetary communication with supervisor. The results failed to support proposed relationships between mandatory budget reports to supervisor and budgetary participation with supervisor, and between mandatory budget reports from supervisor and budgetary explanation from supervisor. Implications of the results for future research and budgetary system design are discussed.

INTRODUCTION

Budgeting is an integral part of short-range planning and control in most organizations (Merchant, 1981). Perhaps the most important factor in the functioning of an organization's budgetary system is the communication that occurs between unit managers who have budget responsibility and their immediate supervisor (Hofstede, 1967). Budgetary communication between a manager and supervisor exists when the manager conveys budget-relevant information to, or receives it from, the supervisor. The budgeting literature has examined several variables that address a manager's budgetary communication with the immediate supervisor and other budget actors, including budgetary participation, budgetary explanation, and budgetary feedback. Budgetary participation is the extent to which a manager has an opportunity to voice opinions about and have influence on his or her budget (cf. Brownell, 1982a). Budgetary explanation is the extent to which a manager receives clear and adequate reasons for decisions pertaining to his or her budget (cf. Tyler & Bies, 1990). Budgetary feedback is the extent to which a manager receives information about his or her achievement of budget goals (cf. Kenis, 1979).

Large organizations typically force managers to become involved in the budgetary process through attendance at mandatory budget meetings and the exchange of mandatory budget reports (Anthony & Govindarajan, 2001). This paper reports the results of a study that explored the extent to which such mandatory budgetary involvement is related to managers' budgetary communication with their immediate supervisor in terms of budgetary participation, budgetary explanation, and budgetary feedback. Mandatory budgetary involvement was addressed in terms of budget meetings that managers must attend with, and budget reports they must prepare for and receive from, the supervisor and budget staff in order to conform to the organization's formal written policies. While a primary purpose of organization-mandated budget meetings and reports is to foster the exchange of budget-relevant information, and thus to enhance budgetary communication, between budget actors such as managers and their immediate supervisor, little empirical research to date has addressed the extent to which mandatory budgetary involvement serves this intended purpose. Shields and Shields (1998, p. 66) recently proposed that future budgeting research should explicitly recognize a "forced (e.g. corporate policy)" dimension of budgetary participation, a recommendation that we believe is also relevant to other budgetary communication variables such as budgetary explanation and budgetary feedback. The current study addresses this recommendation in that it examines whether organizational policies that force managers to become involved in the budgetary process via budget meetings and reports are antecedents of budgetary participation, budgetary explanation, and budgetary feedback.

The remainder of this paper is organized as follows. The next section offers theoretical justification for the relationships examined in the study, as well as hypotheses and research questions. The following two sections present the research method and results of the data analyses, respectively. In the final section, we discuss the results and their implications, future research directions, and limitations of the study.

THEORY, HYPOTHESES, AND RESEARCH QUESTIONS

Organizations seek enhanced budgetary communication between managers and their superiors (e.g. the immediate supervisor) for at least two general reasons. First, enhanced budgetary communication has the potential to reduce information asymmetry within the organization. Economic models of budgeting have emphasized the flow of information up the hierarchy from subordinate managers to their superiors and agents of the superiors such as budget staff (e.g. Baiman & Evans, 1983; Kirby et al., 1991). Subordinate managers generally hold private information regarding their task and task environment which, if acquired by superiors, may allow the superiors to allocate budgetary resources in a more effective manner and to design incentive contracts that better motivate the subordinates to achieve their budgets (Shields & Shields, 1998; Shields & Young, 1993). The budgeting literature has also addressed, albeit to a lesser extent, the flow of information down the hierarchy from superiors to subordinates (e.g. Kren, 1992; Magner et al., 1996). Superiors hold private information regarding budget goals and strategies for achieving budget goals that, if conveyed to subordinates, may facilitate the subordinates' achievement of those goals.

A second general reason that organizations seek enhanced budgetary communication between managers and their superiors is its potential positive effect on the managers' work-related attitudes, morale, and motivation, and, in turn, on behaviors such as job performance (Shields & Shields, 1998; Shields &

Young, 1993). Budgetary communication in terms of budgetary participation, budgetary explanation, or budgetary feedback has been found to be related to a variety of work-related affective and behavioral reactions. These reactions include increased job satisfaction, greater perceived fairness of the budgetary process and its outcomes, a more favorable attitude toward and greater trust in superiors, a more favorable attitude and greater commitment toward the budget and the organization, a reduced propensity to create budgetary slack, and improved job performance (e.g. Bies & Shapiro, 1988; Brownell, 1982b; Chong & Chong, 2002; Dunk, 1993; Govindarajan, 1986; Hirst & Lowy, 1990; Kenis, 1979; Libby, 1999; Magner et al., 1995; Merchant, 1985; Milani, 1975; Wentzel, 2002).

Mandatory budget meetings and mandatory budget reports are two basic types of structural procedures that an organization might implement to promote budgetary communication. Mandatory budget meetings provide for a two-way flow of budget-relevant information between the budget actors involved in the meeting. Mandatory budget reports promote a one-way flow of budget-relevant information, with the direction of the flow depending upon which of the budget actors generated the report and which is (are) the recipient(s) of the report. Our focus in the current study is budgetary communication between two specific budget actors, a unit manager and his or her immediate supervisor. We next discuss how a manager's mandatory budgetary involvement in terms of attending budget meetings and exchanging budget reports not only with the immediate supervisor but also with another category of budget actor, budget staff, might be related to the manager's budgetary communication with the supervisor in terms of budgetary participation, budgetary explanation, and budgetary feedback.

Mandatory Budgetary Involvement with Supervisor

When managers attend mandatory budget meetings with their immediate supervisor, they have a face-to-face forum to voice views and opinions regarding their budget directly to the supervisor. Furthermore, these meetings provide opportunities for supervisors to explain the reasons for their budget decisions directly to the subordinate manager and to provide direct feedback regarding the manager's achievement of budget goals. For these reasons, we propose that as managers have greater mandatory involvement in the budgetary process in terms of budget meetings with their supervisor, they will have greater budgetary participation with, and greater budgetary explanation and budgetary feedback from, the supervisor.

H1a. Mandatory budget meetings with the immediate supervisor will have a positive relationship with a manager's budgetary participation with the supervisor.

H1b. Mandatory budget meetings with the immediate supervisor will have a positive relationship with the budgetary explanation a manager receives from the supervisor.

H1c. Mandatory budget meetings with the immediate supervisor will have a positive relationship with the budgetary feedback a manager receives from the supervisor.

Mandatory budget reports to the immediate supervisor are another avenue by which managers might proffer their budgetary views and opinions directly to the supervisor. Thus, we propose that as a manager has greater mandatory involvement in the budgetary process in terms of budget reports to the supervisor, the manager will participate more fully with the supervisor in budgetary decision making. Because mandatory budget reports from a manager to a supervisor promote a flow of information only up (but not down) the organizational hierarchy, we do not propose a relationship between mandatory budget reports to the supervisor and either the budgetary explanation or the budgetary feedback that a manager receives from the supervisor.

H2. Mandatory budget reports to the immediate supervisor will have a positive relationship with a manager's budgetary participation with the supervisor.

While mandatory budget reports from managers to their immediate supervisor promote a one-way flow of budget-relevant information up the organizational hierarchy, mandatory budget reports from supervisors to subordinate managers promote a one-way flow of budgetary information in the opposite direction. For this reason, we propose that as a manager has greater mandatory involvement in the budgetary process in terms of mandatory reports from the supervisor, the manager will receive greater budgetary explanation and budgetary feedback from the supervisor. However, we do not propose a relationship between mandatory budget reports from the supervisor and a manager's budgetary participation with the supervisor, because the concept of budgetary participation generally relates to a subordinate manager conveying budgetary views and opinions up the hierarchy.

H3a. Mandatory budget reports from the immediate supervisor will have a positive relationship with the budgetary explanation a manager receives from the supervisor.

H3b. Mandatory budget reports from the immediate supervisor will have a positive relationship with the budgetary feedback a manager receives from the supervisor.

Mandatory Budgetary Involvement with Budget Staff

Managers in large organizations typically must interact with the organization's budget staff during the budgetary process. For example, staff members provide assistance to managers in preparing their unit's initial budget, review the budget to determine whether or not it is consistent with organizational objectives and the budgets of other units, and work with managers to make appropriate changes to the budget when inconsistencies are found. Some of this interaction between managers and budget staff is likely to occur by means of organization-mandated budget meetings and reports.

From one perspective, increased mandatory budgetary involvement with budget staff might enhance a manager's budgetary communication with the immediate supervisor if staff members serve as intermediaries in an indirect transfer of budget-relevant information between the two parties. For example, when attending mandatory budget meetings with or submitting mandatory budget reports to budget staff, managers may voice views and opinions regarding their budget that staff members, in turn, transmit in some form and through some medium to the supervisor. Also, the supervisor may through some medium convey explanations or feedback regarding a manager's budget to budget staff that they, in turn, transmit in some form to the manager during mandatory budget meetings or in mandatory budget reports.

From another perspective, increased mandatory budgetary involvement with budget staff may reduce a manager's budgetary communication with the supervisor if it signifies a top-down, bureaucratic budgetary environment in which the supervisor plays a trivial role in establishing the final budget for the manager's unit. In this environment, managers may be less inclined to express their budgetary views and opinions to the supervisor because they do not think their input will have much influence on the final budget. The supervisor, for his or her part, may be less inclined to provide the manager with explanations or feedback regarding the manager's budget both because the supervisor may know little about the rationale used in establishing the budget figures and because he or she feels little responsibility for the budget.

Because the theoretical support is equivocal and prior empirical evidence is lacking, we did not formulate specific hypotheses regarding relationships between mandatory budgetary involvement with budget staff in terms of budget meetings and reports and a manager's budgetary communication with the immediate supervisor in terms of budgetary participation, budgetary explanation, and budgetary feedback. Instead, we examined these relationships in the context of the following research questions.

RQ1. Are mandatory budgetary meetings with budget staff related to a manager's budgetary participation with the immediate supervisor, budgetary explanation from the immediate supervisor, and budgetary feedback from the immediate supervisor?

RQ2. Are mandatory budgetary reports to budget staff related to a manager's budgetary participation with the immediate supervisor, budgetary explanation from the immediate supervisor, and budgetary feedback from the immediate supervisor?

RQ3. Are mandatory budgetary reports from budget staff related to a manager's budgetary participation with the immediate supervisor, budgetary explanation from the immediate supervisor, and budgetary feedback from the immediate supervisor?

RESEARCH METHOD

Sample and Procedures

An initial sample of 766 business operating locations with annual sales exceeding $50 million, each from a unique company, was drawn from a database of over 10,000 operating locations maintained by a large utility for marketing purposes. The minimum of $50 million in sales was applied as large organizations are more likely to have formal budgetary procedures in place (Bruns & Waterhouse, 1975; Merchant, 1981). Two questionnaires were sent to each location's chief accounting officer for distribution to two different managers with significant budget responsibility.

Usable questionnaires were returned by 148 responsibility center managers (a 9.7% response rate) from 94 different companies (representing 12.3% of the companies to which questionnaires were sent). The average respondent was male (92.9%) and 44.5 years old (S.D. = 7.9), had been with the company for 15 years (S.D. = 8.7) and in his current position for 6.1 years (S.D. = 5.7), and had authority over 34 subordinates (S.D. = 70.1). The operating locations for which the respondents worked were principally in manufacturing (87.8%) and their Standard Industry Code (SIC) major group numbers spanned a diverse group of industries, including food, textiles, paper, chemicals, fabricated metal products, industrial machinery, electrical equipment, transportation equipment, and measuring equipment.

Because of the relatively low response rate, we conducted two tests of non-response bias. First, the 94 company operating locations for which the respondents worked were compared to a separately drawn sample with respect to industry composition (SIC major group numbers) and size ($50–$100 million in sales, $100–$500 million in sales, $500 million and over in sales). No significant differences ($p < 0.05$) were detected for industry composition or size. In addition, the first 30 and last 30 respondents were compared on the basis of gender, age, tenure with company, tenure in current position, and number of subordinates. No significant differences emerged between the two groups on any of these demographic variables. These tests provide some assurance that the sample is representative of the population from which it was drawn.

Measures of Mandatory Budgetary Involvement

Six items were developed to measure the respondents' mandatory budgetary involvement with the supervisor and budget staff in terms of meetings and reports. Budget meetings with supervisor and budget meetings with budget staff, respectively, were measured with the following two items: "In the budget preparation process, what is the minimum number of times that you have to meet: (1) with your immediate supervisor (with or without budget officials and/or other managers being present); and (2) with budget officials (with your immediate supervisor not present)?" Budget reports to supervisor and budget reports to budget staff, respectively, were measured with the following two items: "In the budget preparation process, what is the minimum number of budget reports that you have to prepare specifically for: (1) your immediate supervisor; and (2) budget officials?" Budget reports from supervisor and budget reports from budget staff, respectively, were measured with the following two items: "In the budget preparation process, what is the minimum number of budget reports sent to you that have to be prepared primarily by: (1) your immediate supervisor; and (2) budget officials?" To emphasize the request for mandatory meetings and reports, the instructions expressly stated that the respondents should only consider "budget meetings and reports that are necessary under a LITERAL or STRICT INTERPRETATION of written policies (i.e. that are necessary to conform to the LETTER OF THE LAW)." Respondents were also instructed to "assume a ONE YEAR time frame." Budget officials were defined as "company employees, other than your immediate supervisor, who have a role in the budgeting process." Budget reports were defined as including "any formal, written dissemination of financial or non-financial data through paper or electronic media."

Skewness and kurtosis statistics for the six measures of mandatory budgetary involvement indicated serious deviations from normality, with the ratio of the absolute value of the statistic relative to its standard error greater than 9 in each case. Also, we were concerned that the relationships between the measures of mandatory budgetary involvement and the criterion variables in the study would be subject to diminishing returns and therefore nonlinear. For these reasons, we applied a log transformation to the six variables so that their distributions more closely approximated a normal one and to place the variables on a geometric scale to restore linearity.

Measures of Budgetary Communication with Supervisor

Budgetary participation with supervisor was measured with eight items based on those used in previous budgeting studies (Brownell & Merchant, 1990; Bruns & Waterhouse, 1975; Kren, 1992; Merchant, 1981; Milani, 1975; Shields & Young, 1993; Swieringa & Moncur, 1975). The items were phrased to reflect a behavior of the supervisor and so that they were stated in an active voice. Sample items include: "My supervisor seeks my opinions and suggestions when my budget is being set," "My supervisor initiates budget-relevant discussions with me," "My supervisor finalizes my budget only when I am satisfied with it," and "My supervisor includes changes I have suggested in new budgets." Each item had a seven-point scale with the endpoints 1 ("strongly disagree") and 7 ("strongly agree"). Cronbach's alpha reliability coefficient for the measure was 0.92, which exceeds the minimum 0.70 value recommended by Nunnally (1978). Item responses were summed and averaged into a composite score.

Budgetary explanation from supervisor was measured with the following three items that we developed: "My supervisor provides adequate explanations for budget decisions that affect me," "My supervisor gives sufficient justification for important budgetary decisions that affect my unit," and "My supervisor attempts to see that I have a clear understanding of the rationale for budgeting decisions that he/she makes." The endpoints of each item were 1 ("strongly disagree") and 7 ("strongly agree"). Cronbach's alpha was 0.90. Item responses were summed and averaged into a composite score.

Budgetary feedback from supervisor was measured with three-items used by Kenis (1979). The items were: "My supervisor gives a considerable amount of feedback about my achievement concerning my budget goals," "My supervisor provides a great deal of feedback and guidance about my budget variance," and "My supervisor lets me know how well I am doing in terms of achieving my budget goals." Each item had a seven-point scale with the endpoints 1 ("strongly disagree") and 7 ("strongly agree"). Cronbach's alpha in the current study was 0.87. Item responses were summed and averaged into a composite score.

RESULTS

Table 1 contains means, standard deviations, and Pearson bivariate correlations for the variables. Correlations among the mandatory budgetary involvement variables were generally low-to-moderate, ranging from 0.04 to 0.54. Correlations among the budgetary communication variables were moderate-to-high, ranging from 0.45 to 0.69. Correlations between the mandatory budgetary involvement variables and the budgetary communication variables were low-to-moderate, with absolute values ranging from 0.01 to 0.30.

The primary analytical technique was ordinary least-squares regression. Budgetary participation with supervisor, budgetary explanation from supervisor, and budgetary feedback from supervisor were each regressed separately on the six mandatory budgetary involvement variables. Hypothesized relationships between the mandatory budgetary involvement variables and the budgetary communication variables were examined using a one-tailed test of significance, while a two-tailed test of significance was used for examining all other relationships. Table 2 contains the results of the regression analysis. The betas (standardized regression coefficients), which represent the relationship between a given mandatory budgetary involvement variable and a budgetary communication variable after controlling for the other mandatory budgetary involvement variables, were the basis for addressing the hypotheses and research questions of the study.

The hypotheses pertain to relationships between the mandatory budgetary involvement with supervisor variables and the budgetary communication variables. Hypothesis 1a, which proposes a positive relationship between budget meetings with supervisor and budgetary participation with supervisor, was supported at $p < 0.10$. Hypotheses 1b and 1c, which propose that budget meetings with supervisor has positive relationships with budgetary explanation from supervisor and budgetary feedback from supervisor, respectively, were supported at $p < 0.05$. Hypothesis 2 proposes a positive relationship between budget reports to supervisor and budgetary participation with supervisor. It was not supported, as the relationship between the two variables was not statistically significant ($p > 0.10$). Hypothesis 3a, which proposes a positive

Table 1. Means, Standard Deviations, and Pearson Correlations.

Variable	Mean	S.D.	1	2	3	4	5	6	7	8	9
1. Budget meetings with supervisor[a]	1.26	0.68	1.00								
2. Budget reports to supervisor[a]	1.20	0.73	0.54**	1.00							
3. Budget reports from supervisor[a]	0.69	0.69	0.25**	0.34**	1.00						
4. Budget meetings with budget staff[a]	0.91	0.71	0.45**	0.19*	0.23**	1.00					
5. Budget reports to budget staff[a]	1.19	0.69	0.19*	0.38**	0.14	0.34**	1.00				
6. Budget reports from budget staff[a]	0.97	0.71	0.10	0.04	0.37**	0.26**	0.47**	1.00			
7. Budgetary participation with supervisor[b]	5.10	1.26	0.21*	0.09	0.01	0.19*	-0.03	-0.18*	1.00		
8. Budgetary explanation from supervisor[b]	4.76	1.34	0.23**	0.13	0.11	0.18*	0.08	-0.12	0.69**	1.00	
9. Budgetary feedback from supervisor[b]	4.70	1.32	0.30**	0.23**	0.08	0.23**	0.10	-0.10	0.45**	0.58**	1.00

[a] A log transformation was applied to these variables prior to analysis.
[b] The theoretical range of these variables is 1–7.
* Significant at the $p < 0.05$ levels (two-tailed test).
** Significant at the $p < 0.01$ levels (two-tailed test).

Table 2.   Regression Results.

Mandatory Budgetary Involvement Variable[a,b]	Budgetary Communication Variable		
	Budgetary Participation with Supervisor	Budgetary Explanation from Supervisor	Budgetary Feedback from Supervisor
With supervisor			
Budget meetings with supervisor	**0.17**[†]	**0.19**[*]	**0.19**[*]
Budget reports to supervisor	**−0.04**	−0.09	0.06
Budget reports from supervisor	0.04	**0.16**[*]	**0.05**
With budget staff			
Budget meetings with budget staff	0.17[†]	0.11	0.16[†]
Budget reports to budget staff	0.02	0.15	0.08
Budget reports from budget staff	−0.26[**]	−0.30[**]	−0.22[*]
R^2	0.11[**]	0.12[**]	0.14[**]

Note: Boldface coefficients address relationships that were hypothesized to be positive and thus were evaluated with a one-tailed test of significance. Other coefficients were evaluated with a two-tailed test of significance.

[a] A log transformation was applied to these variables prior to analysis.
[b] Betas (standardized regression coefficients) are displayed for these variables.
[†] Significant at the $p < 0.10$ levels.
[*] Significant at the $p < 0.05$ levels.
[**] Significant at the $p < 0.01$ levels.

relationship between budget reports from supervisor and budgetary explanation from supervisor, was supported at $p < 0.05$. Hypothesis 3b proposes that budget reports from supervisor has a positive relationship with budgetary feedback from supervisor. It was not supported as the relationship between these variables was not significant.

The research questions pertain to relationships between the mandatory budgetary involvement with budget staff variables and the budgetary communication variables. Regarding RQ1, budget meetings with budget staff had a positive relationship with both budgetary participation with supervisor and budgetary feedback from supervisor at $p < 0.10$, but did not have a significant relationship with budgetary explanation from supervisor. Regarding RQ2, budget reports to budget staff did not have a significant relationship with any of the budgetary communication variables. Regarding RQ3, budget reports from budget staff had a significant negative relationship with budgetary participation with supervisor ($p < 0.01$), budgetary explanation from supervisor ($p < 0.01$), and budgetary feedback from supervisor ($p < 0.05$).

DISCUSSION

Large organizations typically mandate that unit managers attend budget meetings and exchange budget reports with their immediate supervisor and budget staff in order to promote a flow of budget-relevant information up and down the organizational hierarchy and thus to enhance budgetary communication within the organization. However, few, if any, prior studies have examined the extent to which organization-mandated budgetary involvement is actually related to budgetary communication between the manager and other actors in the budgetary process such as the immediate supervisor. Our study, which addresses this gap in the budgeting literature, indicates that some organization-mandates requiring managers to be involved in the budgetary process enhance communication between the manager and immediate supervisor in terms of budgetary participation, budgetary explanation, and budgetary feedback. As we proposed, mandatory budget meetings with the supervisor, which have the potential for two-way exchanges of budget-relevant information, were found to promote both upward-flowing (budgetary participation with supervisor) and downward-flowing (budgetary explanation and feedback from supervisor) budgetary communication. The face-to-face interaction that occurs during mandatory budget meetings likely provides opportunities for managers and their supervisors to express budget-related facts, views, and opinions directly to each other.

Our findings regarding the effects of exchanging mandatory budget reports with the supervisor were equivocal. As we proposed, mandatory budget reports from the supervisor improved the level of budgetary explanation that a manager received. Mandatory budget reports may be a principal vehicle through which supervisors convey the reasons for their budget decisions to subordinates. Contrary to our expectations, however, mandatory budget reports to the supervisor were not associated with a manager's level of budgetary participation with the supervisor. Moreover, and again contrary to our expectations, mandatory budget reports from the supervisor were not associated with the level of budgetary feedback that a manager received from the supervisor. Organizations may place formal restrictions on the timing and content of mandatory budget reports that limit the degree to which managers can voice their budgetary views and opinions to supervisors and the degree to which supervisors can provide feedback to subordinates regarding their achievement of budget goals. The richer, face-to-face setting offered by budget meetings may be a more conducive environment for managers and their supervisors to exchange these types of information.

The current study also examined whether managers' mandatory budgetary involvement with budget staff was related to their budgetary communication with the supervisor. Budget staff may intermediate the informational exchanges between a manager and supervisor and thereby provide a useful service that enhances budgetary communication. Consistent with this perspective, mandatory budget meetings with budget staff were found to enhance a manager's budgetary communication with the supervisor in terms of budgetary participation and budgetary feedback. However, these benefits of mandatory budgetary involvement with budget staff seem confined to the medium of budget meetings and do not extend to budget reports. In fact, mandatory budget reports from budget staff to the manager were associated with *less* upward- and downward-flowing budgetary communication between the manager and supervisor. This finding may be an artifact of the budgetary environment of organizations where budget staff issue a large number of reports. A large number of staff budget reports suggests a rigid budgetary bureaucracy and an autocratic style of budgeting (Seiler & Bartlett, 1982). A bureaucratic and autocratic budgetary process may allow supervisors little or no role in establishing the final budgets for their subordinates. In this kind of budgetary environment, subordinate managers may feel there is little to be gained by expressing their budgetary views to the supervisor, and the supervisor may either lack enough background information, or instead feel no responsibility, to provide budgetary explanation and feedback to the subordinate.

While we believe the explanations that we have offered for our findings are viable, the study was not designed to identify the actual psychological processes that underlie these phenomena. Future budgeting studies should first test whether the findings generalize beyond the current group of managers and, if so, then investigate the specific processes that account for the findings. Future research might also examine the relationships tested in the study from the perspective of the supervisor, rather than the subordinate manager, to assess whether the supervisor makes similar judgments regarding the degree to which mandatory budget meetings and reports foster budgetary communication between the two parties. Furthermore, future budgeting studies should examine the relative contributions that voluntary vs. mandatory budgetary involvement make to budgetary communication between managers and their supervisors. Voluntary budget meetings and reports may promote relatively more budgetary communication than mandatory budget meetings and reports because they likely have fewer organizational restrictions regarding their timing and content and because formal supervisor-subordinate roles are likely to be de-emphasized.

Our results have practical implications for officials who are involved in designing their organization's budgetary system. For example, they suggest that mandatory budget meetings may be a particularly important structural procedure for enhancing budgetary communication between a manager and supervisor, even if the manager is meeting with budget staff rather than the supervisor. On the other hand, the results also suggest that structural procedures mandating the exchange of budget reports between the manager and supervisor may not always promote the intended flow of budgetary information between the two parties. Moreover, procedures that mandate budget reports from budget staff to managers may even have an unintended negative impact on budgetary communication between the manager and supervisor. The future research that we have suggested aimed at identifying the processes that underlie our results may provide officials with insight as to how to better design mandatory budgetary involvement procedures that will be effective in enhancing budgetary communication within the organization without unintended negative consequences.

The results of the current study must be assessed in light of several limitations. Of greatest concern, the questionnaire had a low response rate. Although we provided evidence suggesting that non-response bias did not seriously undermine the results, the respondents may still have differed in relevant ways from those who did not return a questionnaire. Also, mandatory budget meetings and reports were measured only in terms of frequency of occurrence, which may not fully reflect the extent to which these procedures allowed the respondents to become involved in the budgetary process. Moreover, the budgetary communication with supervisor variables were measured with perceptions and may not adequately capture the objective amount of budgetary participation, budgetary explanation, and budgetary feedback that occurred between the manager and the supervisor. Finally, we have implied a causal sequence from mandatory budget meetings and reports to budgetary communication with the supervisor that cannot be proved with the cross-sectional data used in the study. These limitations notwithstanding, we believe the study provides some of the first empirical evidence regarding how organization-mandated budget meetings and reports are (or are not) related to budgetary communication within organizations.

REFERENCES

Anthony, R. N., & Govindarajan, V. (2001). *Management control systems (10e)*. Boston: McGraw-Hill and Irwin.

Baiman, S., & Evans, J. H. (1983). Pre-decision information and participative management control systems. *Journal of Accounting Research, 21*, 371–395.

Bies, R. J., & Shapiro, D. L. (1988). Voice and justification: Their influence on procedural fairness judgments. *Academy of Management Journal, 31*, 676–685.

Brownell, P. (1982a). Participation in the budgeting process: When it works and when it doesn't. *Journal of Accounting Literature, 1*, 124–153.

Brownell, P. (1982b). A field study examination of budgetary participation and locus of control. *The Accounting Review, 57*, 766–777.

Brownell, P., & Merchant, K. (1990). The budgetary and performance influences of product standardization and manufacturing process automation. *Journal of Accounting Research, 28*, 388–397.

Bruns, W. J., & Waterhouse, J. H. (1975). Budgetary control and organization structure. *Journal of Accounting Research, 13,* 177–203.
Chong, V. K., & Chong, K. M. (2002). Budget goal commitment and informational effects of budget participation on performance: A structural equation modeling approach. *Behavioral Research in Accounting, 14,* 65–86.
Dunk, A. S. (1993). The effect of budget emphasis and information asymmetry on the relation between budgetary participation and slack. *The Accounting Review, 68,* 400–410.
Govindarajan, V. (1986). Impact of participation in the budgetary process on managerial attitudes and performance: Universalistic and contingency perspectives. *Decision Sciences, 17,* 496–516.
Hirst, M. K., & Lowy, S. M. (1990). The linear additive and interactive effects of budgetary goal difficulty and feedback on performance. *Accounting, Organizations and Society, 15,* 425–436.
Hofstede, G. H. (1967). *The game of budget control.* Assen, The Netherlands: Van Gorcum.
Kenis, I. (1979). Effects of budgetary goal characteristics on managerial attitudes and performance. *The Accounting Review, 54,* 707–721.
Kirby, A. J., Reichelstein, S., Sen, P. K., & Paik, T. (1991). Participation, slack, and budget-based performance evaluation. *Journal of Accounting Research, 29,* 109–128.
Kren, L. (1992). Budgetary participation and managerial performance: The impact of information and environmental volatility. *The Accounting Review, 67,* 511–526.
Libby, T. (1999). The influence of voice and explanation on performance in a participative budgeting setting. *Accounting, Organizations and Society, 24,* 125–137.
Magner, N., Welker, R. B., & Campbell, T. L. (1995). The interactive effect of budgetary participation and budget favorability on attitudes toward budgetary decision makers: A research note. *Accounting, Organizations and Society, 20,* 611–618.
Magner, N., Welker, R. B., & Campbell, T. L. (1996). Testing a model of cognitive budgetary participation processes in a latent variable structural equations framework. *Accounting and Business Research, 27,* 41–50.
Merchant, K. (1981). The design of the corporate budgeting system: Influences on managerial behavior and performance. *The Accounting Review, 56,* 813–829.
Merchant, K. (1985). Budgeting and the propensity to create budgetary slack. *Accounting, Organizations and Society, 10,* 201–210.
Milani, K. (1975). The relationship of participation in budget setting to industrial supervisor performance and attitudes: A field study. *The Accounting Review, 50,* 274–284.
Nunnally, J. C. (1978). *Psychometric theory (2e).* New York: McGraw-Hill.
Seiler, R. E., & Bartlett, R. W. (1982). Personality variables as predictors of budget system characteristics. *Accounting, Organizations and Society, 7,* 381–403.
Shields, J. F., & Shields, M. D. (1998). Antecedents of participative budgeting. *Accounting, Organizations and Society, 23,* 49–76.
Shields, M. D., & Young, S. M. (1993). Antecedents and consequences of participative budgeting: Evidence on the effects of asymmetrical information. *Journal of Management Accounting Research, 5,* 265–280.
Swieringa, R., & Moncur, R. (1975). *Some effects of participative budgeting on managerial behavior.* New York: National Association of Accountants.
Tyler, T. R., & Bies, R. J. (1990). Beyond formal procedures: The interpersonal context of procedural justice. In: J. Carroll (Ed.), *Applied Social Psychology and Organizational Settings* (pp. 77–98). Hillsdale, NJ: Lawrence Erlbaum.
Wentzel, K. (2002). The influence of fairness perceptions and goal commitment on managers' performance in a budget setting. *Behavioral Research in Accounting, 14,* 247–271.

BUDGETARY SLACK AND PERFORMANCE IN GROUP PARTICIPATIVE BUDGETING: THE EFFECTS OF INDIVIDUAL AND GROUP PERFORMANCE FEEDBACK AND TASK INTERDEPENDENCE

Clement C. Chen and Keith T. Jones

ABSTRACT

Prior experimental budgeting research has focused primarily on individuals' budget setting and little experimental research has examined budgeting in a group setting. Using a controlled experiment, this study extends prior participative budgeting research by examining the effects of aggregation levels of performance feedback and task interdependence on budgetary slack and the effects of different levels of feedback on group performance in a group participative budget setting.

The results suggest that aggregation levels of performance feedback differentially impact budgetary slack and group performance. Providing both group and individual performance feedback increases group performance

Advances in Management Accounting
Advances in Management Accounting, Volume 13, 183–221
Copyright © 2004 by Elsevier Ltd.
All rights of reproduction in any form reserved
ISSN: 1474-7871/doi:10.1016/S1474-7871(04)13008-6

and reduces budgetary slack compared to providing group performance feedback only. Providing information about other subordinates' performance further increases group performance and reduces budgetary slack beyond the effects of providing individual workers information only about their own performance. The results indicate that task interdependence also affects the level of budgetary slack. Specifically, high task interdependence groups created more budgetary slack than did low task interdependence groups.

INTRODUCTION

Recent changes in business practices have influenced the traditional managerial accounting environment. Among these radically changing practices is the reorganization of business operations to focus on workgroups (Young & Lewis, 1995), spurred by the emergence of quality programs and Japanese management systems. Dumaine (1990) estimated that half of America's largest companies are experimenting with teams. The primary objective of the team approach is to improve performance (Safizadeh, 1991) and to reduce budgetary slack, which refers to the intentional understatement by a subordinate of his or her performance capability (Horngren, 2003; Young, 1985).

Budgetary slack may result in increased pay for subordinates merely as a result of inadequate challenge contained in the budget, leading to suboptimal resource allocation decisions (Merchant, 1985). Thus, it is generally assumed that the presence of slack causes profits to be lower than optimum because the cost function of the firm is not minimized (Onsi, 1973). It should be noted that slack, in and of itself, is not necessarily detrimental to the success of the organization. Frequently, slack is created by design for strategic purposes. For example, slack is created when the organization is performing well and serves to prevent the development of unrealistic expectations. Conversely, slack is used in poor times to maintain aspiration levels. It is important to understand what factors about groups will motivate subordinates to reveal their private information about expected performance in the budget, in order to learn how both planning and control of employee behavior can be improved.

The increased emphasis on workgroups raises questions regarding the appropriate design of accounting systems. Two important questions relate to the desirable degree of task interdependence (Wageman & Baker, 1997) and the aggregation level of performance feedback (Saavedra et al., 1993). In a workgroup setting, task interdependence refers to the degree to which group members must rely on one another to perform their tasks effectively given the design of their jobs (Kiggundu, 1981, 1983). An example of a low interdependence task is the work of a pool of word processing specialists in which each attends to the in-box without regard for the work of others. An example of a high task interdependence task is an assembly-line task in which one person's output becomes another person's input. Shea and Guzzo (1989) suggested that task interdependence potentially has a significant effect on group performance. Subsequent studies have examined this assertion (e.g. Saavedra et al., 1993; Wageman & Baker, 1997) with mixed results, but the effects of task interdependence on budgetary slack have not been tested.

Performance feedback is defined as a subset of performance information available to individuals in their work environment (Nadler, 1979). The information system can provide superiors and subordinates with one or several of three levels of performance feedback identified by Nadler (1979): group, individual, and individuals-in-groups (multi-individual). Group-level feedback is information about group performance only. Individual-level feedback provides information to each group member about his or her own performance. The individuals-in-groups (multi-individual) level feedback provides visibility of each group member's performance to all members of the group.

The investigation of the effects of aggregation levels of performance feedback on performance is needed for several reasons. First, the potential benefits gained from enhanced group performance must be weighed against the investment required to design and implement information systems capable of generating subordinates' individual performance information (Goltz et al., 1989). Second, it is important to examine the effects of multi-individual feedback due to concerns about the potential invasion of personal privacy introduced by the sharing of personal information. Prue and Fairbank (1981) suggest that, while the sharing of private individual performance feedback among group members may enhance group performance, there are potential psychological costs such as distress or embarrassment. Thus, it is unclear whether the public sharing of private information (i.e. multi-individual feedback) truly enhances group productivity.

The current study extends prior participative budgeting research by examining the effects of task interdependence and performance feedback on budgetary slack and the effects of increasing feedback detail on group performance. Specifically, the study uses three types of performance feedback to superiors and subordinates: (1) group feedback only; (2) group and individual feedback; and (3) group and multi-individual feedback. Task interdependence has two levels: (1) low task interdependence, wherein subordinates independently complete a final product; and (2) high task interdependence, wherein subordinates complete specific assigned subassembly tasks in a sequential order.

Results indicate that aggregation levels of performance feedback differentially impact budgetary slack and group performance. The provision of individual and group performance feedback increased group performance and reduced budgetary slack compared to the provision of group performance feedback only. The provision of multi-individual and group performance feedback further improved group performance and reduced budgetary slack. High task interdependence groups created more budgetary slack than low task interdependence groups. Additional analyses disclosed no significant effect of task interdependence on performance.

The study also contributes methodologically by incorporating important aspects of methodological design missing from prior research. Goltz et al. (1989) and Prue & Fairbank (1981) suggest that presenting feedback alone without goals or rewards seems to result in less consistent effects than presenting feedback combined with goals or rewards. Since neither Goltz et al. (1989) nor Tindale, Kulik and Scott (1991) included goals or financial rewards in their studies, the current study incorporates both goals (budgets) and rewards in an attempt to strengthen empirical findings. The study also provides actual performance feedback as opposed to artificial feedback, which may have accounted for the lack of findings in Tindale's (1991) study.

The following sections present the development of hypotheses tested in this study, followed by an explanation of the experimental methods and the results of statistical tests used to test the hypotheses. Finally, the paper provides a discussion of the implications and conclusions drawn from the study, along with a discussion of the study's limitations and suggested areas for future research.

HYPOTHESIS DEVELOPMENT

Compensation Scheme

This study adopts a slack-inducing compensation scheme consistent with prior budgeting research (Chow et al., 1991; Fisher et al., 2000, 2002; Young, 1985). In practice, many subordinates' compensation contracts are slack-inducing in that workers receive a fixed salary for performance up to the budget standard and compensation increases linearly with performance above the budget standard (Crystal, 1993; Henderson, 1989; Merchant & Manzoni, 1989; Waller, 1994). Under these slack-inducing contracts, subordinates have incentives to create budgetary slack in participative budgeting – that is, to set budgets below their expected performance in order to maximize incentive compensation.

Subordinates in this study performed a task for a supervisor and earned a fixed rate for performance up to the budget and a variable rate for performance above the budget (see Eq. (1)). Consistent with Young, Fisher and Lindquist (1993), the compensation contract is group-based such that each member of a three-member group is paid equally and receives one-third of the group compensation based on the group productivity and group budget. The compensation contract is as follows:

$$P = F + V(A - B) \quad if \ A > B : \text{otherwise} \ P = F \tag{1}$$

where P = group compensation; F = fixed compensation; V = variable compensation per unit of production over the budget standard; A = group performance; and B = group budget.

Note that subordinate compensation is maximized when the budget equals zero. However, subordinates are likely to select budgets that are less than their performance capabilities but greater than zero due to behavioral factors such as social pressure and disutility for lying (Chow et al., 1988; Young, 1985). Social pressure creates a feeling that discourages the subordinate from misrepresentation when a superior has information on the subordinate's productive capability (Young, 1985).

Task Interdependence and Budgetary Slack

The existence of task interdependence is viewed as one of the reasons for uncertainty about the effort and pay relationship (Thompson, 1967). Evidence in the budgeting literature suggests that uncertainty in the organization's work environment often impacts subordinates' propensity to create budget slack as a protective device for economic interests. Additionally, when a subordinate's compensation scheme allows, the subordinate may benefit economically by adding in slack because he or she can increase compensation. Onsi (1973) reported that managers bargain for slack as a way of hedging against uncertainties affecting outcomes. Similarly, Bourgeois (1981) and Merchant (1985) argued that slack provides a cushion of spare resources that act as internal shock absorbers to minimize workflow disruptions, thereby providing managers with room to move in response to uncertainty.

As tasks become more interdependent, more coordinated efforts are required for the completion of a task, rendering workers more dependent upon the efforts and skills of others to complete the task. Subordinates in the workgroup may build in more budgetary slack to hedge against uncertainty regarding coworkers' input (efforts and skills). Thus, as task interdependence increases, a subordinate creates slack to hedge not only against the uncertainty about his or her individual performance, but also uncertainty about other group members' performance. Since group slack is a function of individual members' slack, as individual members create more budgetary slack, overall group slack increases.

H1. High task interdependence groups will build in more budgetary slack than low task interdependence groups.

Performance Feedback and Budgetary Slack

In this study, performance feedback refers to performance information on subordinates available to superiors and subordinates in their work environment. Prior feedback research that used laboratory experiments has mostly manipulated feedback to subjects without reference to a superior (Saavedra et al., 1993; Stone, 1971; Tindale et al., 1991). This study incorporated the role of superior in the feedback system to be consistent with prior budgeting literature (Chow et al., 1988; Young, 1985; Young et al., 1993). Superiors and subordinates receive the same performance information from the information system.

Group performance feedback does not provide information about individual subordinates' output to superiors. Therefore, since individual workers have more knowledge of their own performance capability than does the superior, there is a superior-subordinate (vertical) information asymmetry about an individual subordinate's performance capability. Group feedback also leads to the existence of a subordinate-subordinate (horizontal) information asymmetry about coworkers' performance capabilities. Horizontal information asymmetry refers to the existence of private information about a subordinate not known by other subordinates. Thus, the provision of only group performance feedback to subordinates does not discourage subordinates from creating budgetary slack due to lack of identifiability of individual subordinates' output.

The availability of individual performance feedback as well as group performance information to the superior reduces vertical information asymmetry because the superior has information on an individual subordinate's performance capability. As a result, subordinates who receive individual performance feedback will experience social pressure from superiors, referred to as "superior pressure" in this study, because superiors are knowledgeable of the subordinates' performance capability. The feeling of superior pressure discourages subordinates from misrepresenting performance capability (Young, 1985). Thus, group budgetary slack, which is an aggregate of individual group members' budgetary slack, should be reduced by the addition of individual performance feedback.

The disclosure of multi-individual performance information to superiors and subordinates reduces not only the superior's vertical information asymmetry about each subordinate's performance capability but also the horizontal information asymmetry among coworkers. Subordinates experience superior pressure since the superior is able to identify subordinates' individual performance. In addition, the identifiability of each group member's individual performance should result in social pressure from peers, referred to as "peer pressure" in this study. This peer pressure from coworkers should further reduce budgetary slack. In other words, subordinates who receive feedback about both the group's performance and coworkers' performance are likely to build less slack into the budget than subordinates who receive information about the group's performance and their own contribution only. Prior budgeting research has mainly examined the effect of social pressure from superiors on individuals' budgetary slack (Young, 1985). The current study examines the possibility for both superior and peer pressure when individuals' performance information is made available to coworkers.

Consistent with the above arguments, social facilitation theory suggests that budgetary slack will be reduced when an individual's performance is available to all group members. Social facilitation theory posits that the presence of potential evaluators will increase an individual's motivation to maintain a positive image (Erez & Somech, 1996; Guerin, 1986). Thus, in the presence of potential evaluators such as superiors and peers, subordinates in the workgroup should create less budgetary slack to present a positive self-image. These expectations are stated formally in the following hypotheses:

H2a. The level of slack will be lower for groups receiving individual and group feedback compared to groups receiving only group feedback.

H2b. The level of slack will be lower for groups receiving multi-individual and group feedback compared to groups receiving individual and group feedback.

Performance Feedback and Group Performance

Prior studies offer mixed results as to whether providing individual feedback in addition to group feedback increases group performance. Goltz et al. (1989) found an increase in performance when individual-level feedback was added, while Tindale, Kulik and Scott (1991) found no such effect. These mixed results may be partially due to differences in methodology. For instance, Tindale, Kulik, and Scott provided "bogus" feedback to subjects rather than actual feedback based upon the subject's performance. In addition, differing arguments lead to differing expectations. Economic theory suggests that different aggregation levels of performance feedback should not differentially impact group performance since subordinates will always maximize their payoffs by performing up to their performance capability. However, behavioral factors such as superior pressure and peer pressure can influence individual efforts, thereby influencing group performance (Erez & Somech, 1996). Empirical findings suggest that social loafing is decreased by making the performance of individuals in a group more identifiable (Williams et al., 1981).

Group feedback appears to affect the incidence of social loafing and, therefore, the level of effort exerted by individuals performing in group contexts. Research on social loafing (Harkins et al., 1980) indicates that individual levels of effort and performance tend to be lower when individuals' contributions to group performance cannot be identified. The provision of individual performance feedback and group performance feedback to subordinates would impose superior pressure on subordinates since the superior has knowledge of subordinates' individual output. Thus, the identifiability of an individual subordinate's output should increase subordinates' efforts, thereby enhancing group performance.

The disclosure of multi-individual performance information to superiors and subordinates should further increase the group performance. The individual performance information on every group member reduces horizontal information asymmetry about other group members' performance capability. As a result, subordinates should experience both superior pressure and peer pressure since the subordinates are subject to scrutiny not only from the superior, but also from coworkers. In addition, social facilitation theory suggests that individuals are motivated to present a positive self-image in the presence of potential evaluators (Erez & Somech, 1996). Thus, due to concerns about self-presentation and evaluation apprehension, subordinates are motivated to increase individual efforts when their individual performance is made available to their superiors and coworkers. The above arguments suggest the following hypotheses:

H3a. The performance of groups receiving individual and group feedback will be higher than the performance of groups receiving only group feedback.

H3b. The performance of groups receiving multi-individual and group feedback will be higher than the performance of groups receiving individual and group feedback.

METHOD

Subjects and Design

A total of 144 undergraduate management students participated in this study. The use of student subjects is consistent with prior behavioral budgeting studies examining the impact of various factors on budgetary outcomes in a production setting (Chow et al., 1988; Chow et al., 1991; Fisher et al., 2000, 2002; Young et al., 1993). Since the experiment was designed to test general theories about the effects of the variables in question upon human behaviors in a production setting, the use of student subjects was believed appropriate.

The experiment involved a 3 × 2 mixed design. Performance feedback (group feedback only, individual and group feedback, or multi-individual and group feedback) was manipulated between subjects and task interdependence (low or high) was manipulated within subjects. Group-level feedback was used as a baseline for this study because it is believed that, at a minimum, the use of groups in an organization should provide for feedback at the group level in order to monitor a group's progress and performance. The current study seeks to examine whether it is desirable – in terms of the effects on budgetary slack and group performance – to provide feedback that reflects individuals' contributions to the group effort.

Subjects were randomly assigned to groups of three and each group to a feedback experimental condition. Subjects had to participate in two experiments (high and low task interdependence conditions) and new workgroups were formed at the end of the first experiment, resulting in 96 workgroups.

The experimental task, adapted from Drake et al. (1999), involved building a toy castle using LEGO™ blocks. The task was counterbalanced with one-half of the subjects first performing a task of low interdependence, followed by a task of high interdependence. The other half of the subjects performed the tasks in reverse order.

Experimental Procedures

Two experiments were conducted in each session. Experiment 2 followed the same procedures as Experiment 1, with the exception of the task interdependence manipulation. New workgroups were formed at the end of Experiment 1 so that the subjects did not work with the same group members in Experiment 2. Both experiments consisted of three periods: an eight-minute training period, an eight-minute trial production period that fully simulated the actual production period, and an eight-minute production period. The training and trial production periods were used to reduce the effects of differential learning and the group performance from the trial production period was used as a proxy for group performance capability.

The experimental procedure consisted of the following steps:

(1) The experiment was conducted using one large room that served as the "The CCC Company Headquarters" and several smaller rooms were used for

training and as "plants." The experimenter assumed the role of "manager" and the assistants assumed the role of "quality inspector." Each group came to the manager's office and was asked to assume the role of a workgroup to produce toy castles. Each experimenter followed the same detailed script (Appendix A) to maintain consistency across experimenters.

(2) During the orientation, the workgroup was asked to jointly work on constructing a robot using LEGO™ blocks for five-minutes, with a model of a robot displayed. The purpose of this task was to foster group identity and cohesiveness. Following this "ice-breaker exercise," subjects were physically isolated so that no observation of others' work was possible. The subjects were issued file folders and instructed to place all experimental materials in this folder and keep it with them at all times. Each production plant had a set of identical "plant rules" posted within the view of each worker. Plant rules were: (1) To pass quality inspection, colors had to be in the correct location on the finished product; (2) Subjects could not speak with coworkers; (3) Quality inspectors were not allowed to answer questions; (4) Coworkers could not switch assigned roles; (5) Quality inspection occurred at the end of the production process. These rules were highlighted during orientation and again before the training session.

(3) The next phase consisted of a short eight-minute training session in which workers learned the experimental task. The construction of colored subassemblies and toy castles was explained and demonstrated. Subjects were shown how to construct the subassemblies and formed the castle using LEGO™ blocks. Subjects in the low task interdependence condition were asked to independently build all three types of subassembly and form the toy castle. Subjects in the high task interdependence condition were asked to practice building only the assigned subassembly task. Models of each type of subassembly and the final product were displayed at all times. The assistants were always present in the plant to ensure that workers complied with plant rules.

(4) The eight-minute trial production period followed the training session, after which subjects were provided feedback from the manager to ensure that they were aware of their performance capability. Given that most subjects are familiar with assembly of Lego™ blocks and the concern about the length of the experiment, this study used an eight-minute training session. This approach is consistent with Drake et al. (1999), who also used a Lego™ task and had four two-minute training periods. Results of tests for the current study indicate that the performance in the training and trial production periods was not significantly different ($P = 0.56$). Thus, learning did not seem to have an effect on the group performance examined in the hypothesis. Subjects

were asked to produce good quality castles during the trial production period, which simulated the actual production period. They were told they could each earn $0.25 for each good quality castle the group produced. Subjects in the low task interdependence condition were asked to build castles independently during the session. Subjects in the high task interdependence condition were asked to build the subassembly independently and place the completed subassembly in the finished goods storage bin so that the next group member could use it for further processing. The quality inspector counted the number of good-quality castles and recorded the number in a performance report, which was later submitted to the manager.

(5) The research assistant provided each subject a written description of the pay scheme (Appendix B). The pay scheme is described in Eq. (1), with $F = 6.00, $V = 0.25. Both the pay scheme and the procedure for setting the budget were explained and illustrations provided of how pay would vary with different combinations of budgets and group performance.

(6) The manager provided a performance feedback report (Appendix C) to each member of the group and told the subjects that he and the subjects shared the same performance information. Subjects in the group feedback condition received information on group performance (total castles built) and the average group's performance (based on the pilot test). Subjects in the group and individual feedback condition received information on the group performance, average groups' performance, and his or her own individual performance (total castles built in low task interdependence condition and total subassemblies built in high task interdependence condition). Subjects in the group and multi-individual feedback received information on group performance, average group performance and every group member's individual performance.

(7) The budget-setting meeting followed. Subjects in the low task interdependence condition were told that they would work independently in the upcoming production period and they were asked to write down an estimate of their group performance on the group performance target form (Appendix D). Subjects in the high task interdependence condition were told that they would work with their coworkers to jointly build castles and that they should write down an estimate of the group performance on the group performance target form. Subjects in both task interdependence conditions were told that the group budget would be the average of the three group members' estimates of the group performance. Then, all workgroups were told that the performance feedback would be provided at the end of the production session and that they should take all the time needed to determine the group performance target. Subjects were not permitted

to communicate during the budget-setting process. The group performance target forms were later sealed in an envelope by the quality inspector and submitted to the manager.

(8) The manager distributed the group performance target report (Appendix E), which contained the group budget, to each member of the workgroup. The workgroups then completed an eight-minute production period according to task interdependence treatment conditions. Afterwards, subjects were provided feedback for the production period. After the completion of each experiment, subjects filled out exit questionnaires (Appendix F), consisting of demographic questions and items assessing other behavioral variables of interest (i.e. social pressure from superior and peer). New workgroups were formed at the end of the first experiment.

(9) Experiment 2 followed the same procedures as Experiment 1, with the exception of the task interdependence manipulation. Following the completion of Experiment 2, payments were calculated and disbursed. Across all experimental conditions, the average payment was $12.08. Experimental sessions took between 70 and 90 minutes.

Dependent Variables

Budgetary slack was measured as the group's performance capability minus the group budget. The group's performance in the trial production session was used as a proxy for performance capability. Subordinates' group performance in the trial production period serves as an unobtrusive measure of performance capability for an eight-minute production period. Past research found that subordinates set average budgets at more than 70% of performance capability (Chow et al., 1988; Chow et al., 1991). Consistent with past research, the average budget set by workgroups in this study was 23.39 units, which was 73% of the group performance capability. The average group performance in the trial production period was 31.91 units. Group performance was measured as the number of toy castles correctly built in the production period.

Manipulation Checks

Because subjects were assigned to distinctly different treatments by the researcher, no true "manipulation checks" were considered necessary with respect to the experimental treatments involved in this study, i.e. task interdependence and performance feedback. However, in order to assess the validity of the theoretical assumptions regarding the inducement of superior and peer pressure, certain questions were included in a post-experimental questionnaire. First, one item was used to measure subjects' perceptions of the ability of the manager to accurately determine if the subject was setting a budget below his or her production potential (Appendix F, Item 16). Subjects responded on a seven-point Likert scale that ranged from "strongly disagree" (1) to "strongly agree" (7). Subjects' responses to this question indicate a higher perceived superior pressure in the individual and group performance feedback condition than in the group performance feedback condition (5.57 vs. 5.09; $p < 0.05$). Likewise, the results show that subjects receiving multi-individual and group performance feedback perceived more peer pressure (Appendix F, Item 12) than those in the individual and group performance condition (5.18 vs. 4.59; $t = 2.59$; $p < 0.05$). These results suggest that different levels of performance feedback affect subjects' perceived superior and peer pressure in setting a budget.

Second, the post-experiment questionnaire measured perceived superior pressure and peer pressure relative to individual performance. The results suggest that subjects in the group and individual performance feedback condition experienced more superior pressure (Appendix F, Item 17) than subjects in the group performance feedback condition (5.79 vs. 5.41; $t = 1.96$; $p < 0.05$). The responses from subjects in the multi-individual and group performance feedback condition indicate higher perceived peer pressure (Appendix F, Item 13) than subjects in the individual and group performance feedback condition (5.83 vs. 5.46; $t = 1.86$; $p = 0.06$).

A separate item (Appendix F, Item 18) was used to assess whether the manager's opinion of their budget was relatively more important to subjects when more feedback detail was available to the supervisor. There was no significant difference relative to this item when comparing subjects in the group and group plus individual feedback conditions (4.75 vs. 4.90, $p = 0.15$), but subjects in the group and multi-individual feedback treatment indicated a significantly higher importance rating than did those in the group plus individual feedback treatment (5.40 vs. 4.90, $p < 0.05$). The lack of a difference in the first comparison was unexpected and may be due to the fact that subjects were less accountable than they would be in a "real-world" employment situation; that is, they would not be subject to a performance evaluation. In fact, participants were provided an information sheet clearly indicating that they were part of an experiment and no consequences would be forthcoming based on performance. However, this lack of a difference is interesting when one considers that the experimental treatments were effective in inducing more concern with regard to actual performance.

Furthermore, the reason for the significant difference in the second comparison is unclear. It is possible that the pressure felt when subjects knew that peers would review their input made the supervisor's knowledge of their input more salient, but such a conclusion cannot be unequivocally drawn based on the data.

Except for the patterns discussed in the preceding paragraph, the results of all other comparisons were in accordance with expectations. Together, the results discussed above suggest that the experimental treatments were effective in inducing increasing amounts of superior and peer pressure as the level of information asymmetry decreased.

RESULTS

Preliminary Analysis

To ensure that individual differences did not influence the experimental results, certain demographic variables were tested for differences across treatments. Specifically, statistical tests were performed to determine if age, class standing, performance capability, major, and gender were different across experimental conditions. Tests revealed no significant difference across cells for any of these variables, indicating no systematic bias in the experimental results due to assignment of subjects to treatments. However, class standing ($p = 0.14$) and performance capability ($p = 0.13$) more closely approached conventional significance levels than did the other variables. In addition, performance capability and group performance were significantly correlated ($p < 0.05$). Therefore, class standing and performance capability were included as control variables in hypothesis testing.

Order Effects Analysis

Task interdependence is a within-subjects variable with two levels: low and high. Although the experiment was counterbalanced to minimize the possibility of order effects, statistical analysis was necessary to ensure that the order of the treatment did not affect the performance of the workgroups. The results of a one-way ANOVA indicated that the order did not have a significant effect on performance ($F = 0.04$; df $=1$, 94; $p = 0.85$). Additionally, two separate analyses, one for low task interdependence and the other for high task interdependence, were performed to examine the order effect. The results of the ANOVAs also suggested that the order did not have a significant effect on the group performance.

Tests of Hypotheses

Effect of Task Interdependence on Budgetary Slack
Hypothesis 1 predicts that high task interdependence groups will build in more budgetary slack than low task interdependence groups. This hypothesis was tested using a 2 (high/low task interdependence) by 3 (group/group + individual/group + multi-individual feedback) mixed model analysis of covariance with budgetary slack as the dependent variable, task interdependence and performance feedback as independent variables, and performance capability and class standing as covariates. Task interdependence served as a within-subjects factor.

Table 1 contains the results related to budgetary slack. Panel A shows means and standard deviations by experimental cell, while Panel B presents ANCOVA results testing Hypothesis 1, 2a and 2b. Results for the covariates indicate that class standing was not significantly related to budgetary slack ($F = 1.4; p = 0.24$), but that performance capability was significantly and positively related to slack ($F = 7.46; p < 0.01$). However, after controlling for performance capability, task interdependence had a significant main effect on budgetary slack and the effect was in the expected direction ($F = 11.46; p < 0.01$). The interaction between task interdependence and performance feedback was not significant ($F = 1.09$; $p = 0.30$). This result strongly supports H 1.

Effect of Performance Feedback on Budgetary Slack
Hypothesis 2a predicts that the level of slack will be lower for groups receiving individual and group feedback compared to groups receiving only group feedback. Hypothesis 2b predicts that the level of slack will further be lower for groups receiving multi-individual and group feedback compared to groups receiving individual and group feedback. Panel A of Table 1 shows that the mean budgetary slack under group and individual performance feedback is significantly lower than under group performance feedback (8.18 vs. 11.93; $t = -2.78$; $p < 0.01$; one-tailed). This result strongly supports H 2a. The mean budgetary slack under group and multi-individual performance feedback is 5.72 castles compared with a mean of 8.18 castles under group performance feedback. This difference is marginally significant ($t = -1.83; p = 0.07$; one-tailed), providing partial support for H 2b.

Hypothesis 2a and H 2b were further examined using ANCOVA. Consistent with the results discussed in the previous section, the ANCOVA results (Table 1, Panel B) indicate that class standing was not significantly related to budgetary slack, but performance capability was significantly related to budgetary slack and the interaction was not significant. After controlling for the effect of performance capability, performance feedback was significantly associated with the level of

Table 1.   Descriptive Statistics and Statistical Test for Budgetary Slack ($n = 16$ Groups Per Cell with Three Subjects Per Group).

Panel A: Descriptive Statistics

	Performance Feedback (PF)			
	Group	Group and Individual	Group and Multi-Individual	Overall
Task Interdependence (TI)				
Low	9.25	7.06	5.00	7.10
	(6.23)	(4.19)	(3.67)	(5.04)
High	14.62	9.31	6.44	10.12
	(6.97)	(4.71)	(4.50)	(6.39)
Overall	11.93	8.18	5.72	8.61
	(7.05)	(4.53)	(4.10)	(5.92)

Panel B: ANCOVA for Budgetary Slack

Source	Sum of Squares	df	Mean Square	F	p-Value[a]
Performance capability	184.09	1	184.09	7.46	<0.01
Class standing	34.58	1	34.58	1.40	0.24
Task interdependence	282.72	1	282.72	11.46	<0.01
Performance feedback	749.05	2	374.52	15.18	<0.01
Interaction (PF X TI)	54.05	2	27.02	1.09	0.34
Error	2171.42	88	24.67		

Note: Cell data are mean (standard deviation) of budgetary slack in terms of number of castle built. Performance Capability = group performance in the trial production session in terms of number of castles built; Class Standing = average class standing in a group (1 = freshman, 2 = sophomore, 3 = junior, 4 = senior); Task Interdependence = two levels (low or high); Performance Feedback = three levels (group only, group and individual, or group and multi-individual); Budgetary Slack = group performance capability minus group budget in terms of number of castles built.
[a] Two-tail p-value.

budgetary slack and in the expected direction ($F = 15.18$; $p < 0.01$). This result strongly supports H 2a and 2b.

Effect of Performance Feedback on Group Performance
Hypothesis 3a predicts that the performance of groups receiving individual and group feedback will be higher than the performance of groups receiving only group feedback. Hypothesis 3b predicts that the performance of groups receiving multi-individual and group feedback will be higher than the performance of groups receiving individual and group feedback. Group performance mean results are presented in Table 2, Panel A. The mean group performance under the

Table 2. Descriptive Statistics and Statistical Test for Group Performance ($n =$ 16 Groups Per Cell with Three Subjects Per Group).

Panel A: Descriptive Statistics

	Performance Feedback (PF)			
	Group	Group and Individual	Group and Multi-Individual	Overall
Task Interdependence (TI)				
Low	31.06	33.81	36.94	33.94
	(4.31)	(2.76)	(4.12)	(4.44)
High	30.50	32.38	33.81	32.23
	(4.07)	(3.46)	(4.12)	(4.05)
Overall	30.78	33.10	35.38	33.08
	(4.13)	(3.17)	(4.35)	(4.31)

Panel B. ANCOVA for Group Performance

Source	Sum of Squares	df	Mean Square	F	p-Value[a]
Performance capability	408.48	1	408.48	40.28	<0.05
Class standing	8.67	1	8.67	0.86	0.36
Task interdependence	14.78	1	14.78	1.46	0.23
Performance feedback	208.63	2	104.31	10.29	<0.01
Interaction (PF X TI)	24.99	2	12.49	1.23	0.30
Error	892.40	88	10.14		

Note: Cell data are mean (standard deviation) of group performance in terms of number of castle built. Performance Capability = group performance in the trial production session in terms of number of castles built; Class Standing = average class standing in a group (1 = freshman, 2 = sophomore, 3 = junior, 4 = senior); Task Interdependence = two levels (low or high); Performance Feedback = three levels (group only, group and individual, or group and multi-individual); Group Performance = number of toy castles workgroup correctly built in the eight-minute production period.
[a] Two-tail *p*-value.

group and individual performance feedback condition was 33.10 castles, while the mean was 30.78 castles under the group performance feedback condition. This difference is significant ($t = 2.36$; $p < 0.05$; one-tailed), providing strong support for H 3a. The mean group performance under group and multi-individual performance feedback was 35.38 castles, significantly higher than the mean of 33.10 castles built by those in the group and individual performance feedback condition ($t = 2.33$; $p < 0.05$; one-tailed). This result supports H 3b.

Hypothesis 3a and 3b were also examined using ANCOVA. As discussed in the previous section, class standing was not significantly related to group performance while performance capability was significantly related to group performance. The ANCOVA results in Table 2, Panel B indicate a significant main effect for performance feedback ($F = 10.29$; $p < 0.01$). In other words, even after controlling for performance capability, performance feedback significantly affected group performance. Additionally, the interaction between performance feedback and task interdependence was not significant ($F = 1.23$; $p = 0.30$). This result provides further support for H3a and H3b.

Additional Analysis – Task Interdependence and Group Performance
There are potentially positive and negative effects of task independence on group performance. On the one hand, because of increased monitoring resulting from knowing that another group member is waiting on one's output, an increase in performance might reasonably be expected. On the other hand, such factors as bottlenecks could potentially decrease overall production. Because of the lack of a strong theory to make a prediction, no formal directional hypothesis is included regarding the effects of task interdependence on group performance. However, we ran additional analysis to gain additional insights into the impact of task interdependence on group performance.

Panel A of Table 2 shows the means and standard deviations by experimental cell, in terms of number of castles built. Panel B shows the results of a 2×3 ANCOVA with task interdependence and performance feedback as independent variables, group performance as a dependent variable, and class standing and performance capability as covariates. The results for the covariates indicate that class standing was not significantly related to group performance ($F = 0.86$; $p = 0.30$) but that performance capability was significantly and positively related to group performance ($F = 40.28$; $p < 0.05$). Task interdependence did not have a significant main effect ($F = 1.46$; $p = 0.20$). In other words, after controlling for the effect of performance capability on group performance, task interdependence did not significantly affect group performance. However, the direction of the impact of task interdependence on group performance is consistent with Hirst and Yetton (1999), who found group performance to be higher in low task interdependence than high task interdependence.

DISCUSSION AND CONCLUSIONS

This paper extends the participative budgeting literature by examining the effects of task interdependence and performance outcome feedback on budgetary slack and group performance in a group setting. The results suggest that the combination of group and individual performance feedback reduces budgetary slack and improves group performance compared to group performance feedback.

Multi-individual and group feedback further reduces budgetary slack and enhances group performance beyond the effects of merely providing individuals with information about their own performance. The results also suggest that high task interdependence results in higher levels of budgetary slack than does low task interdependence, although the additional analysis indicated no effect of this variable on group performance.

The role of accountants has evolved to include not only interpreting and analyzing information, but also working on cross-functional teams to actively participate in decision making. Therefore, it is useful to understand various task-design factors affecting budgetary outcomes. For instance, it is imperative that managers make decisions regarding appropriate levels of feedback in designing and implementing information systems. Since each type of feedback may differentially motivate and direct behavior, the question of how well feedback performs these functions is relevant for increasing group productivity.

The findings from this study can help educators and managers better understand what levels of interdependence and feedback are desirable in implementing accounting control systems and group-based approaches to job tasks. It appears that merely increasing the extent to which workers must rely upon one another to complete the ultimate task does not necessarily enhance group performance. As noted previously, increasing subjects' mutual dependence on one another (task interdependence) affected slack, but this variable had no measurable effect on performance. If interdependence does affect performance, the effects may be due to such factors as communication and cooperation, factors that were controlled for in the current study to enhance internal validity. In any case, to the extent that task interdependence in practice results in increased slack without a corresponding improvement in group performance, these results would almost certainly be considered suboptimal from the organizational standpoint.

At least with respect to the current study, factors other than task interdependence appear to play a more important role in determining group performance. For instance, providing information about coworkers' contributions to output appears to have an upward impact on group performance and a simultaneous downward impact on budgetary slack, possibly the result of peer pressure. While it cannot be stated unequivocally that pressure from a "superior" and peers is the intervening variable leading to such a result, the results indicate that the experimental treatments were successful both in inducing such pressures and in producing desirable results in terms of slack and performance.

The results of this study must be interpreted in light of certain limitations inherent in experimental research. First, as with all laboratory experiments, the results depend on the specific experimental task, treatments, and parameter values used. These treatments are necessarily somewhat artificial in order to

202 CLEMENT C. CHEN AND KEITH T. JONES

control for the effects of certain "real-world" influences to enhance the internal validity of the experiment. For example, communications among group members vary with such factors as context, relative hierarchical position of members and strength of personalities, and may differentially impact budgets and motivation of group members. The current study controlled for the effects of communication in order to avoid confounding the experimental results. Second, some factors were fixed or not considered in this experimental budget setting that can vary in actual budget setting situations. For example, budgets were set unilaterally by the workgroups even though budgets are often negotiated bilaterally between the superior and subordinates in practice (Fisher et al., 2000, 2002). This study also uses a single-period setting, which prevents the learning and interactions that are possible in real-world, repetitive budget processes. Therefore, the effects obtained in this study do not necessarily generalize to subsequent periods.

There are many other avenues that appear worthwhile for future research on group participative budgeting. First, an area that has been subjected to extensive research in management accounting is that of supervisory style in performance evaluation (e.g. Roberts & Reed, 1996). Future research considering the interaction between variables such as feedback sign (positive vs. negative), feedback frequency, and supervisory style would be worthwhile extensions to this body of research. Prior feedback research has found that individuals behave differently when faced with negative, as opposed to positive feedback (Mesch et al., 1994). Research in accounting could investigate the behavioral impact of different modes of reporting negative performance results. Second, as discussed in the preceding paragraph, this study does not address the effects of feedback and interdependence in a multi-period setting. The direction of the effects, if any, of multi-period participation is not known and appears worthy of investigation. Finally, as previously discussed, there may be psychological costs associated with sharing individual performance information with coworkers. Although providing information to the group about individuals' capabilities enhanced group performance, psychological costs were not measured in this study, and the effects of feedback and interdependence levels on these "costs" remains an empirical question.

ACKNOWLEDGMENTS

The authors wish to thank the anonymous reviewers, John Lee (Ed.), and participants at the 2003 American Accounting Association Midwest and Ohio Region Meetings and the Hawaii International Conference on Business for their comments on earlier versions of this paper.

REFERENCES

Bourgeois, J. (1981). On the measurement of organizational slack. *Academy of Management Review*, 26, 29–39.
Chow, C., Cooper, J., & Waller, W. (1988). Participative budgeting: Effects of a truth-inducing pay scheme and information asymmetry on slack and performance. *The Accounting Review*, 60(January), 111–122.
Chow, C., Cooper, J., & Haddad, K. (1991). The effects of pay schemes and ratchets on budgetary slack and performance: A multiperiod experiment. *Accounting, Organizations, and Society*, 15(January), 47–60.
Crystal, G. S. (1993). Budgets and performance compensation. In: Rachlin & Sweeney (Eds), *Handbook of Budgeting* (3rd ed.). New York: Wiley.
Drake, A., Haka, S., & Ravenscroft, S. (1999). Cost systems and incentive structure effects on innovation, efficiency and probability in teams. *The Accounting Review*, 74(3), 323–345.
Dumaine, B. (1990). Who needs a boss? *Fortune* (May 7).
Erez, M., & Somech, A. (1996). Is group productivity loss the rule or the exception?: Effects of culture and group-based motivation. *Academy of Management Journal*, 39, 1513–1537.
Fisher, J., Frederickson, J. R., & Peffer, S. A. (2000). Budgeting: An Experimental Investigation of the Effects of Negotiation. *The Accounting Review*, 75(1), 93–114.
Fisher, J., Frederickson, J. R., & Peffer, S. A. (2002). The effect of information asymmetry on negotiated budgets: An empirical investigation. *Accounting, Organizations, and Society*, 27, 27–43.
Goltz, S. M., Citera, M., Jensen, M., Favero, J., & Komaki, J. (1989). Individual feedback: Does it enhance effects of group feedback? *Journal of Organizational Behavior Management*, 10(2), 77–92.
Guerin, B. (1986). Mere presence effects in humans: A review. *Journal of Experimental Social Psychology*, 22, 38–77.
Harkins, S. G., Lantane, B., & Williams, K. (1980). Social loafing: Allocating effort or taking it easy? *Journal of Social Psychology*, 19, 259–272.
Henderson, R. (1989). *Compensation management: Rewarding performance*. Virginia: Reston.
Hirst, M. K., & Yetton, P. W. (1999). The effects of budget goals and task interdependence on the level of and variance in performance: A research note. *Accounting, Organizations, and Society*, 24, 205–216.
Kiggundu, M. N. (1981). Task interdependence and the theory of job design. *Academy of Management Review*, 7, 499–508.
Kiggundu, M. N. (1983). Task interdependence and job design: Test of a theory. *Organizational Behavior and Human Performance*, 31, 145–172.
Merchant, K. (1985). Budgeting and the propensity to create budget slack. *Accounting, Organizations, and Society*, 10(2), 201–210.
Merchant, K., & Manzoni, J. (1989). The achievability of budget targets in profit centers: A field study. *The Accounting Review*, 64(3), 539–558.
Mesch, D. J., Farr, J., & Podsakoff, P. M. (1994). Effects of feedback sign on group goal setting, strategies and performance. *Group and Organization Management*, 19, 309–333.
Nadler, D. A. (1979). The effects of feedback on task group behavior: A review of the experimental research. *Organizational Behavior and Human Performance*, 23, 309–338.
Onsi, M. (1973). Factor analysis of behavioral variables affecting budget slack. *The Accounting Review* (July), 535–548.

Prue, D. M., & Fairbank, J. A. (1981). Performance feedback in organizational behavior management: A review. *Journal of Organizational Behavior Management, 3,* 1–16.

Roberts, G., & Reed, T. (1996). Performance appraisal participation, goal setting and feedback: The influence of supervisory style. *Review of Public Personnel Administration, 16*(4), 29–60.

Saavedra, R., Earley, P. C., & Van Dyne, L. (1993). Complex interdependence in task performing groups. *Journal of Applied Psychology, 78,* 61–72.

Safizadeh, M. H. (1991). The case of workgroups in manufacturing operations. *California Management Review, 33*(Summer), 61–82.

Shea, G. P., & Guzzo, R. A. (1989). Group as human resources. *Research in Personnel and Human Resources Management, 5,* 323–356.

Stone, T. (1971). Effects of mode of organization and feedback level on creative task groups. *Journal of Applied Psychology, 55,* 324–330.

Thompson, J. D. (1967). *Organizations in action.* New York: McGraw-Hill.

Tindale, R. S., Kulik, C. T., & Scott, L. A. (1991). Individual and group feedback and performance: An attributional perspective. *Basic and Applied Social Psychology, 12*(1), 41–62.

Wageman, R., & Baker, G. (1997). Incentives and cooperation: The joint effects of task and reward interdependence on group performance. *Journal of Organizational Behavior, 18,* 138–158.

Waller, W. (1994). Discussion of motivating truthful subordinate reporting: An experimental investigation in a two-subordinate context. *Contemporary Accounting Research, 10*(Spring), 721–734.

Williams, K., Harkins, S., & Lantane, B. (1981). Identifiability as a deterrent to social loafing: Two cheering experiments. *Journal of Personality and Social Psychology, 40,* 303–311.

Young, S. M. (1985). Participative budgeting: The effects of risk aversion and asymmetric information on budgetary slack. *Journal of Accounting Research, 23*(Autumn), 829–842.

Young, S. M., Fisher, J., & Linquist, T. (1993). The effects of intergroup competition and intragroup cooperation on slack and output in a manufacturing setting. *The Accounting Review, 68*(3), 466–481.

Young, S. M., & Lewis, B. (1995). Experimental incentive-contracting research in management accounting. In: R. Ashton & A. Ashton (Eds), *Judgment and Decision-Making Research in Accounting and Auditing* (pp. 55–75). Cambridge, England: Cambridge University Press.

APPENDIX A

Study Script

Welcome to this production exercise. During this exercise, you will play the role of production workers for CCC Company that produces toy castles. You will build castles using LEGO™ blocks in plants. You will be working on a team with two other co-workers. This production exercise consists of two parts. Each part consists of four periods: orientation, training, trial-production and production. You will be paid cash at the end of the exercise. The amount you are paid will be based on your performance and the decisions you make.

My name is Clement Chen and I am your manager. Keith Jones and David McIntyre are quality inspectors. They will supervise, examine, and count the number of quality castles built at the end of the training, trial production and production period. I will meet you in my office after the end of trial production period. Please read and sign the consent form. Quality inspectors, please lead your workgroup to designated production plants.

Orientation (Quality Inspectors)
You and two other group members will be working on construction tasks as a workgroup. Now, please construct the toy robot, displayed in front of you, with your co-workers. The groups in the past, on average, can complete this task in four minutes. You will have 5 minutes to complete this task. Time starts at _____ and time finishes at _____. Please stop.

Following this exercise: Please comply with plant rules throughout this exercise. Plant rules are: (1) To pass quality inspection, colors must be in the correct location on the finished product; (2) You may not speak with coworkers; (3) Quality inspectors may not answer questions; (4) You may not switch assigned roles with coworkers; (5) Quality inspection occurs at the end of the production process. The plant rules are posted on the wall in front of you at all times. Each of you will receive a file folder. The group identification code is on the upper right hand corner of the folder. The first digit indicates your group number and the last digit indicates your assigned member ID. Please place all materials in this folder and keep this folder with you at all times.

Training Period (Quality Inspectors)
Please comply with plant rules. Each toy castle consists of three different colored subassemblies. You will be shown how to construct subassemblies and form the castle using LEGO™ blocks. The subassembly or castle is considered "good quality" if it is built the same as the model displayed in front of you. The quality inspector will only count good quality castles as your output at the end of the training period. Although you will not be paid for the output you turn out during the training period, it's to your benefit to learn the task.

- Quality inspector demonstrates how to construct subassemblies and castles (High Task Interdependence) or castles (Low Task interdependence).
- Following the demonstration of construction of toy castles:

Low task interdependence. [Please construct the castle using the Lego blocks in the storage bin sitting on the table. Please place the completed toy castles in the storage bin located to your right] Your individual performance is measured by the number of good quality castles built. The group performance is measured by the total number of good quality castles produced by the group.

High task interdependence. {Please construct only the assigned subassembly task using the Lego blocks in the storage bin sitting on the table. Please place your finished subassembly in the storage bin located to your right so your co-worker next in the sequence can complete his or her subassembly task using your finished subassembly.} Your individual performance is measured by the number of good quality subassemblies built. The group performance is measured by the total number of good quality castles produced by the group.

"The training period will last 10 minutes." Please stop your production when asked.

Time starts at _____ and finishes at _____.

Please stop your production.

- Quality inspectors move storage bins (3) that contain completed subassemblies and/or castles to an area where workers cannot observe the counting and recording of completed subassemblies and castles.
- Quality inspectors count and record (1) only the "good quality" castles as individual performance (Low TI with Individual Feedback); only the "good quality" subassemblies as individual performance output (High TI with Individual feedback) (2) only the "good quality" castles as output for the workgroup (all TI conditions).
- Quality inspectors then take apart all assembled pieces and place them in storage bins where these pieces came from.
- Quality inspectors provide performance reports to the manager.

Trial Production Period (Quality Inspectors)
Please comply with plant rules and produce as many good quality castles as you can. Your group will earn $0.25 for each good quality castle the group produces. The castle is considered "good quality" if it is built the same as the model castle displayed in front of you. The quality inspector will only count good quality castles as your output at the end of the trial production period.

Low task interdependence. [Please construct the castle using the Lego blocks in the storage bin sitting on the table. Please place your completed toy castles in the storage bin located to your right]

High task interdependence. {Please build only the assigned subassembly task using the Lego blocks in the storage bin sitting on the table. Please place your completed subassembly in the storage bin located to your right so that your coworker next in sequence can complete his or her subassembly task using your finished subassembly.}

The trial production will last 10 minutes. Please stop your production when asked.

Time starts at _____ and finishes at _____.

Please stop your production.

- Quality inspectors move storage bins (3) that contain completed subassemblies and/or castles to an area where workers cannot observe the counting and recording of completed subassemblies and castles.
- Quality inspectors count and record (1) only the "good quality" castles as individual performance (Low TI with Individual Feedback); only the "good quality" subassemblies as individual performance output (High TI with Individual feedback) (2) only the "good quality" castles as output for the workgroup (all TI conditions).
- Quality inspectors then take apart all assembled pieces and place them in storage bins where these pieces came from.
- Quality inspectors provide performance reports to the manager.

Explanation of the Pay Scheme (Quality Inspectors)
Please take out the written description of the "pay scheme" from your folder. The pay scheme will be explained. Your group performance in the upcoming 10-minute production session will be paid for in cash according to your pay scheme and performance target selected. Group performance is measured by the total number of castles built exactly like the model castle displayed in front of you. I will now take you to the manager's office.

Feedback Manipulations (the Manager)
- The manager distributes a performance report to each member of the workgroup.

Please take a look at your performance report.

- The manager announces one of the following:

Group feedback condition. You are provided with exactly the same information I have. I only have information on your group performance for the production period. I do not know your individual performance for the production period.

Group and individual feedback condition. You are provided with exactly the same information I have. I have information on your group performance and individual performance for the production period.

Group and multi-individual feedback condition. You are provided with exactly the same information I have. I have information on your group performance and individual performance for the production period. Your group member also has information about your individual performance for the production period.

I will provide another performance report at the end of your production period. Please return to your plants.

Group Performance Target-Setting (Quality Inspectors)
Please take out the "performance target form" from your folder. Please take as much time as you need to determine the estimate. Please do not write your name on the paper. Your estimate will be sealed in an envelope and submitted to the manager.

Low task interdependence. [You will work independently on building castles in the upcoming production session. Please write down an estimate of your individual performance. Your group performance target will be the sum of your estimates of individual performance]

High task interdependence. {You will work with co-workers to jointly build castles in the upcoming production session. Please write down your estimate of your group performance. Your group performance target will be the lowest estimate of the three estimates made by group members.}

• Quality inspectors gather and seal envelopes, which are submitted to the manager.

Disclosure of the Group Performance Target to Workgroups (Manager and Quality Inspectors)
• The manager distributes "group performance target report" to each member of the workgroup at the plants.

Please have it faced down until everyone receives it.

• The manager leaves the room
• Quality inspectors allow about 1 minute (Time Watch) before proceeding to the production period.

Production Period (Quality Inspectors)
Please comply with plant rules and produce as many good quality castles as you can. You will be paid cash based on your production performance.

Low task interdependence. [Please construct the castle using the Lego blocks in the storage bin sitting on the table. Please place your completed toy castles in the storage bin located to your right]

High task interdependence. {Please build only the assigned subassembly task using the Lego blocks in the storage bin sitting on the table. Please place the completed subassembly in the storage bin located to your right so that your coworker next in sequence can complete his or her subassembly task using your finished subassembly.}

The production period will last 10 minutes. Please stop your production when asked.

Time starts at _____ and finishes at _____. Please stop your production.

- Quality inspectors move storage bins that contain completed subassemblies and/or castles to an area where workers cannot observe the counting and recording of completed subassemblies and castles.
- Quality inspectors count and record (1) only the "good quality" castles as individual performance (Low TI with Individual Feedback); only the "good quality" subassemblies as individual performance output (High TI with Individual feedback) (2) only the "good quality" castles as output for the workgroup (all TI conditions).
- Quality inspectors then take apart all assembled pieces and place them in storage bins where these pieces came from.
- Quality inspectors provide performance reports to the manager.
- The manager distributes performance reports to workers.

At the end of Experiment 1. Part I of the production exercise is now completed. Please take out the Questionnaire from your folder and place it in your folder when you have completed it.

Break
- New workgroups are formed.

At the end of Experiment 2. Part II of the production exercise is now completed. Thank you all for participating in this study. I appreciate your help. Please take out the Questionnaire from your folder and place it back in your folder when you have completed it. After you have placed your completed questionnaire in your folder, please wave for the quality inspector to come to the table.

• The manager pays the subjects.

APPENDIX B

The CCC Pay Scheme

You will earn one-third of the group pay. Your group will earn at least $6.00 for completing the production session. In addition, you will have a performance target for the number of castles correctly built. Your group will earn an additional $0.25 for each castle correctly built above the performance target. Your pay depends on two things: (1) the number of castles correctly built by the group during the production session; and (2) your performance target. Specifically, the group pay function is as follows:

$$\text{Group Pay} = \$6.00 + \$0.25 \times (\text{number of castles correctly built}$$
$$- \text{group performance target})$$

This means, Your individual pay = 1/3 of the group pay.

If the total number of castles correctly built by the group is *less than or equal to* the group performance target:

$$\text{Group pay} = \$6$$

Or

$$\text{Individual pay} = \$2(\$6.00/3)$$

If the total number of castles correctly built the group is *greater than* the group performance target:

$$\text{Group pay} = \$6 + \$0.25 \times (\text{number of castles correctly built}$$
$$- \text{group performance target})$$

Or

$$\text{Individual pay} = \text{one-third of the group pay}$$
$$\text{Group Pay} = \$6.00 + \$0.25 \times (\text{number of castles correctly built}$$
$$- \text{group performance target})$$

This means, Your individual pay $= 1/3$ of the group pay.

Example 1
Assume that your group has correctly built 30 castles and your group's target performance is 30 castles. Because the number of castles correctly built was *equal to* your group's performance target, the group pay for the production session would be $6.00 and your pay for the production session would be $2.00 ($6.00/3).

Example 2
Assume that your group has correctly built 25 castles and your group's target performance is 35 castles. Because the number of castles correctly built was *less than* your group's performance target, the group pay for the production session would be $6.00 and your pay for the production session would be $2.00 ($6.00/3).

Example 3
Assume that your group has correctly built 50 castles and your group's target performance is 20 castles. Because the number of castles correctly built was *greater than* your group's performance target, the group's pay for the production session would be $13.50:

$$\text{Group pay} = \$6.00 + \$0.25 \times (50 - 20) = \$13.50$$

Your individual pay, one-third of the group pay, for the production session would be $4.50 ($13.50/3).

APPENDIX C

Performance Report

Group Identification Number: _____

Group Performance

Castles

Average Groups' Performance

28 Castles

Group Identification Number: _____

Group Performance

Castles

Average Groups' Performance

28   Castles

Your Individual Performance

Castles

Group Identification Number: _____

Group Performance

Castles

Average Groups' Performance

28   Castles

Your Individual Performance

Subassemblies

Group Identification Number: _____

Group Performance

Castles

Average Groups' Performance

28   Castles

Your Individual Performance

Castles

Other Members' Individual Performance

Member A	Castles
Member B	Castles

Group Identification Number: _____

Group Performance

Castles

Average Groups' Performance

28	Castles

Your Individual Performance

Subassemblies

Other Members' Individual Performance

Member A	Subassemblies
Member B	Subassemblies

Group Identification Number: _____

Group Performance

Castles

Average Groups' Performance

28   Castles

Your Individual Performance

Castles

Other Members' Individual Performance

Member B	Castles
Member C	Castles

Group Identification Number: _____

Group Performance

Castles

Average Groups' Performance

28   Castles

Your Individual Performance

Subassemblies

Other Members' Individual Performance

Member B	Subassemblies
Member C	Subassemblies

Group Identification Number: _____

Group Performance

Castles

Average Groups' Performance

28	Castles

Your Individual Performance

Castles

Other Members' Individual Performance

Member A	Castles
Member C	Castles

Group Identification Number: _____

Group Performance

Castles

Average Groups' Performance

28   Castles

Your Individual Performance

Subassemblies

Other Members' Individual Performance

Member A	Subassemblies
Member C	Subassemblies

APPENDIX D

Group Performance Target Form

Group Identification Number: _____

You will work independently on building castles in the upcoming production session. Please write down an estimate of your individual performance. Your group performance target will be the sum of your estimates of individual performance.

As a reminder, your group pay function is as follows:

Group Pay = \$6.00 + \$0.25 × (number of castles correctly built

− group performance target)

Please provide your estimate of your individual performance: _____ castles

Group Identification Number: _____

You will work with co-workers to jointly build castles in the upcoming production session. Please write down your estimate of your group performance. Your group performance target will be the average of the three estimates made by group members.

As a reminder, your group pay function is as follows:

$$\text{Group Pay} = \$6.00 + \$0.25 \times (\text{number of castles correctly built}$$
$$- \text{group performance target})$$

Please provide your estimate of your group performance: _____ castles

APPENDIX E

Group Performance Target Report

Group Identification Number: _____

Your Group Performance Target: _____ castles

APPENDIX F

Questionnaire

Directions: Please complete the questionnaire below, answering each question as accurately and honestly as you can.

(1) Three digit identification number (shown on the folder) _____
(2) Sex (circle one): M F
(3) Age (20, 21, 22, etc.) _____
(4) Race (Caucasian American, Black American, other) _____
(5) Major (accounting, management, finance, etc.) _____
(6) Year in school (freshman, sophomore, junior, senior, other) _____
(7) If you had produced 8 units and set your group performance target at 20 units in a given period, what would your group earnings and individual earnings have been according to the CCC compensation contract? Group Pay _____ or Individual Pay _____

(8) If you had produced 20 units and set your group performance target at 20 units in a given period, what would your group earnings and individual earnings have been according to the CCC compensation contract? Group Pay _____ or Individual Pay _____

(9) If you had produced 80 units and set your group performance target at 20 units in a given period, what would your group earnings and individual earnings have been according to the CCC compensation contract? Group Pay _____ or Individual Pay _____

For Question 10 and 11, please circle yes or no.

(10) During the group performance target-setting meeting, coworkers knew the performance target I set.

Yes/No

(11) At the end of the trial production period and before I received the performance report, I knew how many subassemblies or castles each co-worker produced during the trial production period

Yes/No

For the following statements, please circle the number or response that best describes your level of agreement or disagreement, from (1) "Strongly Disagree," to (7) "Strongly Agree."

(12) During the group performance target-setting meeting, it was important to me that the co-workers thought I was setting a target that was appropriate given my production potential.

Strongly Disagree			Neutral			Strongly Agree
1	2	3	4	5	6	7

(13) During the production period, it was important to me that the coworkers thought I was doing a good job on my production.

Strongly Disagree			Neutral			Strongly Agree
1	2	3	4	5	6	7

(14) The manager knew the performance target I set.

Strongly Disagree			Neutral			Strongly Agree
1	2	3	4	5	6	7

(15) The manager knew how many units I produced.

Strongly Disagree			Neutral			Strongly Agree
1	2	3	4	5	6	7

(16) The manager could accurately evaluate if I was setting the performance target below my production potential.

Strongly Disagree			Neutral			Strongly Agree
1	2	3	4	5	6	7

(17) During the production period, it was important that the manager thought I was doing a good job on my production.

Strongly Disagree			Neutral			Strongly Agree
1	2	3	4	5	6	7

(18) It was important to me that the manager thought I was setting performance target that was appropriate given my production potential.

Strongly Disagree			Neutral			Strongly Agree
1	2	3	4	5	6	7

(19) I liked exerting effort on the production task.

Strongly Disagree			Neutral			Strongly Agree
1	2	3	4	5	6	7

(20) I did my best to produce a large number of units.

Strongly Disagree			Neutral			Strongly Agree
1	2	3	4	5	6	7

(21) What type of performance report did you receive? (Please check only one answer.)

_____ I received only group performance information.

_____ I received information on both group and my individual performance.

_____ I received information on both group performance and every member's individual performance.

Thank you for your participation in this exercise. Please place your questionnaire in your folder and wave for the quality inspector to come to the table.

DO PERCEPTIONS OF FAIRNESS MITIGATE MANAGERS' USE OF BUDGETARY SLACK DURING ASYMMETRIC INFORMATION CONDITIONS?

Kristin Wentzel

ABSTRACT

Prior research demonstrates a positive relationship between information asymmetry and managers' use of budgetary slack and thereby suggests that minimizing managers' private information is a potential tactic for reducing slack in budgets. Asymmetric information, however, often cannot be avoided when specialized technical expertise is required to operate a particular responsibility area. This study contributes to the literature by investigating whether favorable perceptions of fairness mitigate managers' use of budgetary slack during participative environments in which managers hold private information. Overall, the findings demonstrate the benefits of fair budgeting practices. In particular, survey results suggest that the presence of budgetary slack in efficiency targets is lower for managers who hold favorable fairness perceptions. A gender effect is also demonstrated between perceptions of fairness and the presence of budgetary slack in spending targets. Factor analytical evidence toward the development of a more refined measure of budgetary slack is provided.

Advances in Management Accounting
Advances in Management Accounting, Volume 13, 223–244
© 2004 Published by Elsevier Ltd.
ISSN: 1474-7871/doi:10.1016/S1474-7871(04)13009-8

INTRODUCTION

Budgetary slack refers to budgeted goals that are intentionally made easier. Since the primary goal of organizational budgeting is efficient resource allocation, the inclusion of slack into budget targets is typically viewed as dysfunctional and undesirable.[1] Numerous studies in the accounting literature therefore focus on understanding the factors which contribute to the creation of budgetary slack. In particular, prior research demonstrates that slack is easier to incorporate into budgets when subordinate managers (hereafter referred to as "managers") possess superior information to supervisors; i.e. when information asymmetry exists (Chow et al., 1988; Dunk, 1993; Young, 1985). Minimizing information asymmetry is therefore a potential option for reducing managers' use of budgetary slack. Unfortunately, asymmetric information often cannot be avoided in settings which require specialized expertise. In such instances, managers maintain an advantage over superiors when budget targets are set participatively since such asymmetric information provides greater opportunities for the inclusion of slack.

The purpose of this study is to explore whether fairness perceptions effectively mitigate managers' use of budgetary slack during participative environments in which managers hold private information. Prior accounting research shows that several factors impact the relationship between information asymmetry and slack in experimental settings. For instance, Chow et al. (1988) find that truth-inducing pay schemes reduce slack when information asymmetry is present, while Young (1985) and Waller (1988) demonstrate that risk preferences influence the effectiveness of such pay schemes on slack reduction. More recently, Fisher et al. (2002) report that under asymmetric information conditions, budgets contain more slack when negotiations between supervisors and subordinates end in agreement. This study contributes to this body of literature by using questionnaire data collected from one field site to investigate whether fairness perceptions influence managers' use of budgetary slack in work settings characterized by asymmetric information. Recent research demonstrates that fairness perceptions influence performance during budgeting (Libby, 1999; Wentzel, 2002) and managers' propensities to create slack (Little et al., 2002). No study, however, has directly examined whether favorable fairness perceptions are able to mitigate managers' use of budgetary slack during asymmetric information conditions favoring managers. Investigation of this issue is important because it may provide guidance for minimizing slack when asymmetric information cannot be avoided. Specifically, if fairness perceptions significantly influence the use of budgetary slack when managers hold private information, then the inclusion of slack into budget targets could be reduced through practices which foster fair budgeting environments.

Overall, the results of this study support this proposition by demonstrating that significantly less slack is present during asymmetric information conditions when managers hold relatively higher perceptions of fairness.

The remainder of this paper is organized as follows: the relevant literature is reviewed in the next section and the hypotheses are developed. The research method and the results of data analyses follow. Concluding remarks and suggestions for future research are presented in the final section.

LITERATURE REVIEW AND HYPOTHESIS DEVELOPMENT

Managers' use of budgetary slack has been widely studied in the accounting literature. Much of the research in this area stems from Argyris' (1952) seminal study in which he asserts that budgeting processes benefit from managerial involvement and participation during the setting of budget goals. Recognizing that managers are motivated by self-interest, concerns that participatory environments provide managers with opportunities to set easier budget goals for themselves (i.e. create budgetary slack) are well documented in the literature (Chow et al., 1988; Collins, 1978; Kim, 1992; Lukka, 1988; Schiff and Lewin, 1970; Waller, 1988, Young, 1985). Conversely, though, participation has also been shown to reduce managers' need to create slack in certain contextual settings by creating positive communication between superiors and subordinates (Dunk & Lal, 1999; Govindarajan, 1986; Kren, 2003; Merchant, 1985; Nouri, 1994; Nouri & Parker, 1996; Onsi, 1973). Overall, the mixed evidence regarding the role of budgetary participation on slack creation suggests that, while participatory environments provide opportunities for the inclusion of budgetary slack, additional factors influence whether slack will indeed be used during budgeting. The purpose of this study is to investigate the interaction of two such factors, fairness perceptions and information asymmetry, on managers' use of budgetary slack during participatory environments.

Regarding fairness perceptions, recent accounting research considers two primary types of fairness: distributive justice and procedural justice.[2] *Distributive justice* refers to the fairness of an *outcome*, while *procedural justice* relates to the fairness of the *process* used to determine an outcome. Furthermore, research in the managerial domain establishes a link between fairness perceptions and performance during budgeting. Such findings suggest that managers exhibit particularly positive organizational behaviors when they view budgetary procedures as fair. For instance, Libby's (1999) experimental results show that performance increases under high justice conditions, while Wentzel (2002) demonstrates that fairness perceptions improve performance ratings by increasing managers' commitment to budgetary goals. Since the inclusion of slack into budget targets is viewed as a dysfunctional response attitude which hampers performance (Collins, 1978), a negative relationship is expected between an individual's perception of fairness and the presence of budgetary slack, such that more slack is present in budgetary goals when either the budgeting process or the distributive outcomes of the process are deemed unfair. Little et al. (2002) find support for this premise by demonstrating that managers' propensities to create budgetary slack are lower when they perceive that both the organization's formal budgetary procedures and their supervisors' enactment of these procedures are fair. Asymmetric information conditions, however, were not considered.

This study extends Little et al. (2002) in two primary ways. First, this study tests whether Little et al.'s findings regarding the relationship between fairness and slack extend to settings in which asymmetric information is present. Such an investigation is important because asymmetric information is often inherent in organizational settings which require specialized technical expertise. This study contributes to research in this area by investigating whether an additional benefit of fair budgeting practices is the mitigation of managers' use of budgetary slack in work settings characterized by private information. Second, while Little et al. consider the role of procedural fairness in managers' use of budgetary slack, this paper examines the role of *both* the procedural and distributive facets of fairness. Prior research suggests that both facets of justice impact attitudes and performance in budget settings (e.g. Lindquist, 1995; Wentzel, 2002) and in other domains (see Greenberg, 1990 for a comprehensive review), while also asserting that procedural and distributive fairness are separate and distinct constructs (Greenberg, 1990).

More specifically, this study examines whether perceptions of distributive and procedural fairness influence the use of budgetary slack during asymmetric information conditions favoring managers. Prior research suggests that slack is easier to incorporate into budgets when subordinates possess superior information relative to supervisors; i.e. when information asymmetry in favor of subordinate managers exists (Chow et al., 1988; Dunk, 1993; Young, 1985). Specifically, managers who hold private information regarding the technical requirements and efficiency capabilities of their responsibility areas maintain an advantage over superiors when budget targets are set participatively since such asymmetric information provides greater opportunities for the inclusion of slack. The primary purpose of this study is to explore whether favorable fairness perceptions are able to mitigate managers' use of budgetary slack during situations of asymmetric information. When information asymmetry is present during participatory budget settings, opportunities exist for managers to incorporate slack into budgetary targets. Managers who hold favorable perceptions of distributive and procedural fairness, however, should be less likely to take advantage of their private information since resentment and outcome negativity tend to be lower for employees who view outcomes and procedures as fair (Brockner et al., 1994). Formally stated, this paper tests the following hypotheses:

H1a. Distributive justice moderates the relationship between information asymmetry and budgetary slack such that, in the presence of asymmetric conditions favoring managers, less slack is included in participatory budgets when managers' perceptions of distributive justice are high.

H1b. Procedural justice moderates the relationship between information asymmetry and budgetary slack such that, in the presence of asymmetric conditions favoring managers, less slack is included in participatory budgets when managers' perceptions of procedural justice are high.

In general, budgetary slack is a complex phenomenon that is difficult to capture (Lukka, 1988; Nouri & Parker, 1996; Van der Stede, 2000). While objective measures of actual budgetary slack are desirable, such measures are difficult to obtain (Dunk, 1993; Nouri & Parker, 1996). Surrogates for slack therefore are typically utilized in field research. Specifically, some studies measure a manager's *propensity* to create slack (Govindarajan, 1986; Little et al., 2002; Merchant, 1985; Onsi, 1973), relying on the presumption that managers with a greater *propensity* to create slack will indeed create greater *actual* slack given the opportunity (Kren, 2003). Other studies utilize *perceptual* measures of budgetary slack and rely on managers' perceptions of the actual level of slack contained in their budgets (Dunk, 1993; Dunk & Wright, 1998; Van der Stede, 2000). While neither measure has been deemed superior in the literature, this study utilizes the latter form and measures managers' *perceptions* of actual slack present in budget targets to investigate whether fairness perceptions influence the presence of slack when asymmetric information conditions exist in a participatory budget setting.

RESEARCH METHOD

Description of Site, Sample, and Data Collection Procedures

All responsibility area managers holding budgeting responsibilities at a large urban hospital were asked to participate in the study. Several factors contributed to the appropriateness of this site for testing the relationship between information asymmetry, fairness perceptions, and managers' use of budgetary slack.

First, interviews with top executives at this field site revealed that information asymmetry varies between supervising vice presidents (VPs) and responsibility area managers (i.e. subordinates) because of the vast technical knowledge required to operate each division of the hospital. VPs readily admitted during interviews that they rarely question budget revision requests in some of the specialized divisions under their control because it is difficult to stay abreast of the latest advancements in these areas.

Second, this hospital was in the midst of a five-year restructuring program involving downsized resources at the time the survey was administered. Leventhal et al. (1980) argue that the salience of allocation procedures is increased when a system is being reorganized in response to pressures for change (e.g. downsizing), while Brockner et al. (1995, 1994) find that fairness perceptions formed during downsizing significantly impact the productivity and morale of surviving employees. Fairness issues are thus expected to be particularly salient in this sample group.

Third, incentives to create slack exist since budget targets are set participatively and since budget performance is included as a facet of managers' performance appraisals. In particular, budget variances are measured and distributed in report form on a monthly basis. Explanations for large variances are required by VP's and thus help hold responsibility area managers accountable for their budgetary performance.

Data for the study were collected shortly after the operating budgets for the third year of the restructuring program had been finalized. The survey was administered through the site's inter-office mailing system in three mailings. A letter of support from the COO was included with the first mailing of the questionnaire. A thank-you/reminder postcard was distributed in the second mailing. Finally, a second copy of the questionnaire was distributed during the final mailing. To promote honest and candid responses, confidentiality was guaranteed and participants were instructed to return the completed survey directly to the researcher, rather than to the COO's office. To encourage participation, a postcard addressed to the COO was included with the questionnaires so the managers could notify the COO when the survey had been completed and returned to the researcher. Eighty-eight surveys were distributed and eighty-one surveys were completed and returned for a 92% response rate.

Measures

The survey measures are described next. Seven point Likert scales were used for all the measures. Descriptive statistics for the survey measures are provided in Table 1 and the survey items are shown in the Appendix. The following

Table 1. Summary of Descriptive Statistics.

Variable	N	Min	Max	Mean	S.D.
ASYM	74	4.17	7.00	5.58	0.84
BUDPART	77	1.00	7.00	3.93	1.61
DJ	77	1.20	7.00	4.67	1.26
PJ	76	1.43	7.00	4.04	1.27
SLACK-EFF	77	1.00	7.00	3.70	1.51
SLACK-SPND	77	1.00	7.00	2.69	1.30

Note: ASYM = information asymmetry; BUDPART = budgetary participation; DJ = distributive justice; PJ = procedural justice; SLACK-EFF = efficiency facet of budgetary slack; SLACK-SPND = spending facet of budgetary slack.

descriptive data were also collected: gender, age, educational level, and tenure with hospital. Table 2 summarizes the results of this descriptive information. A correlation matrix is provided in Table 3. Finally, the data were analyzed for the presence of late response bias; no systematic difference between the timeliness of responses and an individual's perception of fairness was found.

Distributive justice (DJ) was measured by averaging managers' responses to five items. Four items were based on Magner and Johnson's (1995) scale which

Table 2. Description of Survey Respondents.

Variable	Percentage
Age	
30 or under	1
31–40	25
41–50	56
Over 50	18
Gender	
Female	69
Male	31
Education	
Business	26
Medical	32
Combined business/medical	34
Other	8
Tenure with hospital	
2 years or less	7
3–4 years	9
5 or more years	84

Table 3.   Pearson Correlation Coefficient Matrix.

	ASYM	BUDPART	DJ	PJ	SLACK-EFF	SLACK-SPND
ASYM	1.000	−0.070	−0.025	−0.055	0.206[*]	−0.072
BUDPART	−0.070	1.000	0.427[**]	0.502[**]	−0.365[**]	−0.315[**]
DJ	−0.025	0.427[**]	1.000	0.616[**]	−0.646[**]	−0.109
PJ	−0.055	0.502[**]	0.616[**]	1.000	−0.535[**]	−0.117
SLACK-EFF	0.206[*]	−0.365[**]	−0.646[**]	−0.535[**]	1.000	0.206[*]
SLACK-SPND	−0.072	−0.315[**]	−0.109	−0.117	0.206[*]	1.000

Note: ASYM = information asymmetry; BUDPART = budgetary participation; DJ = distributive
justice; PJ = procedural justice; SLACK-EFF = efficiency facet of budgetary slack; SLACK-
SPND = spending facet of budgetary slack.
[*] Correlation is significant at the 0.05 level (1-tailed).
[**] Correlation is significant at the 0.01 level (1-tailed).

assesses various comparative bases (needs, expectations, and what is deserved)
that managers may use when judging the fairness of distributions, while one item
addressed the interpersonal facet of distributive justice (Greenberg, 1993). The
Cronbach alpha in this sample was 0.8679.

Procedural justice (PJ) was assessed using managers' average response score
to seven procedural justice statements. Six items were adapted from Magner and
Johnson's (1995) scale which pertains to five of Leventhal's (1980) six rules for
determining the fairness of allocation procedures (consistency across persons and
time, accuracy, correctability, ethicality, and bias suppression), while an additional
item addressed the informational facet of procedural justice (Greenberg, 1993).
The Cronbach alpha for this measure was 0.8838.

The amount of *information asymmetry* (ASYM) existing between cost center
managers and supervising vice presidents was assessed using Dunk's (1993)
six-item measure. This measure asks subordinates to indicate on a seven-point
likert scale whether the individual or the supervisor holds more information
regarding activities relating to the responsibility center. A response of (1) indicates
that the supervisor holds better information than the manager, while a response
of (4) indicates equal information between both parties, and a response of (7)
signifies that the manager is more knowledgeable. Since there are six items in
the information asymmetry scale, a total score of more than 24 suggests that the
manager holds private information, while a score of exactly 24 indicates information symmetry, and a score below 24 reveals that the supervisor holds superior
information to the manager.

As suggested during planning interviews with site executives, the results showed
that superior-subordinate relationships were characterized by a significant degree
of private information in favor of the managers. Actual responses on this scale

ranged from 19 to 42 with an average score of 32.85. A *t*-test indicated that the mean was significantly greater than an information symmetry score of 24 ($t = 13.86$, $p = 0.00$). Only four managers scored less than 24 on this measure. Since the purpose of this study is to investigate the impact of fairness perceptions during asymmetric information conditions that favor managers, these four observations were deleted from the data set. The Cronbach alpha for this measure was 0.7789.

Budgetary participation (BUDPART) was also measured. Budgetary participation was assessed by averaging managers' responses to Milani's (1975) five-item scale in which respondents were asked to rate their level of involvement with the budgetary process. The Cronbach alpha for the measure was 0.8677.

The dependent variable, *budgetary slack* (SLACK), was measured using 6 items based on Dunk's (1993) and Van der Stede's (2000) research. The items are intended to assess the ease with which budgetary targets can be achieved, such that higher scores indicate higher levels of perceived slack. The Cronbach alpha in this sample was 0.3393.

Given the low internal reliability of the budgetary slack scale, a factor analysis was performed employing maximum likelihood estimation with varimax rotation. The results of the factor analysis are shown in Table 4. Two factors emerged from this analysis. Factor 1 had an eigenvalue of 1.26 and accounted for 20.95% of the variance, while factor 2 held an eigenvalue of 1.12 and accounted for 18.69% of the variance. Together these factors accounted for 39.63% of the variable's variance. Items 1 and 2 loaded on factor 1, while items 3, 4, 5, and 6 loaded on the second factor. Based on the factor loading scores, item 1 (factor loading $= 0.987$) was selected to capture the first factor, while item 4 (factor loading $= 0.732$) was

Table 4. Factor Analysis Results of Budgetary Slack Scale.

	Factor Loadings
Items loading on factor 1	
1. Standards set by the budget induce high productivity in my responsibility area.	0.987
2. The budget set for my responsibility area is safely attainable.	0.427
Items loading on factor 2	
3. The budget for my responsibility area is not particularly demanding.	0.460
4. I have to carefully monitor costs in my area of responsibility because of budgetary constraints in my area's budget.	0.732
5. Budgetary targets have not caused me to be particularly concerned with improving efficiency in my area of responsibility.	0.315
6. Cost targets incorporated in my responsibility area's budget are difficult to reach.	0.484

selected to capture the second factor. The first factor appears to describe the level of *productivity* induced by budget targets, while the second factor refers to the level of *cost monitoring* required by employees to meet budgetary goals.

Overall, the results of the factor analysis are intuitively appealing since they appear to describe the *efficiency* and *spending* aspects of budget variances. More specifically, the inclusion of slack helps managers meet budget targets. When budget targets are met, differences between actual performance levels and budgeted levels are minimized; in other words, variances between actual and budgeted data are reduced. For managerial purposes, variances are typically broken into two components: differences in expected levels of productivity (i.e. efficiency variances) or changes in budgeted costs (i.e. spending variances). The budgetary slack scale appears to capture both the efficiency and spending facets of budget variances and suggests that these factors should be considered separately as distinct facets of budgetary slack, rather than combined into a single measure. Throughout the remainder of this paper, the efficiency facet is referred to as "SLACK-EFF" and the spending facet is referred to as "SLACK-SPND."

Hypothesis Testing

The proposed relationships were examined using moderated regression analysis. The primary purpose of this study is to investigate whether fairness perceptions mitigate managers' use of budgetary slack during participatory environments in which managers hold private information. The variable of interest is the interaction between information asymmetry and managers' perceptions of fairness. Separate regression models were run using the two facets of slack as dependent variables (SLACK-EFF, SLACK-SPND) and perceptions of distributive (DJ) and procedural (PJ) fairness as independent variables. Interaction terms (ASYMDJ, ASYMPJ) were formed by multiplying individuals' information asymmetry scores with measures of distributive and procedural justice, respectively. Budgetary participation (BUDPART) was also included in each of the models. The tested models were as follows:

(1) $\text{SLACK-EFF} = a + b_1\text{ASYM} + b_2\text{DJ} + b_3\text{ASYMDJ} + b_4\text{BUDPART} + e$;
(2) $\text{SLACK-EFF} = a + b_1\text{ASYM} + b_2\text{PJ} + b_3\text{ASYMPJ} + b_4\text{BUDPART} + e$;
(3) $\text{SLACK-SPND} = a + b_1\text{ASYM} + b_2\text{DJ} + b_3\text{ASYMDJ} + b_4\text{BUDPART} + e$;
(4) $\text{SLACK-SPND} = a + b_1\text{ASYM} + b_2\text{PJ} + b_3\text{ASYMPJ} + b_4\text{BUDPART} + e$.

Various forms of the interaction term are possible. Hartmann and Moers (1999) emphasize the importance of properly specifying interactive models, while Sharma et al. (1981) recommend a technique for identifying the type of interactive relationship contained in moderator models. The method requires the examination of the following equations:

(1) $y = a + b_1 x + e$;
(2) $y = a + b_1 x + b_2 z + e$;
(3) $y = a + b_1 x + b_2 z + b_3 xz + e$;

where y = slack, x = information asymmetry, and z = fairness perceptions. According to Sharma et al. (1981), if equations (6) and (7) are not significantly different (i.e. $b_3 = 0$; $b_2 \neq 0$), then z is not a moderator variable, but simply an independent predictor variable. If z is a *pure* moderator variable, then it interacts with the predictor variable to modify the form of the relationship between y and x, but has a negligible correlation with the criterion variable. Mathematically, in the case of the pure moderator, equations (5) and (6) are not different from each other, but are different from Eq. (7) (i.e. $b_2 = 0$, $b_3 \neq 0$). If z is a *quasi-moderator*, then it not only interacts with the predictor variable to affect the relationship between y and x, but it is also a predictor variable itself. In the quasi-moderator case, Eqs (5), (6), and (7) are all different from each other (i.e. $b_2 \neq b_3 \neq 0$).

The regression results for the *efficiency* facet of slack (SLACK-EFF) are discussed first. Panel A of Table 5 indicates a significant positive relationship between the presence of information asymmetry and slack ($t = 1.67$, $p = 0.05$). The question of interest, however, is whether fairness mitigates the presence of slack during these asymmetric conditions. The results of Panel B suggest that a significant negative relation exists between perceptions of distributive justice and perceptions of slack ($t = -6.15$, $p < 0.00$). The interaction term in Panel C, however, is not significant at conventional probability levels ($t = -0.041$, $p = 0.34$). Taken together, these results suggest that distributive justice is an independent predictor, rather than a moderator, of the efficiency facet of budgetary slack such that higher levels of distributive fairness are associated with lower levels of slack. Regarding perceptions of procedural justice, Panel D shows that higher perceptions of procedural fairness are associated with lower levels of slack ($t = -3.76$, $p < 0.00$). Furthermore, the interaction term (ASYMPJ) is also significant in Panel E ($t = -1.92$, $p = 0.03$) suggesting that procedural fairness is a quasi-moderator of the efficiency facet of slack. Overall, support is found for the proposed hypothesis in that both distributive and procedural fairness appear to influence the presence of budgetary slack in efficiency targets.

The regression results for the *spending* facet of slack are shown in Table 6. The results of Panels B and C, respectively, show that neither distributive justice ($t = 0.66$, $p = 0.26$) nor the interaction term ($t = 1.06$, $p = 0.15$) are significant at conventional probability levels. Similar results are obtained in Panels D and E, respectively, for PJ ($t = 0.94$, $p = 0.18$) and ASYMPJ ($t = 0.07$, $p = 0.47$).

Table 5.   Regression Results for SLACK-EFF.

Panel A: SLACK-EFF $= a + b_1$ASYM $+ b_2$BUDPART $+ e$

	Sum of Squares	df	Mean Square	F	Sig.
Regression	25.07	2	12.54	6.45	0.00
Residual	138.02	71	1.94		
Total	163.10	73			

$R^2 = 0.15$
Adj. $R^2 = 0.13$

	Coefficients			
	B	Std. Error	t	Sig.
Constant	3.18	1.19	2.67	0.00
ASYM	0.32	0.19	1.67	0.05
BUDPART	−0.31	0.10	−3.05	0.00

Panel B: SLACK-EFF $= a + b_1$ASYM $+ b_2$DJ $+ b_3$BUDPART $+ e$

	Sum of Squares	df	Mean Square	F	Sig.
Regression	73.52	3	24.51	19.15	0.00
Residual	89.58	70	1.28		
Total	163.10	73			

$R^2 = 0.45$
Adj. $R^2 = 0.43$

	Coefficients			
	B	Std. Error	t	Sig.
Constant	5.23	1.02	5.13	0.00
ASYM	0.38	0.16	2.43	0.01
DJ	−0.72	0.12	−6.15	0.00
BUDPART	−0.07	0.09	−0.79	0.22

Panel C: SLACK-EFF $= a + b_1$ASYM $+ b_2$DJ $+ b_3$ASYMDJ $+ b_4$BUDPART $+ e$

	Sum of Squares	df	Mean Square	F	Sig.
Regression	72.36	4	18.09	13.95	0.00
Residual	86.91	67	1.30		
Total	159.28	71			

$R^2 = 0.45$
Adj. $R^2 = 0.42$

Table 5. (*Continued*)

	Coefficients			
	B	Std. Error	t	Sig.
Constant	3.91	3.39	1.16	0.13
ASYM	0.62	0.59	1.05	0.15
DJ	−0.45	0.70	−0.64	0.26
ASYMDJ	−0.05	−0.12	−0.41	0.34
BUDPART	−0.06	0.09	−0.63	0.27

Panel D: SLACK-EFF $= a + b_1$ASYM $+ b_2$PJ $+ b_3$BUDPART $+ e$

	Sum of Squares	df	Mean Square	F	Sig.
Regression	48.66	3	16.22	9.78	0.00
Residual	114.38	69	1.66		
Total	163.04	72			

$R^2 = 0.30$
Adj. $R^2 = 0.27$

	Coefficients			
Constant	4.52	1.17	3.88	0.00
ASYM	0.32	0.18	1.76	0.04
PJ	−0.53	0.14	−3.76	0.00
BUDPART	−0.10	0.11	−0.95	0.17

Panel E: SLACK-EFF $= a + b_1$ASYM $+ b_2$PJ $+ b_3$ASYMPJ $+ b_4$BUDPART $+ e$

	Sum of Squares	df	Mean Square	F	Sig.
Regression	54.52	4	13.63	8.54	0.00
Residual	108.52	68	1.60		
Total	163.04	72			

$R^2 = 0.33$
Adj. $R^2 = 0.30$

	Coefficients			
Constant	−2.22	3.70	−0.60	0.28
ASYM	1.52	0.65	2.33	0.01
PJ	1.11	0.87	1.28	0.10
ASYMPJ	−0.29	0.15	−1.92	0.03
BUDPART	−0.10	0.11	−0.96	0.17

Note: ASYM = information asymmetry; BUDPART = budgetary participation; DJ = distributive justice; PJ = procedural justice; SLACK-EFF = efficiency facet of budgetary slack; SLACK-SPND = spending facet of budgetary slack.

Table 6. Regression Results for SLACK-SPND.

Panel A: SLACK-SPND $= a + b_1$ASYM $+ b_2$BUDPART $+ e$

	Sum of Squares	df	Mean Square	F	Sig.
Regression	13.35	2	6.68	4.34	0.02
Residual	109.24	71	1.54		
Total	122.60	73			

$R^2 = 0.11$
Adj. $R^2 = 0.08$

	Coefficients			
	B	Std. Error	t	Sig.
Constant	4.56	1.06	4.31	0.00
ASYM	0.15	0.17	−0.84	0.20
BUDPART	−0.26	0.09	−2.88	0.00

Panel B: SLACK-SPND $= a + b_1$ASYM $+ b_2$DJ $+ b_3$BUDPART $+ e$

	Sum of Squares	df	Mean Square	F	Sig.
Regression	14.02	3	4.67	3.01	0.04
Residual	108.57	70	1.55		
Total	122.60	73			

$R^2 = 0.11$
Adj. $R^2 = 0.08$

	Coefficients			
	B	Std. Error	t	Sig.
Constant	4.32	1.12	3.84	0.00
ASYM	−0.15	0.17	−0.88	0.19
DJ	0.08	0.13	0.66	0.26
BUDPART	−0.29	0.10	−2.87	0.00

Panel C: SLACK-SPND $= a + b_1$ASYM $+ b_2$DJ $+ b_3$ASYMDJ $+ b_4$BUDPART $+ e$

	Sum of Squares	df	Mean Square	F	Sig.
Regression	14.55	4	3.64	2.32	0.07
Residual	104.95	67	1.57		
Total	119.50	71			

$R^2 = 0.12$
Adj. $R^2 = 0.07$

Table 6. (*Continued*)

| | Coefficients | | | |
	B	Std. Error	t	Sig.
Constant	8.17	3.72	2.20	0.16
ASYM	−0.84	0.65	−1.30	0.10
DJ	−0.72	0.77	−0.93	0.18
ASYMDJ	0.14	0.13	1.06	0.15
BUDPART	−0.29	0.10	−2.77	0.00

Panel D: SLACK-SPND = $a + b_1$**ASYM** + b_2**PJ** + b_3**BUDPART** + e

	Sum of Squares	df	Mean Square	F	Sig.
Regression	14.85	3	4.95	3.19	0.03
Residual	107.21	69	1.56		
Total	122.06	72			

$R^2 = 0.12$
Adj. $R^2 = 0.08$

| | Coefficients | | | |
	B	Std. Error	t	Sig.
Constant	4.30	1.13	3.81	0.00
ASYM	−0.15	0.17	−0.88	0.19
PJ	0.13	0.14	0.94	0.18
BUDPART	−0.31	0.11	−2.94	0.00

Panel E: SLACK-SPND = $a + b_1$**ASYM** + b_2**PJ** + b_3**ASYMPJ** + b_4**BUDPART** + e

	Sum of Squares	df	Mean Square	F	Sig.
Regression	14.85	4	3.71	2.36	0.06
Residual	107.20	68	1.58		
Total	122.06	72			

$R^2 = 0.12$
Adj. $R^2 = 0.07$

| | Coefficients | | | |
	B	Std. Error	t	Sig.
Constant	4.55	3.67	1.24	0.11
ASYM	−0.20	0.65	−0.30	0.38
PJ	0.07	0.86	0.08	0.47
ASYMPJ	0.01	0.15	0.07	0.47
BUDPART	−0.31	0.11	−2.92	0.00

Note: ASYM = information asymmetry; BUDPART = budgetary participation; DJ = distributive justice; PJ = procedural justice; SLACK-EFF = efficiency facet of budgetary slack; SLACK-SPND = spending facet of budgetary slack.

Sensitivity analyses were also conducted to determine whether any of the descriptive variables significantly impacted individuals' perceptions of justice. Gender was the only characteristic which proved statistically significant at conventional probability levels. Overall, the results suggest that female managers tend to hold significantly lower perceptions of fairness than their male counterparts ($t = 3.29$, $p = 0.00$). Similar gender differences are evident in prior studies (for instance, see Armstrong-Stassen, 1998 or Sweeney & McFarlin, 1997). To test whether these gender differences impacted the results of this study, the data were partitioned into male and female groups and the models were re-run. The results remained qualitatively unchanged with the exception of Eq. (3): SLACK-SPND = $a + b_1$ASYM $+ b_2$DJ $+ b_3$ASYMDJ $+ b_4$BUDPART $+ e$. For the female group, a significant interaction between perceptions of distributive justice and information asymmetry emerged ($t = 2.06$, $p = 0.05$), along with a significant negative relationship between DJ and SLACK-SPND ($t = -2.00$, $p = 0.05$). The results suggest that perceptions of distributive fairness moderate the relationship between information asymmetry and spending facets of budgetary slack for females, but not for male managers, such that less slack is used as perceptions of distributive justice increase during asymmetric information conditions.

SUMMARY AND CONCLUDING REMARKS

The primary objective of this study was to investigate whether favorable perceptions of fairness are able to mitigate managers' use of budgetary slack in participative environments in which managers hold private information. This research is important because asymmetric information favoring subordinates often cannot be avoided when specialized technical expertise is required to operate a particular responsibility area. The results suggest that significantly less slack is present in efficiency targets when managers hold more favorable perceptions of fairness. Furthermore, significantly less slack is present in spending targets for female managers who hold more favorable perceptions of distributive fairness. Evidence toward the refinement of a budgetary slack measure is also provided.

In general, the inclusion of slack in a budget helps managers meet budget targets. When budget targets are met, differences between actual and budgeted performance levels are minimized. In other words, variances between actual and budgeted data are reduced. Principles of management accounting theory maintain that variances are comprised of two elements: differences in expected levels of productivity (i.e. efficiency variances) and differences in budgeted costs (i.e. spending variances). Factor analytical evidence presented in this study supports this basic accounting principle and seems to suggest that budgetary slack is appropriately viewed as a two-dimensional variable containing both efficiency and spending facets.

Several limitations of this study should be considered in interpreting the results. First, this study surveyed managers from a large urban hospital utilizing a non-random sampling technique. While there is no evidence to suggest that the data collection procedure may have introduced systematic bias, the findings are limited to the extent that the results do not generalize beyond the sample group. Caution also should be exercised when interpreting the results given the low reliability score initially achieved for the budgetary slack scale in this sample group. While factor analysis supported the two-factor split, one-item measures of each facet were utilized to test the hypothesis. Further research is needed to enhance these scales. In general, budgetary slack is a difficult construct to capture (Lukka, 1988; Van der Stede, 2000). As in prior research, this study examined *perceived* slack, rather than *actual* slack. Debate over the use of self-reported vs. objective measures is longstanding. Evidence suggests, however, that biases in self-ratings are unlikely to confound research findings (Brownell & Dunk, 1991; Nunnally, 1981). Finally, this study was conducted at a field site which was in the midst of downsizing. Since fewer opportunities for slack exist when resources are scarce, this study provides a conservative test of the proposed hypotheses.

In conclusion, the findings are consistent with prior justice research which demonstrates the benefits of fair budgeting practices. Overall, the results suggest that the presence of budgetary slack in efficiency targets is significantly lower when managers perceive both the budgeting procedures and resource allocations to be fair. A gender effect was also noted. While similar gender effects have been reported in prior organizational behavior research, not much attention has been given to date to possible gender issues in fairness studies in the budgeting domain. Further consideration of such effects may prove fruitful in future accounting research. Overall, the findings in this study hold practical relevance for managers involved in participative budgeting environments characterized by downsized resources and superior-subordinate information asymmetry, while also extending Little et al.'s (2002) prior findings to a new setting. Specifically, the results suggest that the use of fair budgeting practices can mitigate managers' use of budgetary slack even when the managers hold private information over their superiors.

The results of this study also provide suggestions for honing the budgetary slack construct to better fit accounting theory. Prior field studies have predominately relied on a uni-dimensional measure of slack which combines both cost management and efficiency facets. Such studies have generally produced modest Cronbach-alpha scores at the lower limits of acceptability.[3] While further validation of the efficiency and spending facets beyond this sample group is clearly necessary, future field research may benefit from the pursuit of a two-dimensional budgetary slack measure. In particular, a two-dimensional measure recognizes the possibility that managers may not have equal opportunities to build slack into efficiency and spending targets. For instance, prices of goods and services may be fairly fixed in the short-run, thus providing managers with little discretion over spending targets. More discretion, however, may be possible over efficiency targets since managers can control their departments' levels of productivity. Separate consideration of the spending and efficiency facets therefore may enhance future research efforts in the budgetary slack area.

NOTES

1. Some studies note that slack can be beneficial in certain settings by providing managers with flexibility to respond to changes in operating conditions (e.g. Dunk, 1995; Govindarajan, 1986; Merchant & Manzoni, 1989; Nouri, 1994; Schiff & Lewin, 1970).
2. The terms *fairness* and *justice* are used interchangeably throughout the paper.
3. For instance, Van der Stede, 2000 ($\alpha = 0.68$), Dunk and Wright, 1998 ($\alpha = 0.69$), Dunk, 1993 ($\alpha = 0.68$).

ACKNOWLEDGMENTS

This paper is based on my dissertation at Temple University. I would like to thank those who served on my dissertation committee for their guidance: David Ryan (Chair), Alison Konrad, Roland Lipka, Janice Mereba, and Joe Ugras. Also, I am grateful for the helpful suggestions provided on earlier drafts by Chris Agoglia, Rick Hatfield, Nace Magner, participants at the 2003 AAA Mid-Atlantic Regional meeting, and the anonymous reviewers.

REFERENCES

Argyris, C. (1952). *The impact of budgets on people*. New York: School of Business and Public Administration.
Armstrong-Stassen, M. (1998). The effect of gender and organizational level on how survivors appraise and cope with organizational downsizing. *The Journal of Applied Behavioral Science, 34*(2), 125–142.
Brockner, J., Konovsky, M., Cooper-Schneider, R., Folger, R., Martin, C., & Bies, R. J. (1994). Interactive effects of procedural justice and outcome negativity on victims and survivors of job loss. *Academy of Management Journal, 37*(2), 397–409.

Brockner, J., Wiesenfeld, B. M., & Martin, C. L. (1995). Decision frame, procedural justice, and survivors' reactions to job layoffs. *Organizational Behavior and Human Decision Processes*, *63*(1), 59–68.

Brownell, P., & Dunk, A. S. (1991). Task uncertainty and its interaction with budgetary participation and budget emphasis: Some methodological issues and empirical investigation. *Accounting, Organizations and Society*, *16*(8), 693–703.

Chow, C. W., Cooper, J. C., & Waller, W. S. (1988). Participative budgeting: Effects of a truth inducing pay scheme and information asymmetry on slack and performance. *The Accounting Review*, *63*(1), 111–122.

Collins, F. (1978). The interaction of budget characteristics and personality variables with budgetary response attitudes. *The Accounting Review*, *53*(2), 324–335.

Dunk, A. S. (1993). The effect of budget emphasis and information asymmetry on the relation between budgetary participation and slack. *The Accounting Review*, *68*(2), 400–410.

Dunk, A. S. (1995). The joint effects of budgetary slack and task uncertainty on subunit performance. *Accounting and Finance* (November), 61–75.

Dunk, A. S., & Lal, M. (1999). Participative budgeting, process automation, product standardization, and managerial slack propensities. *Advances in Management Accounting*, *8*, 139–157.

Dunk, A. S., & Wright, S. (1998). A multi-method examination of the effect of budget emphasis on the relation between extrinsic valence and managerial performance: The influence of budgetary slack and task programmability. *Pacific Accounting Review*, *10*(1), 1–25.

Fisher, J., Frederickson, J. R., & Peffer, S. A. (2002). The effect of information asymmetry on negotiated budgets: An empirical investigation. *Accounting, Organizations and Society*, *27*(1/2), 27–43.

Govindarajan, V. (1986). Impact of participation in the budgetary process on managerial attitudes and performance: Universalistic and contingency perspectives. *Decision Sciences*, 496–516.

Greenberg, J. (1990). Organizational justice: Yesterday, today, and tomorrow. *Journal of Management*, *16*(2), 399–432.

Greenberg, J. (1993). The social side of fairness: Interpersonal and informational classes of organizational justice. In: R. Cropanzano (Ed.), *Justice in the Workplace: Approaching Fairness in Human Resource Management* (pp. 79–103). Hillsdale, NJ: Lawrence-Erlbaum.

Hartmann, F. G. H., & Moers, F. (1999). Testing contingency hypotheses in budgetary research: An evaluation of the use of moderated regression analysis. *Accounting, Organizations and Society*, *24*(4), 291–315.

Kim, D. C. (1992). Risk preferences in participative budgeting. *The Accounting Review*, *67*(2), 303–318.

Kren, L. (2003). Effects of uncertainty, participation, and control system monitoring on the propensity to create budget slack and actual budget slack created. *Advances in Management Accounting*, *11*, 143–167.

Leventhal, G. S. (1980). What should be done with equity theory? In: K. J. Gergen, M. S. Greenberg & R. H. Willis (Eds), *Social Exchange: Advances in Theory and Research* (pp. 27–55). New York: Plenum Press.

Leventhal, G. S., Karuza, J., & Fry, W. R. (1980). Beyond fairness: A theory of allocation preferences. In: G. Mikula (Ed.), *Justice and Social Interaction* (pp. 167–218). New York: Springer-Verlag, New York.

Libby, T. (1999). The influence of voice and explanation on performance in a participative budgeting setting. *Accounting, Organizations and Society*, *24*, 125–137.

Lindquist, T. M. (1995). Fairness as an antecedent to participative budgeting: Examining the effects of distributive justice, procedural justice and referent cognitions on satisfaction and performance. *Journal of Management Accounting Research*, *7*(Fall), 122–147.

Little, H. T., Magner, N. R., & Welker, R. B. (2002). The fairness of formal budgetary procedures and their enactment: Relationships with managers' behavior. *Group and Organization Management*, 27(2), 209–225.

Lukka, K. (1988). Budgetary biasing in organizations: Theoretical framework and empirical evidence. *Accounting, Organizations and Society*, 13(3), 281–301.

Magner, N., & Johnson, G. G. (1995). Municipal officials' reactions to justice in budgetary resource allocation. *Public Administrative Quarterly*, 18(4), 439–456.

Merchant, K. A. (1985). Budgeting and the propensity to create budgetary slack. *Accounting, Organizations and Society*, 10(2), 201–210.

Merchant, K. A., & Manzoni, J. F. (1989). The achievability of budget targets in profit centers: A field study. *The Accounting Review* (July), 539–558.

Milani, K. (1975). The relationship of participation in budget-setting to industrial supervisor performance and attitudes: A field study. *The Accounting Review*, 50(2), 274–284.

Nouri, H. (1994). Using organizational commitment and job involvement to predict budgetary slack: A research note. *Accounting, Organizations and Society*, 19(3), 289–295.

Nouri, H., & Parker, R. J. (1996). The effect of organizational commitment on the relation between budgetary participation and budgetary slack. *Behavioral Research in Accounting*, 8, 74–90.

Nunnally, J. C. (1981). *Psychometric theory*. New Delhi: Tata, McGraw Hill.

Onsi, M. (1973). Factor analysis of behavioral variables affecting budgetary slack. *The Accounting Review* (July), 535–548.

Schiff, M., & Lewin, A. Y. (1970). The impact of people on budgets. *The Accounting Review*, 45(2), 259–268.

Sharma, S., Durand, R. M., & Gur-arie, O. (1981). Identification and analysis of moderator variables. *Journal of Marketing Research*, 18, 291–300.

Sweeney, P. D., & McFarlin, D. B. (1997). Process and outcome: Gender differences in the assessment of justice. *Journal of Organizational Behavior*, 18, 83–98.

Van der Stede, W. A. (2000). The relationship between two consequences of budgetary controls: Budgetary slack creation and managerial short-term orientation. *Accounting, Organizations and Society*, 25(6), 609–622.

Waller, W. S. (1988). Slack in participative budgeting: The joint effect of a truth-inducing pay scheme and risk preferences. *Accounting, Organizations and Society*, 13(1), 87–98.

Wentzel, K. (2002). The influence of fairness perceptions and goal commitment on managers' performance in a budget setting. *Behavioral Research in Accounting*, 14, 247–271.

Young, M. (1985). Participative budgeting: The effects of risk aversion and asymmetric information on budgetary slack. *Journal of Accounting Research*, 23(2), 829–842.

APPENDIX
SURVEY MEASURES

Budgetary Participation (1 = very little, 7 = very much)

(1) The portion of my responsibility area's budget that I am involved in setting.
(2) The frequency of budget-related discussion with superiors initiated by me.
(3) The amount of influence I have on the final budget for my responsibility area.

(4) The importance of my contribution to my area of responsibility's budget.
(5) The frequency of budget-related discussions initiated by my superior when budgets for my area of responsibility are being set.

Distributive Justice (1 = strongly disagree, 7 = strongly agree)

(1) My responsibility area received the budget that it deserved.
(2) The budget allocated to my responsibility area adequately reflects my needs.
(3) My responsibility area's budget was what I expected it to be.
(4) I consider my responsibility area's budget to be fair.
(5) My supervisor expresses concern and sensitivity when discussing budget restrictions placed on my area of responsibility.

Procedural Justice (1 = strongly disagree, 7 = strongly agree)

(1) Budgeting procedures are applied consistently across all responsibility areas.
(2) Budgeting procedures are applied consistently across time.
(3) Budgetary decisions for my area of responsibility are based on accurate information and well-informed opinions.
(4) The current budgeting procedures contain provisions that allow me to appeal the budget set for my area of responsibility.
(5) The current budgeting procedures conform to my own standards of ethics and morality.
(6) Budgetary decision makers try hard not to favor one responsibility area over another.
(7) Budgetary decision makers adequately explain how budget allocations for my responsibility area are determined.

Budgetary Slack (1 = strongly disagree, 7 = strongly agree;
R = reverse scoring used)

(1) Standards set by the budget induce high productivity in my responsibility area (R).
(2) The budget set for my responsibility area is safely attainable.
(3) The budget for my responsibility area is not particularly demanding.
(4) I have to carefully monitor costs in my area of responsibility because of budgetary constraints in my area's budget (R).

(5) Budgetary targets have not caused me to be particularly concerned with improving efficiency in my area of responsibility.
(6) Cost targets incorporated in my responsibility area's budget are difficult to reach (R).

Information Asymmetry (1 = superior, 4 = equal, 7 = manager)

(1) In comparison with your immediate superior, who is in possession of better information regarding the activities undertaken in your area of responsibility?
(2) In comparison with your immediate superior, who is more familiar with the input-output relationships inherent in the internal operations of your area of responsibility?
(3) In comparison with your immediate superior, who is more certain of the performance potential of your responsibility area?
(4) In comparison with your immediate superior, who is more familiar technically with the work in your area of responsibility?
(5) In comparison with your immediate superior, who is better able to assess the potential impact on your activities of factors external to your responsibility area?
(6) In comparison with your immediate superior, who has a better understanding of what can be achieved in your responsibility area?

EFFECTS OF RESPONSIBILITY AND COHESIVENESS ON GROUP ESCALATION DECISIONS

Woody M. Liao, David R. Finley and William E. Shafer

ABSTRACT

This paper reports the results of an experimental study examining the joint effect of two group characteristics, responsibility and cohesiveness, on escalation of commitment in an ongoing unsuccessful project. Two levels (high/low) of group responsibility and group cohesiveness were manipulated to examine their effects on group escalation decisions. Forty-eight 3-member decision groups were formed and randomly assigned to four treatment cells with 12 groups in each cell. The results of a 2 × 2 ANOVA reveal a significant main effect of responsibility on escalation of commitment, as well as a significant interaction of responsibility and cohesiveness. Specifically, groups with both high responsibility and high cohesiveness committed the largest amount of resources to an ongoing unsuccessful project. These results provide support for the proposition that group responsibility and cohesiveness exert significant joint effects on group escalation of commitment in an ongoing unsuccessful project. The findings suggest that periodic changes of group membership to shift responsibility and cohesiveness may generate new attitudes and views to reduce group escalation of commitment.

Advances in Management Accounting
Advances in Management Accounting, Volume 13, 245–259
© 2004 Published by Elsevier Ltd.
ISSN: 1474-7871/doi:10.1016/S1474-7871(04)13010-4

INTRODUCTION

Escalation of commitment to ongoing unsuccessful projects has received a great deal of attention in general management and management accounting research. In general, this research addresses situations in which decision makers are given negative feedback on an ongoing project, and are asked to make a decision regarding the amount of additional funds to commit to the project. Empirical results indicate that managers tend to escalate their commitment if they are responsible for the initial investment decision (Arkes & Blumer, 1985; Garland, 1990; Staw, 1976, 1981; Staw & Fox, 1977; Staw & Ross, 1978; Teger, 1979). In a real case, Kull (1986) reports an escalation of commitment in the design and implementation of a complex computer-based information system for the New Jersey Division of Motor Vehicles. At an early stage, there were clear indications that the proposed system could not perform the assigned tasks. Nevertheless, the managers continued the project to its completion at a considerable cost. Most experimental research on escalation of commitment has focused on individual (rather than group) escalation behavior and suggested individual self-justification as the driving force for this decision strategy.

However, many management decisions are group rather than individual decisions and group decisions often differ from those of individuals due to dynamic interactions among group members (Arnold et al., 2000; Bedard et al., 1998; Henry, 1995; Sutton & Hayne, 1997; Whyte, 1993). There is a long history of research that addresses the effects of various group characteristics on group interaction, risk shift, and performance (e.g. Conlon & Wolf, 1980; Evans & Dion, 1991; Janis, 1972; Mullen & Cooper, 1994; Russell, 1971; Schachter et al., 1951; Seashore, 1954; Stein, 1976; Zander, 1979). Researchers have also extended the study of escalation of commitment to group settings, finding that groups are also subject to the escalation phenomenon if they are responsible for the initial funding decision (Bazerman et al., 1984).

In addition to group responsibility, another factor that potentially influences escalation of commitment is group cohesiveness. It is well-documented that groups are often prone to the "risky shift" phenomenon, i.e. groups tend to make decisions that are more risky than the mean of the individual decisions of the group members (Bazerman et al., 1984). We argue that more cohesive groups will be more likely to experience this type of risky shift if group norms favor persistence in an ongoing unsuccessful project, and consequently will be more likely to escalate their commitment to such a project. This leads to the prediction that the greatest escalation of commitment will occur under conditions of high group responsibility and high group cohesiveness. Our findings, based on an experimental study of group decision making by business students, confirm this expectation. Specifically, the results reveal a significant main effect of group responsibility on escalation of commitment, and a significant group responsibility/group cohesion interaction.

The remainder of the paper is organized as follows. The next section reviews literature on group responsibility and group cohesiveness and develops research hypotheses. This is followed by a description of the research methodology and presentation of the empirical findings. The final section of the paper provides a summary and discussion of the findings and limitations of the study.

LITERATURE REVIEW AND HYPOTHESIS DEVELOPMENT

Group Responsibility

An extensive body of research has documented individual escalation of commitment to ongoing unsuccessful projects (Arkes & Blumer, 1985; Staw, 1976, 1981; Staw & Fox, 1977; Staw & Ross, 1978). Specifically, individual decision makers have a tendency to justify their initial investment decisions by committing additional resources to such projects. Since groups are composed of individuals, groups like individuals may be prone to escalate their commitment after a setback in a project for which they feel responsible (Brockner & Rubin, 1985; Janis, 1982; Teger, 1979). Several studies have documented evidence related to the extension of individual escalation to group escalation of commitment (e.g. Bazerman et al., 1984; Rutledge, 1994; Rutledge & Harrell, 1994). In general, they found that, if a group feels responsible for an initial investment decision, it is likely that the group will defend and further justify the ongoing project. However, if a group is not responsible for the initial investment decision, it is unlikely that the group will have an incentive to further justify the ongoing project. Therefore, we anticipate a significant main effect of group responsibility on escalation of commitment to an ongoing unsuccessful project, as reflected in the following hypothesis.

H1. Group responsibility will have a significant main effect on decisions to escalate commitment to an ongoing unsuccessful course of action.

Group Cohesiveness

Many studies have documented the "risky shift" phenomenon, which is the tendency of groups to make riskier decisions than individuals (e.g. Brandstatter, 1981; Cartwright, 1968; Dion et al., 1978; Isenberg, 1986; Lamm & Myers, 1978;

Mackie, 1986; Moscovici & Zavalloni, 1969; Rutledge & Harrell, 1994). Decisions to escalate commitment to an ongoing unsuccessful project may be viewed as more risky than decisions not to escalate. If commitment is not escalated, a smaller, sure loss is accepted. In contrast, escalation results in the risk of a bigger loss in exchange for the possibility of making up for the smaller initial loss (Bazerman et al., 1984). Consequently, groups that are more prone to the risky shift phenomenon should be more likely to escalate their commitment to an unsuccessful project.

It can also be argued that more cohesive groups will exert more influence on their members, and under certain conditions will be more prone to experience a risky shift that exacerbates the tendency toward escalation of commitment. Janis (1982) suggests that two factors will affect the propensity of groups to become entrapped in escalation of commitment dilemmas: (1) group cohesiveness; and (2) group norms. Janis (1972, 1982) viewed group cohesiveness as the primary antecedent of groupthink, which occurs when group members' desire for unanimity overrides their motivation to realistically appraise alternative courses of action. Small group research demonstrates that highly cohesive groups are more likely to exert pressure on members to adhere to group norms or standards (Staw, 1976). However, group cohesiveness alone is not a sufficient condition for escalation of commitment to occur. As observed by Janis, cohesive groups may be *unlikely* to escalate their commitment to ongoing unsuccessful projects if group norms favor "open minded scrutiny of new evidence and willingness to admit errors" (Janis, 1982, cited in Brockner and Rubin, 1985, p. 98). In contrast, if group norms favor persistence in an unsuccessful course of action, then escalation of commitment should be more likely in more cohesive groups. Based on this line of reasoning, Brockner and Rubin (1985) suggested that controlled experiments should examine the joint effects of group cohesiveness and group norms on escalation of commitment, and predicted that escalation should be most pronounced for highly cohesive groups that have group norms favoring persistence. However, the joint effects of group cohesiveness and group norms on escalation of commitment have not been addressed empirically.

Although empirical tests of the effects of cohesiveness on groupthink have provided mixed results, there is some evidence that indicates that more cohesive groups exert more influence on their members and discourage dissent within the group. For example, Courtright (1978) and Callaway and Esser (1984) found that more cohesive groups exhibited less disagreement among group members and made poorer decisions than less cohesive groups. Moorhead and Montanari (1986) also found that cohesive groups were more discouraging of dissent among their members than noncohesive groups, which implies that cohesion is likely to lead to consensus-seeking behavior such as groupthink. Turner et al. (1992) found that cohesive groups were more confident in their decisions and perceived

their decisions to be less risky than did noncohesive groups; thus, more cohesive groups should be more prone to making risky decisions such as those involved in the escalation of commitment. Taken together, these findings suggest that more cohesive groups should be more susceptible to escalation of commitment, particularly if group norms favor persistence in an ongoing project. As discussed, it is widely documented that group responsibility is a primary determinant of escalation of commitment; thus, group responsibility for an initial funding decision should contribute to a group norm that favors ongoing commitment to a project. Consequently, escalation of commitment should be greatest under conditions of high group cohesiveness and high group responsibility for an initial funding decision, as reflected in the following hypothesis.

H2. Group responsibility and group cohesiveness will have a significant interactive effect on decisions to escalate commitment to an ongoing unsuccessful course of action. Specifically, groups with high responsibility and high cohesiveness will exhibit greater escalation than groups with high responsibility and low cohesiveness.

RESEARCH METHOD

Participants

Participants were 144 junior business administration students at a major state university. At the time of the experiment, participants had completed two quarters of principles of accounting and were taking management accounting and corporate finance. Participation in the experiment was a requirement of the students' management accounting class. For the class, in addition to three lectures a week, students were required to register and attend one of four discussion sections which met 75 minutes once a week. A graduate teaching assistant was assigned as the leader in each discussion section. Group responsibility (High, Low) and group cohesiveness (High, Low) were manipulated in a 2 × 2 design, and each of the four discussion sections was randomly assigned to one of the four treatment cells. Forty-eight three-person groups were formed, with twelve groups in each treatment cell.

Procedure

The group decision task is a modification of Staw's (1976) R&D funding case. This task was originally developed by Staw to test the self-justification theory in individual escalation decisions. Participants were told that the current study was designed to investigate the use of accounting information in a group decision task. Also, they were told that they would play the role of a member of a Financial Management Committee whose responsibility is to make R&D funding recommendations in a large manufacturing firm consisting of two product divisions. Immediately following the instructions, participants were given an experimental instrument consisting of three parts.

The instrument described the history and the operating situation of the firm and its two product divisions, industrial products and consumer products. Participants were provided with financial data regarding sales and earnings for each division for the past 10 years, which indicated declining profitability. The case indicated that as a result of the declining profitability, the company's directors had appropriated 10 million dollars for R&D to improve the situation. The case also stipulated that the total R&D funds of 10 million dollars should be invested in only one of the two divisions. Each group's decision task at this stage was to determine which division should receive the entire 10 million dollars. It is important to note here that the choice of product division for the initial funding at this stage is not a relevant factor for study of group escalation. Thus, group choices between the industrial and consumer product divisions are not included in our data analysis.

Subsequent to the initial investment decision, groups in the High Responsibility condition were informed that the board of directors had approved the R&D investment in their chosen divisions. In contrast, groups in the Low Responsibility condition were informed that the directors had decided to invest the 10 million dollars in the other division rather than their chosen division. In addition, the instrument provided the funded division's financial data showing steady negative earnings for the 5-year period since the initial R&D funding decision. Groups were informed at this point that the directors had allocated an additional 20 million dollars for R&D to be distributed between the previously funded division and other purposes. In other words, each group's decision at this stage was to recommend how much of the 20 million dollars should be allocated to the previously funded division and to other purposes.

Groups were not given a time limit for group discussion, and were given no specific instructions concerning how they should reach a decision except that the group decision must be unanimous. After the group funding decisions, each participant was asked to complete a questionnaire to assess group responsibility and cohesiveness. After finishing the questionnaire, subjects were debriefed and dismissed.

Cohesiveness Manipulation

Cohesiveness has been traditionally used to measure the strength of the forces that bind members to a group, including both liking for the group as a whole and the attraction of each member to every other member (Cartwright, 1968). In order to increase the strength of the experimental manipulation (McGrath, 1993; Hollingshead et al., 1993), group cohesiveness was manipulated in the weekly discussion classes for the entire academic quarter. Groups in the High Cohesiveness condition formed three-member groups according to the students' personal preferences and choices at the beginning of the quarter. These groups worked class exercises as a team in the discussion class every week. In addition, five group projects were assigned by the discussion leader to each High Cohesiveness group during the quarter to provide the opportunity for further development of cohesion among group members. On the other hand, groups in the Low Cohesiveness condition were randomly formed at the end of the quarter immediately before the administration of the experiment. They were not given the opportunity to work on class exercises as a team, and the discussion leader did not assign any additional group projects to them during the quarter.

Dependent Variable

The dependent variable was the group's escalation of commitment to the previously chosen division. We measured this variable by the amount of new R&D funds allocated by each group in the second funding decision to the previously funded division. This allocation of new R&D funds to the division could range from $0 to $20 million. The higher the amount allocated to the previously funded division, the greater the group's escalation of commitment.

RESULTS

Manipulation Checks

The post-experimental questionnaire was used to measure participants' perceptions of responsibility for the initial funding decision and group cohesion. These measures were used to test the effectiveness of the experimental manipulations. Table 1 summarizes the mean responses for responsibility and cohesion by experimental condition. The mean perceived responsibility for the High

Table 1. Manipulation Checks.

Group Responsibility	Group Cohesiveness		
	High	Low	Pooled
Panel A: Perceived responsibility			
High	7.29	5.67	6.48
	(1.31)	(1.34)	(1.33)
Low	3.87	3.25	3.56
	(1.07)	(1.01)	(1.05)
Pooled	5.58	4.46	5.02
	(1.21)	(1.18)	(1.20)
Panel B: Perceived cohesiveness			
High	7.01	5.56	6.28
	(1.69)	(0.78)	(1.33)
Low	5.75	2.93	4.34
	(1.24)	(1.09)	(1.20)
Pooled	6.38	4.24	5.31
	(1.51)	(0.96)	(1.28)

Notes: (1) Reported numbers are mean values. Numbers in parentheses are standard deviations.
(2) All responses were provided on nine-point scales.

Responsibility groups was significantly greater than that for the Low Responsibility groups (6.48 vs. 3.56, $p < 0.05$), which indicates that the manipulation was effective. Similarly, the mean perception of group cohesiveness for the High Cohesiveness groups was significantly greater than that for the Low Cohesiveness groups (6.38 vs. 4.24, $p < 0.05$), again indicating that the manipulation was effective. It is also interesting to note that the perceptions of group cohesiveness were significantly higher under conditions of High Responsibility (6.28 vs. 4.34, $p < 0.05$). This result is consistent with the suggestion of Bazerman et al. (1984) that responsibility will increase group cohesiveness.

Hypothesis Tests

Table 2 summarizes the new R&D funds allocated to the ongoing unsuccessful division, which serves as the measure of escalation of commitment. As is apparent from the table, there was a large difference between the funds allocated in the High and Low Responsibility conditions. Across both responsibility conditions, group cohesiveness did not have a very large effect on funds allocated. However, group cohesiveness did have a relatively large effect in the High Responsibility

Table 2. New R&D Funds Allocated.

Group Responsibility	Group Cohesiveness		
	High	Low	Pooled
High	14.48	10.37	12.42
	(4.65)	(4.70)	(4.68)
Low	4.87	6.28	5.57
	(4.17)	(4.54)	(4.39)
Pooled	9.67	8.32	8.99
	(4.45)	(4.67)	(4.56)

Notes: (1) Reported numbers are mean values. Numbers in parentheses are standard deviations.
(2) Values could range from 0 to 20.

condition. As indicated, escalation of commitment was greatest under conditions of both high responsibility and high cohesion.

The results of a 2×2 analysis of variance (ANOVA) model, summarized in Table 3, confirm the statistical significance of these observed effects. The main effect of group responsibility on escalation of commitment was highly significant ($p = 0.0001$), which is consistent with Hypothesis 1. Tests of the mean differences between experimental cells indicate that escalation of commitment under both group cohesiveness conditions was significantly greater ($p < 0.01$) in the High Responsibility vs. the Low Responsibility conditions. The ANOVA results indicate that the main effect for group cohesion was not significant, but there was a statistically significant interaction of group responsibility and group cohesion, as predicted by Hypothesis 2. Tests of mean differences indicated that, as hypothesized, the mean escalation of commitment was significantly greater ($p < 0.05$) in the High Responsibility/High Cohesiveness cell vs. the High Responsibility/Low Cohesiveness cell. It is also interesting to note that the mean escalation of commitment in the Low Responsibility/High Cohesiveness condition was actually lower than that in the Low Responsibility/Low Cohesiveness condition. However, this difference was not statistically significant.

Table 3. ANOVA Results.

Source	SS	df	MS	F	p
Group responsibility (GR)	489.1038	1	489.1038	24.11	0.0001
Group cohesiveness (GC)	16.6485	1	16.6485	0.82	0.3722
GR × GC	84.6736	1	84.5359	4.13	0.0480
Error	819.4628	44	18.6429	–	–

Supplemental Analysis

We also performed supplemental analysis of certain dissonance measures to obtain further insight into participants' decision-making processes. According to Wicklund and Brehm's (1976) dissonance theory, the processes underlying escalation of commitment can be explained by dissonance arousal and dissonance reduction variables. In order to explain the group escalation of commitment in our study, we consider "commitment" and "relatedness" as dissonance arousal variables and "confidence" and "reversal" as dissonance reduction variables. Commitment is a measure of a group's feeling of how committed it is to an ongoing project. Greater commitment by the group to a project normally drives more need for self-justification and thus greater escalation of commitment. Relatedness is a measure of a group's perception of the extent to which the initial and the subsequent funding decisions on a project are related. Perceptions of greater relatedness of the two funding decisions is expected to drive dissonance arousal and thus escalation of commitment in an ongoing unsuccessful project. On the other hand, confidence is a measure of a group's assurance of the decision quality in the second funding decision. Reversal is a measure of a group's belief in the ability of the second decision to turn the project around. Therefore, more confidence in the quality of the second funding decision and a greater belief in the ability to reverse the situation are likely to result in dissonance reduction by escalation of commitment.

We measured the four dissonance variables (commitment, relatedness, confidence, and reversal) by asking each subject to complete a questionnaire after their group funding decisions. For each group, the dissonance variables were measured based on the average response from its three members. All responses were provided on nine-point scales anchored on "Not at all" and "Extremely." Averages for each dissonance variable were computed by treatment cell to help explain the differences in escalation of commitment among the experimental conditions. Table 4 summarizes the dissonance measures by treatment cell. As shown, all the dissonance measures were higher in the cells where more escalation of commitment occurred. Pair comparisons of cell means for each dissonance variable showed that High Responsibility groups experienced significantly higher arousal and reduction of dissonance than Low Responsibility groups. Also, participants in the High Responsibility/High Cohesiveness conditions experienced greater dissonance arousal and reduction than participants in the High Responsibility/Low Cohesiveness groups. However, group cohesiveness did not have a significant effect on dissonance arousal or reduction in the Low Responsibility conditions. These findings provide further insight into the factors that drive group escalation of commitment by demonstrating that the pattern of

Table 4. Dissonance Measures.

Group Responsibility	Group Cohesiveness		
	High	Low	Pooled
Panel A: Commitment			
High	7.31	5.55	6.43
	(1.33)	(2.35)	(1.89)
Low	3.77	3.22	3.49
	(2.04)	(1.88)	(1.99)
Pooled	5.54	4.38	4.96
	(1.72)	(2.18)	(1.94)
Panel B: Relatedness			
High	6.91	5.27	6.09
	(1.61)	(2.20)	(1.92)
Low	3.73	3.18	3.45
	(1.81)	(2.12)	(2.01)
Pooled	5.32	4.22	4.77
	(1.74)	(2.18)	(1.96)
Panel C: Confidence			
High	7.67	6.62	7.14
	(1.33)	(1.34)	(1.34)
Low	5.64	6.14	5.89
	(1.12)	(0.61)	(0.89)
Pooled	6.65	6.38	6.52
	(1.24)	(0.99)	(1.12)
Panel D: Reversal			
High	6.90	5.56	6.23
	(1.48)	(2.09)	(1.83)
Low	3.61	3.59	3.60
	(2.04)	(2.31)	(2.25)
Pooled	5.25	4.57	4.91
	(1.78)	(2.24)	(2.04)

Notes: (1) Reported numbers are mean values. Numbers in parentheses are standard deviations.
(2) All responses were provided on nine-point scales.

dissonance arousal and reversal were consistent with the observed pattern of escalation of commitment.

SUMMARY AND DISCUSSION

The results of this study indicate that, as hypothesized, group responsibility had a significant main effect on escalation of commitment. This finding confirms previous research demonstrating that groups personally responsible for initial funding decisions are more likely to escalate commitment to an ongoing unsuccessful project (e.g. Bazerman et al., 1984). Also as hypothesized, we found a significant interactive effect of group responsibility and group cohesiveness on escalation of commitment. Specifically, groups in the High Responsibility/High Cohesiveness condition were more likely to escalate commitment than groups in the High Responsibility/Low Cohesiveness condition. This finding is consistent with suggestions by Janis (1982) and Brockner and Rubin (1985) that group cohesiveness and group norms will have a joint effect on escalation of commitment. Groups with a high level of responsibility for an initial funding decision should be predisposed to group norms that favor persistence in ongoing projects. When such group norms are combined with a high level of group cohesiveness, this should exacerbate the tendency toward a "risky shift" that underlies escalation of commitment to unsuccessful ventures.

To obtain further insight into the decision processes underlying group escalation of commitment, we also measured certain cognitive dissonance arousal and reduction variables. These measures revealed a pattern of dissonance arousal and reduction that reflected groups' escalation of commitment, i.e. groups with greater (lesser) escalation of commitment experienced greater (lesser) levels of dissonance arousal and reduction. These results suggest that the arousal and reduction of cognitive dissonance underlies group decisions to escalate commitment to ongoing projects.

The results of this study present some interesting implications for management control of escalation of commitment or de-escalation strategies (Ghosh, 1997; Heath, 1995; Staw & Ross, 1987). Because group responsibility and group cohesiveness appear to have a significant joint effect on escalation decisions, one possible strategy would be to influence group responsibility and cohesiveness by changing group membership. An effective way to achieve this may be to replace some group members periodically to reduce perceptions of both group responsibility and group cohesiveness and increase consideration of different views. This approach should provide not only the benefit of receiving different views from the new members and reducing group feelings of responsibility for the project, but also the benefit of continuity of some members of the original group. Because new members are not responsible for the initial decision and because the group as a whole should feel less cohesive, escalation of commitment to unsuccessful ventures may be reduced. Thus, a possible direction for future research is to investigate whether and how a replacement of a portion of group members would reduce non-rational escalation of commitment.

In addition to group responsibility and cohesiveness, other group characteristics such as group leadership style, group members' risk attitudes, and group goals may also affect group decisions and thus should be the subject of future research on escalation of commitment. A limitation of the current study is that we used a task that had no direct consequences for the decision-making groups. Therefore, future research on these issues should provide significant incentives to groups for successful performance. Finally, due to the desirability of an experimental approach, participants in the current study were non-experts. Future studies should examine the decisions of expert groups in actual companies to determine the effects of variables such as group responsibility and cohesiveness in more ecologically valid settings.

REFERENCES

Arkes, H. R., & Blumer, C. (1985). The psychology of sunk cost. *Organizational Behavior and Human Decision Processes, 35*(February), 124–140.

Arnold, V., Sutton, S. G., Hayne, S. C., & Smith, C. (2000). Group decision making: The impact of opportunity-cost, time pressure and group support systems. *Behavioral Research in Accounting, 12,* 69–96.

Bazerman, M. H., Giuliano, T., & Appelman, A. (1984). Escalation of commitment in individual and group decision making. *Organizational Behavior and Human Decision Processes, 33,* 141–152.

Bedard, J. C., Biggs, S. F., & Maroney, J. J. (1998). Sources of process gain and loss from group interaction in performance of analytical procedures. *Behavioral Research in Accounting, 10*(Suppl.), 207–233.

Brandstatter, H. (1981). Recent research on group decision making. In: H. Brandstatter, J. H. Davis & G. Stocker-Kreichgauer (Eds), *Group Decision Making.* New York: Academic Press.

Brockner, J., & Rubin, J. Z. (1985). *Entrapment in escalating conflicts: A social psychological analysis.* New York: Springer-Verlag.

Callaway, M., & Esser, J. (1984). Groupthink: Effects of cohesiveness and problem-solving procedures on group decision making. *Social Behavior and Personality, 12,* 157–164.

Cartwright, D. (1968). *Group dynamics.* New York: Row, Peterson and Company.

Conlon, E. J., & Wolf, G. (1980). The moderating effects of strategy, visibility, and involvement on allocation behavior: An extension of Staw's escalation paradigm. *Organizational Behavior and Human Decision Processes, 26,* 172–192.

Courtright, J. (1978). A laboratory investigation of groupthink. *Communication Monograph, 45,* 229–246.

Dion, K. L., Baron, R. S., & Miller, N. (1978). Why do groups make riskier decisions than individuals? In: L. Berkowitz (Ed.), *Group Processes.* New York: Academic Press.

Evans, C. R., & Dion, K. L. (1991). Group cohesion and performance: A meta-analysis. *Small Group Research, 22,* 175–186.

Garland, H. (1990). Throwing good money after bad: The effect of sunk costs on the decision to escalate commitment to an ongoing project. *Journal of Applied Psychology, 75*(6), 728–731.

Ghosh, D. (1997). De-escalation strategies: Some experimental evidence. *Behavioral Research in Accounting, 9,* 88–112.

Heath, C. (1995). Escalation and de-escalation of commitment in response to sunk costs: The role of budgeting in mental accounting. *Organizational Behavior and Human Decision Processes*, *62*, 38–54.

Henry, R. A. (1995). Improving group judgment accuracy: Information sharing and determining the best member. *Organizational Behavior and Human Decision Processes*, *62*, 190–197.

Hollingshead, A. B., Mcgrath, J. E., & O'Connor, K. M. (1993). Group task performance and communication technology: A longitudinal study of commuter-mediated vs. face-to-face groups. *Small Group Research*, *24*(August), 307–333.

Isenberg, D. J. (1986). Group polarization: A critical review and meta-analysis. *Journal of Personality and Social Psychology*, *50*, 1141–1151.

Janis, I. L. (1972). *Victims of groupthink*. Boston: Houghton-Mifflin.

Janis, I. L. (1982). *Groupthink*. Boston: Houghton-Mifflin.

Kull, D. (1986). Anatomy of a 4GL disaster. *Computer Decisions* (February 11), 58–65.

Lamm, H., & Myers, D. G. (1978). Group-induced polarization of attitudes and behavior. In: L. Berkowitz (Ed.), *Advances in Experimental Social Psychology*. New York: Academic Press.

Mackie, D. M. (1986). Social identification effects in group polarization. *Journal of Personality and Social Psychology*, *50*, 720–728.

McGrath, J. E. (1993). Introduction: The JEMCO workshop-description of a longitudinal study. *Small Group Research*, *24*(August), 285–306.

Moorhead, G., & Montanari, J. (1986). An empirical investigation of the groupthink phenomenon. *Human Relations*, *39*, 399–410.

Moscovici, S., & Zavalloni, M. (1969). The group as a polarizer of attitudes. *Journal of Personality and Social Psychology*, *12*, 125–135.

Mullen, B., & Cooper, C. (1994). The relation between group cohesiveness and performance: An integration. *Psychological Bulletin*, *115*(2), 210–227.

Russell, D. (1971). Group-induced shift toward risk: A critical appraisal. *Psychological Bulletin* (October), 252–270.

Rutledge, R., & Harrell, A. (1994). The impact of responsibility and framing of budgetary information on group shifts. *Behavioral Research in Accounting*, *6*, 92–107.

Schachter, B., Ellerston, N., McBride, D., & Gregory, D. (1951). An experimental study of cohesiveness and productivity. *Human Relations*, *4*, 229–238.

Seashore, S. E. (1954). *Group cohesiveness in the industrial workforce*. Ann Arbor: University of Michigan Press.

Staw, B. M. (1976). Knee-deep in the big muddy: A study of escalating commitment to a chosen course of action. *Organizational Behavior and Human Decision Processes*, *16*, 27–44.

Staw, B. M. (1981). The escalation of commitment to a course of action. *Academy of Management Review*, *6*, 577–587.

Staw, B. M., & Fox, F. (1977). Escalation: Some determinants of commitment to a previously chosen course of action. *Human Relations*, *30*, 431–450.

Staw, B. M., & Ross, J. (1978). Commitment to a policy decision: A multi-theoretical perspective. *Administrative Science Quarterly*, *23*, 40–64.

Staw, B. M., & Ross, J. (1987). Knowing when to pull the plug. *Harvard Business Review*, *65*(2), 68–74.

Stein, A. (1976). Conflict and cohesion: A review of the literature. *Journal of Conflict Resolution* (March), 143–172.

Sutton, S. G., & Hayne, S. C. (1997). Judgment and decision making, Part III: Group processes. In: V. Arnold & S. G. Sutton (Eds), *Behavioral Accounting Research: Foundation and Frontiers*. Sarasota, FL: American Accounting Association.

Teger, A. I. (1979). *Too much invested to quit: The psychology of the escalation of conflict*. New York: Pergamon.

Turner, M. E., Pratkanis, A. R., Probasco, P., & Leve, C. (1992). Threat, cohesion, and group effectiveness: Testing a social identity maintenance perspective on groupthink. *Journal of Personality and Social Psychology, 63*, 781–796.

Whyte, G. (1993). Escalating commitment in individual and group decision making: A prospect theory approach. *Organizational Behavior and Human Decision Processes, 54*, 430–455.

Wicklund, R. A., & Brehm, J. W. (1976). *Perspectives on cognitive dissonance*. Hillsdale, NJ: Erlbaum.

Zander, A. (1979). The psychology of group process. In: M. R. Rosenweig & L. W. Porter (Eds), *Annual Review of Psychology*. Palo Alto, CA: Annual Reviews.